North Carolina Waterfalls

North Carolina Waterfalls

Where to Find Them, How to Photograph Them

Kevin Adams

JOHN F. BLAIR, PUBLISHER
Winston-Salem, North Carolina

Third Printing, 1998

DESIGN BY DEBRA LONG HAMPTON
PRINTED AND BOUND BY R. R. DONNELLEY & SONS

*The paper in this book meets the guidelines for permanence
and durability of the Committee on Production Guidelines for
Book Longevity of the Council on Library Resources.*

Cover photograph—
Looking Glass Falls, Pisgah National Forest

Library of Congress Cataloging-in-Publication Data
Adams, Kevin, 1961—
   North Carolina waterfalls : where to find them, how to photograph them / Kevin Adams.
        p.   cm.
   Includes index.
   ISBN   0-89587-110-6 (pbk.)
   1. Waterfalls—North Carolina.   I. Title.
GB 1425.N8A33   1994
551.48'4'09756—dc20   93–35021

To my father, Bill,
for teaching me the difference
between a robin and a blue jay, an oak and a hickory.

And to my mother, Phoebe Lorretta,
for teaching me to love and respect
all of nature, especially waterfalls.

Contents

Acknowledgments

I am greatly indebted to many people who offered their time and knowledge and helped to make this book a reality.

Professionals from the United States Forest Service contributed substantially to the content of this book. Thanks go to Chad Boniface, Paul Bradley, Kimberly Brandel, Sally Browning, Linda Byers, Ronnie Carnes, Dave Cawrse, James Crisp, Sue Elderkin, Frank Findley, Jr., Judy Green, Dale Holland, Ray Johns, Grant Keener, Richard Kincaid, L. Phillip Kromer, Bill Lea, Dolly McCall, Marshall McClung, Glenn McConnell, David McFee, Joe Nicholson, James Ouzts, Max Riddle, Jr., Ralph Rogers, Spencer Rollins, Charlie Sanders, Vicki Snipes, Marty Southard, and Rick Wilson.

Other professionals to whom I am indebted include Allen Rogers of South Mountains State Park; John Garrison of Great Smoky Mountains National Park; Virgil Crowe of the Bureau of Indian Affairs, Qualla Indian Reservation; Chris May of the town of Blowing Rock; Larry Bloomer of Crescent Resources, Inc.; and Lowell Rauch, president of Carolina Camera Center.

The following authorities gave unselfishly of their time: Dr. J. Dan Pittillo, professor of biology at Western Carolina University; and Bill Lea of Franklin, who offered suggestions pertaining to photography.

Individuals who provided valued assistance include Joe Keller of Brevard Motor Lodge, Al Raulston, Carlton McNeil, Jim Stewart, Coy Williard, Mike Haydon, Luther Sudderth, John Spencer, Marc Parsons, and my brothers, Steve Adams and Laurie Adams, who deserve special credit.

I am deeply thankful to the staff of John F. Blair, Publisher—Sue Clark, Margaret Couch, Debbie Hampton, Steve Kirk, Carolyn Sakowski, Anne Schultz, Heath Simpson, and Lisa Wagoner—for their confidence in me and the knowledge and dedication they gave to this project.

Finally, and most important, this book would not have been possible without the love and support of my wife, Jane, who not only tolerated an absentee husband but also helped type and proofread the manuscript.

Introduction

Waterfalls have always been a fascination for me. When I was a child, my family's vacations were always to the mountains in general and to waterfalls in particular. We derived great pleasure from searching out particular waterfalls, even though we were often frustrated by the vague directions that were available. Inevitably, our conversations turned to how we would one day write a book and sort out this confusion once and for all.

As we grew older and stopped taking vacations together, this talk was shelved. But I always knew that someday I would write the book we talked about. That someday began nine years ago, when my wife, Jane, gave me my first camera as a birthday present. That present rekindled my great love for the out-of-doors and for waterfalls.

Since I tend to take everything to extremes, I could not be satisfied with a typical guidebook. I wanted to include *every* waterfall in North Carolina that is accessible to the public, along with information on geology, flora and fauna, and photography. Of course, including every waterfall in the state was impossible, but I believe I have come about as close as you can get. It's a safe bet that if you have heard of a major waterfall that is not listed here, it is on private property. The information on photography is designed to fill a need of readers who would like to create the best waterfall pictures possible.

Early on, it became obvious that the waterfalls should be given a geographical organization. After all, if you are planning a vacation to the extreme southwestern portion of North Carolina, you will only be interested in waterfalls in that region. My solution was to list each waterfall under a specific "hub." These hubs are usually the nearest town, and they may contain several or few waterfalls, depending on their location. The Lake Toxaway hub, in the heart of waterfall country, contains well over twenty falls, while the Columbus hub, on the edge of the foothills, has only one. The hubs are presented in a more or less clockwise progression around western North Carolina, beginning with Morganton. Each hub has a map showing the roads and waterfalls in that area, and most have a starting point from which all road directions are given.

For each waterfall, the most widely accepted name is given first, with any other currently used names listed underneath. A number of waterfalls have no name and are distinguished by the rivers that form them. It is interesting to note the many High Falls in the book. Often, waterfalls have not been given specific names but are simply called, for example, "High Falls of the Horsepasture," which distinguishes them from other, usually smaller falls on the same river.

This book contains many waterfalls of all sizes, beauty ratings, and trail lengths and difficulties. Deciding which ones to visit in a one-week vacation can be frustrating for someone not familiar with the area. To help you make a decision, I have recommended particular waterfalls based on beauty and accessibility. These falls are marked by an asterisk (*) following their names. This may spare you from hiking 5 miles to a mediocre waterfall when you could have walked 0.5 mile to a nice one.

Next come listings for the river each waterfall is located on, the county where it is located, and the specific USGS quadrangle you should consult. These maps show elevation by means of contour lines and are the most accurate and detailed you can buy. If you are planning on doing any cross-country hiking, it is wise to carry one of these maps. If you are on national-forest land, make sure the map is modified for Forest Service use. Such maps are the most up-to-date available and have trails, property boundaries, and other features listed. They are available at the various ranger stations (see the appendix).

The landowner of each waterfall is also listed. The addresses of all listed agencies are in the appendix. With few exceptions, all of the private falls in this book are visible from the road. If you leave the road right-of-way for a closer look, you will be trespassing.

An entire book could be written on the process behind measuring a waterfall. See the chapter entitled "North Carolina Waterfalls" for a discussion of this process. Please note that the measurements I have given are not to be considered fact. They should be used for comparison only.

The beauty rating for each waterfall is my opinion based on a number of factors, including viewing restrictions, surroundings, water flow, and distractions. You will not want to bother visiting waterfalls with a rating of 1 to 3 unless you're already in the vicinity. Falls rated from 4 to 6 are recommended and can be quite nice in the right conditions. Those rated from 7 to 9 are always worth the effort, and anything rated a 10 should be considered a must-see.

All trail lengths are given in feet or miles and are one-way distances. The difficulty rating for the trail to each waterfall assumes a healthy, average person, with *average* being the operative word. If you are of average fitness, you can expect a trail rated 1 to 3 to be very easy, 4 to 6 to be moderate, and 7 to 9 to be difficult. A rating of 10 means a suicidal trail. Very young or old persons or those in poor health will need to adjust these figures accordingly. It should also be noted that the difficulty rating has nothing to do with the trail length. A number of trails have multiple difficulty ratings. Only if a trail is fairly consistent over its entire length will it have a single rating. A trail rated 4–8, for example, will be fairly easy over most of its length but

will have some difficult sections.

On March 12 and 13, 1993, the "blizzard of the century" swept across western North Carolina, dumping up to 5 feet of snow and leaving tens of thousands of downed trees. The blizzard affected most of the trails and waterfalls in this book to some extent. A few trails will remain closed for years, and a number of waterfalls will remain an unsightly mess of fallen branches and trees. Unfortunately, I completed much of the research for this book before the storm struck, and I have not been able to rehike all of the trails. Visitors should be aware that some trails may be impassable due to fallen trees, or the waterfalls unphotogenic. I have rehiked most of the trails, and the difficulty ratings reflect the amount of tree-hopping that must be done. The trails are gradually being cleared, and as a result, a trail may be much easier than I have rated it. However, it is very unlikely that any of the fallen trees will be cleared from the waterfalls.

Road directions are given in miles and are usually rounded to the nearest tenth. They can easily vary depending on the accuracy of your odometer (and mine). You will notice that I have not made a distinction between paved and gravel roads. If you do not want to travel on gravel roads, then you will not see most of the falls in this book. A few primary state roads, many, if not most, secondary state roads, and practically all forest roads are unpaved. Unless it is indicated otherwise, they are all suitable for passenger cars. All Forest Service roads are subject to closure due to logging, mining, or other activities.

In most cases, I have given only one of several routes to the falls. You are encouraged to study road and trail maps to determine other routes and loop options.

Many waterfalls in this book are accessible to persons in a wheelchair. These are designated after the trail length and difficulty information as "Handicapped Accessible" in bold type. They are usually, but not always, waterfalls that are next to a road. Handicapped persons not confined to a wheelchair will find numerous other falls accessible to them. Use the trail lengths and difficulty ratings to guide your decisions.

Next, you will find photo tips and a short general-information section. Last comes a listing of nearby waterfalls—my solution to including those falls that are ugly, small, inaccessible, or otherwise unworthy of a full listing. Most nearby waterfalls are on private property but are visible from the road.

People die every year from falling over waterfalls. These tragedies can be prevented by using a little common sense. Wet and moss-covered rocks are extremely slippery, and river currents are stronger than people realize. Stay away from the brink of a waterfall, and never try to climb onto one. It's easy to spot the people who won't follow these simple precautions. They lie motionless at the base of the falls.

Of particular concern to me are the devastating environmental effects brought about by ignorant visitors to waterfalls. A brook trout can easily choke on a carelessly tossed cigarette butt, birds become tangled in fishing line, and litter creates an eyesore for those of us desiring a wilderness experience. Off-trail hiking presents a severe threat to the environment, especially at waterfalls. Climbing around the banks destroys vegetation and dislodges loose soil. No photograph is worth that. Stay on the trail unless you are sure that your presence is not causing an impact.

It is not enough that visitors only concern themselves with their own actions. Mountainsides are being clear-cut and development is taking place at an alarming rate in western North Carolina. Air pollution and introduced pests are destroying entire ecosystems. People must get involved and protect the land and the creatures that inhabit it. If they don't, this book may one day be found in your library's history section, an account of the way things were.

In preparing this book, I drove over 20,000 miles, hiked over 800 miles, exposed over 150 rolls of film,

and explored nearly 300 waterfalls. I also led several waterfall photo tours during this period. I'm often asked, "Don't you get bored with falling water?" My answer is a resounding no. Waterfalls have an irresistible appeal that draws me to them time and again. I've heard people remark, "I'm not hiking to that waterfall. I saw it last year." Last year? That waterfall will not look the same as it did last week, or even yesterday. Weather, seasons, water flow, and lighting are constantly changing a waterfall's appearance. Each time I visit one, it's a new experience for me.

Go to Whitewater Falls in early spring when the leaves have a "virgin" look, in late spring during the rhododendron bloom, in autumn when the forest is ablaze, and in winter just after a snowstorm. You will not see one waterfall four times. You will have four distinct experiences of nature, and the waterfall will be different in each one. Visit a waterfall during the first light of dawn and return at dusk. You will have two distinct memories of that waterfall, each special in its own way.

As you might guess, there are several waterfalls I return to on a regular basis. Linville Falls, Whitewater Falls, the falls of Graveyard Fields, the falls of the Horsepasture River, the falls of the Cullasaja Gorge, and the falls in the Harper Creek/Lost Cove area are all special to me. I don't really have a favorite, but there are few experiences in nature I find as moving as viewing Rainbow Falls by the light of a full moon.

Experience waterfalls. Immerse yourself in their sight and sound. And maybe, for a brief moment, nothing else will matter. Then you will find yourself, like me, wanting to return time and again.

Upper Catawba Falls
Nikon F3, 28-70mm zoom lens, polarizing filter
stacked on warming filter, f/22 at 4 seconds,
Fujichrome Velvia.

The bright overcast sky at the top of the falls was very
distracting. With careful positioning on the right bank, I was
able to eliminate most of the sky. The 28-70mm zoom lens
proved indispensable for this critical composition.

North Carolina Waterfalls

Upper Catawba Falls

Waterfall Distribution in North Carolina

The dots represent every major waterfall that I know of in the state, both public and private. The dashed line represents the Blue Ridge Escarpment. Notice the dense concentration of waterfalls in the southwestern section of the state, in Transylvania, Jackson, and Macon counties.

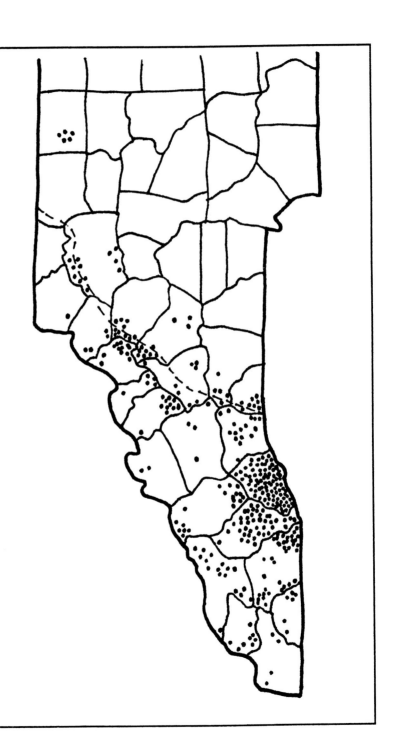

North Carolina Waterfalls

Geology

People are naturally inquisitive, and seeing a waterfall brings to mind all sorts of questions. How old is it? Has it always looked like this? Will it always look like this? How did it get here? How many waterfalls are there in North Carolina?

Although little actual research has been done on North Carolina's waterfalls, several generalizations can be made about them. Waterfalls are formed by any of several situations, and it is these situations that some geologists use to categorize them.

Some waterfalls are attributable to differential erosion of rock. In basic terms, this means that when certain rock erodes slower than the surrounding rock, the harder rock tends to stand higher and form a precipice, over which the stream flows.

Other waterfalls are attributable to a discordance in the river profile. Of course, by their very nature, all waterfalls are located at a discordance in the river profile, but this category is reserved for those waterfalls that do not fit in either of the other two categories. These include waterfalls that form along fault scarps, high plateaus, cliffs, caves—except the rimstone falls discussed in the third category—and where streams flow over canyon walls. The majority of North Carolina's waterfalls belong in this category, although there are a few examples from the first category as well.

The third type of waterfall is attributable to constructional processes. This may be due to lava flow or landslides that block streams, glacial activity, or deposits of calcium carbonate that has precipitated from solution in ground water. The most common example of the latter case is a lip forming around a pool in a limestone cave. Over time, this lip increases in size and forms a "rimstone waterfall" on the downstream side.

The formation process began with the birth of the Appalachian Mountains. According to the widely accepted theory of plate tectonics, the Appalachians were formed approximately 200 million years ago as a result of continental collisions. The incredible force of these collisions caused a mountainous upheaval in the earth's surface. These mountains, originally several thousand feet higher than at present, have been subjected to 280 million years of erosion to create the peaks, valleys, and waterfalls that we see today.

Where major streams flowed over soft, easily erodible rock, the erosion process probably reduced the flow to mere rapids and riffles. This could explain why there are few waterfalls in Cherokee and Clay counties, in the extreme southwestern part of the state. This area is composed mainly of altered sedimentary rock, which is easily erodible. In contrast, Macon, Jackson, and Transylvania counties are composed of harder metamorphic and igneous rock. Thus, it is no coincidence that these counties contain numerous waterfalls.

It would be misleading to say that all of North Carolina's waterfalls are a result of hard rock. Numerous other factors come into play, the most important of which are topography and precipitation. When the Appalachians were created, a fault scarp formed a boundary between the high mountains of North Carolina and the foothills of North Carolina, South Carolina, and Georgia. This escarpment has a southwest-to-northeast configuration and causes a definite discordance in river profiles. Naturally, any streams flowing over this escarpment will form waterfalls where hard rock is present.

A factor that contributes immensely to the size of North Carolina's waterfalls is the presence of a plateau region. If the streams flowing over the escarpment run a short course before reaching the edge, or if they spring from the escarpment itself, the waterfalls will likely be very small and their flow severely restricted during the dry season. Examples of this type of waterfall are Hickory Nut Falls, Glassmine Falls, and Betseys Rock Falls. But in the plateau region, streams flow a greater distance before reaching the escarpment, allowing them to achieve a greater volume. The result is powerful waterfalls with a much greater erosive capability. Many of the major waterfalls in Macon, Jackson, and Transylvania counties can be attributed to the existence of such plateaus. A few examples are Rainbow Falls, Whitewater Falls, and Toxaway Falls. The three rivers that form these falls flow in a southerly direction over the plateaus and escarpment and into the foothills region.

An interesting feature of Macon and Jackson counties is the presence of major waterfalls on the *other* side of the plateaus. These plateaus not only rise above the foothills, but also above the surrounding highlands. Thus, major waterfalls are present along the entire periphery of the plateaus. Examples of waterfalls flowing off the northern side are Cullasaja Falls, Onion Falls, and Flat Creek Falls.

Traveling to North Carolina's mountains from the south or east, you will encounter an obvious point along the route where you must make a steep ascent for a considerable distance. You are climbing the escarpment at this point. Once you cross the escarpment—and the plateau regions of Macon, Jackson, and Transylvania counties, if you're coming from the south—and enter the heart of the mountains, you will no longer find optimal topography for the presence of waterfalls. There are plenty of streams and steep mountains, but without a plateau to build up the stream and an escarpment for it to flow over, there is less chance that a major waterfall will form. The streams leave the steep terrain before they gain appreciable size, then enter directly into flat drainage valleys. You might think that if you continue westward, you will have to climb down the other side of the escarpment at some point, but this is not exactly the case. The transition from the high mountains of North Carolina to the lowlands farther west is much more gradual.

Of course, without water, there would only be cliffs, not waterfalls. A high amount of rainfall produces many small branches, which flow into larger creeks, which in turn flow into larger streams, which create the most aesthetic waterfalls. Precipitation contributes to the size of waterfalls but has little to do with the actual number of them. *That* is determined by topography and the nature of the rock.

A number of terms are used to describe waterfalls, among them cataract, cascade, rapid, shoal, and slide. While no formally accepted usage of these terms exists, a few generalizations can be made. Cataract is usually applied to waterfalls that have a large volume of flow. Cascade refers to small waterfalls, particularly ones that bounce along the rock without free-falling. Rapids are small, interrupted sections of a river that exhibit white water. Broad waterfalls much wider than they are high are referred to as shoals. Inclined falls of water that never leave the rockface and are not appreciably interrupted by rocks are called slides.

Most large waterfalls develop a plunge pool, the size of which is determined by the rock's hardness, the force of the water, and the amount of time the waterfall remains in one place. The natural tendency of any river is to achieve as level a flow as possible. Thus, all waterfalls experience erosion that could someday reduce them to mere riffles, if the volume of flow is great enough.

While all waterfalls erode, one special type also moves. Caprock falls form where resistant rock overlies softer rock. The erosive action of the water tends to undercut the falls, creating an open space behind. Over time, chunks of the harder "cap" break off, and the process begins again. In this manner, the waterfall literally migrates upstream. In the southern Appalachians, this type of waterfall is most common along the Cumberland Plateau in Tennessee and Kentucky, although North Carolina has a few examples, most notably Linville Falls. It is believed that Linville Falls was once 12 miles downstream from its present location. Over many years, the waterfall gradually receded, cutting the Linville Gorge as it went. At its present location, the hard quartzite rock extends to the base of the falls, which will make further migration occur at a much slower pace.

Linville Falls is not the ideal example of a caprock waterfall. Those along the Cumberland Plateau are. The waterfalls of the Cumberland Plateau form where hard sandstone overlies softer limestone and shale. The undercutting is noticeably evident. Caprock waterfalls in North Carolina are composed of different types of rock and are not nearly as evident.

Also, just because a waterfall is undercut does not mean that it is a caprock waterfall. Numerous undercut waterfalls in North Carolina are merely the result of topography or of rock fracturing, from the constant freezing and thawing of the bedding planes. A few examples are Dry Falls, Moore Cove Falls, and Douglas Falls. In fact, if you visit the latter two, it should be evident that they would not be capable of undercutting even if very soft rock were present. The streams are simply too small.

The most famous example of a caprock waterfall is probably Niagara Falls, on the border of the United States and Canada. Surveys made there in 1842, 1875, 1886, 1890, 1905, 1927, and 1950 determined an average rate of recession of about 3 feet per year. At that rate, in less than 2,000 years, the cataract will be a mile farther upstream. Niagara Falls has the third-greatest annual volume of flow of any of the world's waterfalls. Only Guaíra Falls, on the border of Brazil and Paraguay, and Khone Falls, on the border of Kampuchea and Laos, have a greater annual discharge. The tremendous erosive force of these waterfalls cannot be used as a comparison. The waterfalls of North Carolina and the caprock falls along the Cumberland Plateau are eroding at a much slower rate.

The map on page 2 has a dot representing every waterfall I am aware of, public or private, in North Carolina. It is certain that additional falls exist, particularly on private property. Much more information is available for the national forests, national parks, and state parks than is available for private property, so it may be assumed that private lands contain a greater number of unknown waterfalls. Considering that the northern section of the North Carolina mountains is practically all under private ownership, it may also be assumed that several more waterfalls are present there.

This brings up the most often-asked question I hear: How many waterfalls are there in North Carolina?

No one will ever know for sure, but I'll try to give an estimate. The map shows the location of over 325 waterfalls. Factoring in information on geology, topography, precipitation, and property ownership, I would guess there to be at least an additional 200. This suggests over 500 significant waterfalls in North Carolina, and I would not be surprised if there are more. Notice that I said *significant* waterfalls. There are literally thousands of smaller drops and cascades all over the mountains.

Flora and Fauna

Waterfalls are not typically associated with plants and animals, yet a few falls are directly responsible for providing habitat for a number of species, some extremely rare. Several waterfalls in North Carolina support spray cliffs, globally rare natural communities that exist only in the constant spray of waterfalls. There are at least forty-three rare plant species in North Carolina associated with spray cliffs. Many of these plants are endemic, and several are disjunct from tropical regions. At least one, the dwarf polypody fern (*Grammitis nimbata*), is found nowhere else in North America.

You might assume that these plants would thrive in the constant spray, but this is not the case. Most plants are like people; they don't like to be continually bombarded with water. The plants of the spray cliff live in what might be referred to as the "spray zone," which lies just outside the area of heavy spray. The spray zone provides constant or near-constant moisture and a fairly constant temperature. A study at Dry Falls discovered a forty-two-degree difference between the open-air environment at the brink and the protected environment of the spray zone. It is this stable climate that contributes most to the presence of the plants.

It is human presence that contributes most to their decline. Fortunately for the plants' sake, most species are unattractive and easily overlooked. However, a few are showy and have been removed by people intent on transplanting them. These plants can exist only in the specific habitat in which they are found—certainly not in a backyard. The biggest threat is from trampling by people scrambling around the base and behind the falls. If you are concerned about protecting the environment, assume that all plants are rare and important, and use extreme care around waterfalls. If you are not concerned about protecting the environment, please do not visit any waterfall listed in this book.

Rock cliffs are home to a number of animal and plant species, including swallows, phoebes, hawks, bats,

salamanders—including the rare green salamander *Aneides aeneus*—a number of invertebrates, and a host of grasses, sedges, and wildflowers. This association is not a result of the waterfalls themselves, but rather of the environment in which they exist.

Waterfalls and cascades are also important for healthy stream life, as they oxygenate the water. The oxygenated water and deep plunge pools provide ideal habitat for mountain streams' most popular inhabitants—trout. Trout can be purchased at dozens of private farms across the mountains, but there is nothing like the thrill of catching one at a beautiful waterfall.

Of the three species of trout normally caught in North Carolina's streams, only the brook trout is native. Rainbow and brown trout were introduced in the late 1800s and have driven the smaller, less aggressive "brookies" farther and farther from their original range. As a result, harvesting of brook trout is strictly regulated.

Measuring Waterfalls

It may seem unusual to devote an entire section to measuring waterfalls, but a detailed treatment is necessary to clear up a few inconsistencies and some false information. For any given waterfall, it seems that every book, pamphlet, trail guide, and newspaper article gives a different measurement, some of which vary considerably. Depending on the source, Looking Glass Falls is between 60 and 85 feet, Rainbow Falls and Cullasaja Falls are either 150 or 200 feet, and Toxaway Falls varies from 123 to over 250 feet. And these are just a few examples.

You might think that even careless observation would result in more consistent measurements than these. The problem is that few waterfalls have been accurately measured, and it is very difficult to estimate their height. Our perception of distance is distorted when we look up or down, much the same way a lens distorts an image if it is not held perpendicular to the subject. Additionally, our judgment is often skewed by outside factors. The effort exerted to reach a waterfall, preconceived notions of its height, and even the beauty of the waterfall can affect judgment. But the main reason for widely different measurements is that most people are just not good at estimating distances, especially height.

Making accurate measurements presents unique challenges. The first problem is determining the top and bottom of a waterfall. This is obvious at some falls but impossible at most. Should the cascades at the top and bottom of the waterfall be included, or only the main drop? Almost every waterfall in North Carolina consists of cascades and slides, so they must be included, but at what point are they not part of the falls? If you have two distinct drops separated by a small pool, do you have one waterfall or two? How much distance must be between the drops for them to be considered two separate waterfalls? Suppose they are separated by cascades. How steep must these cascades be to unite the drops into one continuous waterfall?

These questions cannot be answered. Even if guidelines existed, they could not be applied to the great variety of North Carolina's waterfalls. And even if every waterfall had an obvious top and bottom, accurate measurement would still be a challenge.

Assuming a perfectly vertical waterfall with a distinct top and bottom, a number of approaches might be taken. An altimeter will measure the difference in elevation, but only very expensive ones are accurate to within less than a few feet. Most pocket models are graduated from 10 feet to a completely useless 200 feet. You could drop a line over the falls and get a very accurate measurement, but this would require climbing to the edge, which obviously is *not* an option.

If the distances from the viewer to the base and the top of the falls are known, a geometric formula—A equals the square root of C squared minus B squared, where C is the distance from the viewer to the top, B is the distance to the base, and A is the height of the waterfall—can be used to determine the height. The distances to the base and the top of the falls can be determined by using a surveyor's transit or a pocket rangefinder. Crude distances can be determined using your camera; focus on the top and bottom and read the distance scale on the lens barrel.

If the distance from the viewer to the base is the only known measurement, a special stick used by foresters to estimate the height of trees can help determine the height of the waterfall. Simply hold the stick at a specified distance and read the scale.

Another method is to attach a mirror to the end of a stick so that when you stand it up, the mirror is level with your eyes. Lay the stick on flat ground with the mirror pointing toward the falls and the end of the stick even with your heel. While standing erect, look into the mirror. Move back and forth—repositioning the stick at your heel each time you move—until you can see the top of the falls in the mirror. Then measure the distance from the mirror to the base of the falls. That measurement will be the same as the height.

All of these methods will give fairly close measurements. Extremely accurate measurements can be made using lasers and satellites, but few of us consider this an option. Remember that the methods described above are only accurate on the "perfect" waterfall, one that is absolutely vertical and has an obvious top and bottom. Also, for most of these methods, there has to be an unobstructed path from the base to the viewer, and the viewer must be at the same elevation as the base. Fewer than five waterfalls in this book meet these criteria.

The point of this discussion is to suggest that any

attempt to give accurate measurements of North Carolina's waterfalls would be futile. Even if I tried, the results could only be considered *my* measurements, not *the* measurements. Anyone else measuring the same waterfall using the same technique would likely arrive at a different conclusion because of their opinion of where to begin and end the measurements.

So how did I arrive at the figures given in this book? Consider them my best guess. I used different methods at different waterfalls, but overall, I simply estimated. For cascades and slides that do not have a steep vertical drop, the measurement usually represents the distance of the run, rather than the loss of elevation. All measurements should be considered accurate for comparison only. A waterfall listed at 50 feet will be higher than one listed at 40 feet and shorter than one listed at 60 feet. This may seem elementary, but given the problems detailed above, it will have to suffice. Anyway, it is not necessary to know a waterfall's height to the nearest foot to enjoy it.

Several waterfalls are reputed to be the highest in the southern Appalachians, with North Carolina's Whitewater Falls most often cited. Others are Amicalola Falls in Georgia, Crabtree Falls in Virginia, and Fall Creek Falls and Buckeye Falls, both in Tennessee. Glassmine Falls in North Carolina is listed by the National Park Service at over 800 feet, which definitely puts it in contention. All of these waterfalls except Fall Creek Falls and Glassmine Falls are of the cascading type and are thus practically impossible to measure accurately. There is simply no way to determine the proper starting and stopping points, and whether the drop can be considered one single waterfall. If each of these examples is to be considered a single waterfall, then I can add several to the list. Flat Laurel Creek and Thompson River, both in North Carolina, have a series of falls and cascades that extend over 0.5 mile. Also, Raven Cliff Falls in South Carolina is a very high combination of drops and cascades that would surely have to be considered.

I realize this discussion has created more questions than it has answered, so I'll try to reach a conclusion as to which is the highest waterfall in the southern Appalachians.

First, we can eliminate Glassmine Falls and Buckeye Falls. Both are on tiny creeks that completely dry up at times. The highest single, free-falling waterfall in the East is probably Fall Creek Falls in Tennessee, with a vertical drop of 256 feet. A few waterfalls have vertical drops that are higher, but the water hugs the rock on the way down. The highest vertical drop that is not free-falling is probably Hickory Nut Falls in North Carolina, even though I believe it is shorter than its "officially" listed height of 404 feet. Among cascading-type waterfalls, there are simply too many variables to determine whether one is higher or longer than another.

My choice is Whitewater Falls. It may not be technically as high or long as a few others, but considering the large volume of flow, the large mass of solid, continuous rock, the high, free-falling drops, and the unrestricted viewing from top to bottom, there can be no argument that it is one massive waterfall over its entire 411 feet.

Photograph on opposite page—

Elk Falls
Nikon F3, 75-300mm zoom lens, polarizing filter stacked on warming filter, f/22 at 1 second, Fujichrome Velvia.

This photo was made from the large rock just downstream of the falls. I mounted the zoom lens on my tripod, sat down at a comfortable spot, and shot several rolls of film from this one vantage point. The lens covers such a range that I was able to shoot numerous compositions with just this one setup.

Photographing
Waterfalls

Elk Falls

Photographing Waterfalls

Waterfalls are among the most popular of nature subjects to photograph. Nearly everyone who visits them brings a camera of some sort. Their photographic knowledge and the equipment they own vary considerably, but they all share a common goal: to take the best possible pictures of waterfalls.

To some, it may seem that waterfalls should be easy to photograph. After all, they are always there. Animals move, fall colors may be drab, and wildflowers may not be in bloom, but waterfalls can always be counted upon to "pose" for the photographer as long as he needs. It is true that waterfalls are not going anywhere—at least not fast enough to be of concern—but experienced photographers know that it is not a simple matter to photograph them. Equipment, film, exposure, lighting, and composition are but a few of the factors that contribute to the quality of the photograph.

This chapter explains photography as it applies to waterfalls only. It also assumes a basic knowledge of photography. Details on general nature photography are beyond the scope of this book. For background reading on the subject, I recommend *The Nature Photographer's Complete Guide to Professional Field Techniques*, by John Shaw, published by Amphoto and available at your local camera store.

Do not think that just because you only have a point-and-shoot camera, your photographs cannot be improved. Much of the information presented here applies to all equipment, from disposable cameras to large-format systems costing thousands of dollars. However, the 35mm photographer will gain the most from this discussion.

Equipment

Cameras

The most often-asked question among people interested in photographing waterfalls is, What camera should I use? If you only take pictures a few times a year for the family photo album, I recommend a simple point-and-shoot camera. Good-quality ones can be bought for around $100. If you only shoot landscapes and want the best possible image quality for reproduction in books, calendars, and wall prints, consider a view camera system. A good system costs several thousand dollars. In my opinion, the best all-around, and certainly the most versatile, camera is the 35mm Single-Lens Reflex (SLR). These cameras accept interchangeable lenses and a wide variety of accessories for nearly anything you might wish to photograph.

Deciding which 35mm SLR to buy is another question altogether. The most important consideration is not which brand to choose—all of the major companies have dependable products—but which one offers the features you need and the accessories you may need later on. Listed below are the main features I look for in a camera.

Manual Exposure

Nearly every camera manufactured today features automatic exposure. Make sure that the one you buy also has a manual override. This is very important in many situations, and especially so for waterfalls. I only rarely use my cameras in the fully automatic mode.

Depth-of-Field Preview

Indispensable for serious photography, this feature allows you to see the depth of field by means of manually stopping the lens down to the shooting aperture. It is also useful for determining if there are any distracting hotspots in the scene, such as sunlight reflecting off wet rocks.

Mirror Lock

When you take a picture with an SLR, at the instant the shutter is released, the mirror which directs light to the viewfinder moves up out of the way to allow light to reach the film. Because it must move very quickly, it slaps against the pentaprism, increasing the possibility of camera shake. A mirror lock allows you to move the mirror up before the shutter is released, eliminating the possibility of a blurred picture. The vibration is most evident when using shutter speeds in the range of $1/4$ to $1/30$ of a second, and especially so in closeup photography. It is not as crucial to lock the mirror for wide-angle scenes such as waterfalls, but it's a good habit to get into. Unfortunately, only the most expensive cameras offer this feature.

Long Shutter Speeds

Some cameras only offer shutter speeds as long as one second. This is very limiting, especially in waterfall photography, when exposures can be several seconds. Choose a camera which goes down to at least eight seconds, and preferably thirty seconds. It's true that the bulb setting on most cameras allows you to manually open the shutter as long as desired, but it's much easier to use the camera's preset speed.

ISO Override

Most cameras today have what is called DX Film Coding. An internal scanner reads the bar code on the film canister to determine the proper ISO (film speed) setting. If, after running an exposure test, you discover your camera is overexposing or underexposing your pictures, you can use the ISO override to correct the problem. If, for example, you are using ISO 50 film and your camera always overexposes by $1/2$ stop, you would simply change the ISO setting to 80. You will have fooled the camera into allowing $1/2$ stop less light to reach the film.

If you want to "push" your film (expose it at a value greater than its ISO setting), an ISO override saves you from having to make additional calculations.

Ability to Accept an External Shutter Release

Either a cable, an electronic, or a wireless remote shutter release is essential for vibration-free photography when using a tripod.

100-Percent Viewing

Most cameras only allow you to view approximately 90 percent of what will actually be recorded on film. This can be quite annoying if you frame tightly; you might get your film back only to discover some unwanted object at the edge of the scene. This is why I much prefer those cameras with full viewing. Unfortunately, as with mirror lock, only the most expensive cameras have this feature.

These are the features which will be useful in waterfall photography. There are others which I consider important for general use. I recommend that you carefully examine the type of photography you want to do and determine which features you need to accomplish this. Among the other features I prefer are a built-in motor drive, the ability to accept TTL flash, a built-in spotmeter, and an exposure-compensation dial.

Lenses

A big advantage of the 35mm SLR is the wide range of lenses available for it. When choosing which one to buy, it is important to remember that it is the lens which is responsible for the sharpness of the photo. It is true that today's lenses are quite close in sharpness from brand to brand, but there are some lemons out there. However, you cannot go wrong with the lenses from the major companies, such as Nikon or Canon. And if price is a major consideration, it is hard to beat the aftermarket lenses from Sigma, Tamron, and Tokina.

For waterfall photography, the most often-used lens is a wide-angle. Several focal lengths fall into this range: 20mm, 24mm, 28mm, and 35mm. If I could have only one lens for waterfalls, it would be a 24mm. Longer lenses, such as 35mm and 50mm, are useful with small falls and those you can't get close to. The 20mm is often used to frame an entire waterfall when the photographer is too close to use a 24mm. I have often wished that I owned an even wider lens.

Telephoto lenses in the 100mm to 300mm range are useful for what I refer to as "isolation" shots—that is, compositions which include only a small portion of a larger scene. This usually means isolating the cascades at the bottom of a waterfall.

Zoom lenses can be a lifesaver in situations which don't allow you to move closer to or farther from the subject. This is often the case with waterfalls, where changing your position may mean getting wet or falling off a cliff. Zooms in the range of 80mm to 200mm and 75mm to 300mm are great for isolation shots, while the 20mm to 35mm lens is ideal for overall pictures.

The big disadvantages of most zooms are the lack of depth-of-field scales and the rotation of the front element during focusing. The latter is an aggravation when using polarizers and other filters which must remain in a fixed position. Fortunately, manufacturers are beginning to hear the pleas of photographers, and a few now offer zooms which remain stationary. The depth-of-field scale is a means of determining the depth of field without looking through the lens. It is most helpful with wide-angle lenses when you want to get as close as possible to the foreground and still keep everything in focus.

Another disadvantage of zooms is their susceptibility to flare due to the increased number of glass elements. This is especially noticeable when shooting sunrises and sunsets. A lens hood helps reduce flare and should be used on all lenses, fixed and zoom.

Specialty Lenses

The 50mm lens most closely matches the angle of view seen by the human eye. A photograph taken with this lens held perpendicular to the subject will appear normal, with no apparent distortions. With a wide-angle lens, this is not always the case. If you have ever photographed a 100-foot waterfall only to have it appear 10 feet on film, you have learned a fundamental lesson in optics: the wider the angle of view, the more distorted the image. This is most often seen in photos of buildings that look as though they are falling over backward, or with trees and lighthouses which appear to be leaning left or right. The effect is greatly pronounced when the lens is tilted up or down.

There is little you can do. Centering the lighthouse will eliminate it from leaning left or right but not from leaning backward. Holding the lens perpendicular will stop it from leaning backward, but unless you are far away, you will not be able to include all of it. Besides, you do not want to be restricted to only a few possible compositions.

With waterfalls, photographers often use a wide-angle lens from the base of the falls and tilt it up to include the top. If you look through the viewfinder when planning such a shot, you will notice that as you tilt the lens up, the waterfall appears to lean backward. Taking the picture from a point midway up the falls with a 50mm lens would eliminate all apparent distortions, but this is rarely possible.

Otherwise, the only way to prevent these distortions would be to keep the film plane perpendicular to the waterfall and somehow shift only the lens. This is one reason why view cameras are so popular; they actually have this capability. Lenses can be moved in complete independence of the film plane, allowing for almost unlimited control of distortions and depth of field.

Short of buying a view camera system, is there anything the 35mm photographer can do? Yes. There actually are a few lenses made specifically for this purpose. Canon's Tilt/Shift (T/S) lenses and Nikon's Perspective Control (PC) lenses permit the lens to be shifted off-center to the film plane. With one of these lenses, that 100-foot waterfall will look 100 feet on film. Nikon offers 35mm and 28mm lenses, while Canon's line includes 24mm, 35mm (shift only), 45mm, and 90mm lenses.

Anything over 28mm is often too long for waterfalls, so I recommend either the Nikon 28mm PC or the Canon 24mm T/S lens. The Canon lens has a few advantages. Besides being the ideal focal length, it is an auto-diaphragm lens, as opposed to Nikon's manual-diaphragm lens; with a manual-diaphragm lens, you have to manually open the aperture to its widest setting for composing, then manually close it to the chosen setting for metering and shooting. More important, the Canon lens incorporates a tilting feature. While this feature is not useful on waterfalls, the possibilities for other applications are alluring. By tilting the lens, you can achieve complete depth of field in, say, a field of wildflowers at a wide-open aperture.

Of course, these lenses are not interchangeable; the Canon lens only works on a Canon body. This means that if you are a Nikon shooter, as I am, you not only have to buy a $1,000-plus lens, but also a body to go with it. Still, for serious waterfall work, I consider the 24mm T/S lens to be indispensable.

Tripods

After the camera and lens, the most important piece of equipment for photographing waterfalls is the tripod. Don't think you can achieve satisfactory results without one. You cannot. A tripod is necessary for most nature photography and absolutely essential for waterfalls.

Tripods offer several advantages besides ensuring sharp images during long exposures. Too often, people approach a scene and, after a few seconds of admiring it, pull out their camera, snap a picture, and go on their way. Quality work is achieved with a slow, studied approach. A tripod demands this. It slows you down and forces you to think about what you are doing. It allows you to carefully scan a scene for composition and to make sure there are no distracting elements jutting in on the edges. This is not possible if you hand-hold the camera.

Just as important as using a tripod is choosing the right one. Lightweight, flimsy models are almost worse than nothing at all. As a general rule, the larger and heavier a tripod is, the better support it will give, though there are a few good medium-sized ones available. The best for the money is the Bogen 3021, a very popular model and my standard tripod for years until I upgraded to the ten-pound Slik Professional. I still use the 3021 for long backpacking trips.

Filters

Filters are perhaps the most misunderstood and improperly used of all photo accessories. I recommend using them only when you have a specific reason to do so and avoiding any filter which drastically alters the scene. Also, you should always buy the best filter you can afford. It just doesn't make sense to place a cheap piece of glass in front of an expensive lens. Though I own quite a few filters, I use only five for my waterfall photography.

Polarizing Filter

This is by far my most often-used filter. It is essential for eliminating distracting reflections from water, wet rocks, and leaves. It also creates an image with greater color saturation.

Warming Filter

Scenes photographed on overcast days or in open shade sometimes have a cool, bluish tint. Warming filters eliminate this coolness. They come in three strengths, designated 81A, 81B, and 81C, with 81A having a faint amber tint, while 81C has a definite yellow cast. I use an 81B for most of my work.

Neutral-Density Filter

If you shoot waterfalls on sunny days, you may discover that there is simply too much light to allow the slow shutter speed required to produce a silky effect. In that case, you need a neutral-density filter, which will cut the amount of light reaching the film while not altering the color. They are available in a variety of strengths, with one-, two-, and three-stop densities being the most common. I rarely use these filters. I try to avoid shooting on sunny days, and when I do, I almost always use a polarizing filter, which itself cuts about two stops of light.

Skylight Filter

Many photographers keep a skylight filter on their lens at all times for protection. I do not. Any filter, regardless of quality, degrades the image to some extent and increases the likelihood of flare. Besides, I am very careful with my cameras. Shooting in the spray of a waterfall is a situation when I *do* use a skylight filter. At those times, I need to protect the front element from moisture and from scratches due to continuous wiping.

Graduated Neutral-Density Filter

Unlike neutral-density filters, these filters are ½ clear and ½ neutral density. They are most useful in shooting sunrises and sunsets, when you need to darken the sky while not affecting the foreground. I have found them to be occasionally useful for waterfalls as well. During early-morning or evening hours, the sun often illuminates the foliage at the top of the falls while the falls and the foreground are in shade. A carefully placed graduated neutral-density filter can save the day. They are available in one-, two-, and three-stop densities and in square and round shapes. I recommend using a square filter (sized to fit the Cokin Filter Holder), because you will need to adjust it up and down. I have found the three-stop filter to be the most useful.

Film

The most often-asked question after, What camera should I use? is, What film should I use? This is not easily answered, because it depends on what your needs are. I can tell you that if you have any desire to sell your photos for use in books, magazines, and calendars, you will need to shoot slide film. Editors demand it. I also like slides because I know the exposures will be exactly as I created them, good or bad. With negative film, you never know when the lab technician has altered the final print to match *his* standards.

Regardless of whether you shoot prints or slides, you definitely want to use a fine-grained film (ISO 25–100). My film of choice is Fujichrome Velvia, which has an ISO rating of 50, though I believe it is actually closer to 40. To my eyes, this is the finest film on the market in terms of color and sharpness.

Exposure

Choosing the proper exposure can be tricky and is best learned by trial and error. If you are not comfortable with the basics, I recommend reading *How to Photograph Birds*, by Larry West (see appendix). Though it is a book on photographing birds, the section on exposure is the best I've seen anywhere.

One thing you should not do is blindly rely on your camera's automatic-exposure system to make the decision for you. Automatic cameras give correct exposures only with average-toned subjects. If you photograph something that is lighter or darker than average in tonality, you will have to compensate. This is why you need a camera with manual override. Some of the newer cameras have highly sophisticated metering systems that can actually compensate on their own if the light or dark area does not take up a large portion of the frame. These cameras work well in most situations, but you should learn exposure for those times when they don't.

The problem with waterfalls is that they are usually large in size and rarely medium in tone. White water, reflections, dark rocks, and dark leaves all "fool" automatic cameras. The easiest method to determine the correct exposure is to meter a medium-toned object that is in the same light as the waterfall. Foliage and dry rocks are a possibility. If there is no medium-toned object, you can meter an object of a different tone and compensate. I often meter the whitest portion of the waterfall and compensate by opening up (increasing exposure) from $^2/_3$ to $1^2/_3$ stops. Another possibility is to meter the rhododendron leaves which are found at most falls. They are generally $^1/_2$ stop darker than medium, so I compensate by stopping down (decreasing exposure) $^1/_2$ stop. I avoid metering dark and wet rocks, as it is difficult to determine the proper amount of compensation. Be sure to place any filters on the lens *before* taking a meter reading.

When I meter the water itself, I never use a spotmeter. Spotmeters read only a very small portion of the scene, and the readings can fluctuate wildly with moving white water. It's impossible to determine an accurate exposure. I use the center-weighted metering pattern, which tends to average things out. Of course, I still have to compensate for the white tonality by opening up from $^2/_3$ to $1^2/_3$ stops. Likewise, the matrix and multisegment metering patterns will not give a proper exposure of a waterfall without compensating, but I find it difficult to determine how much compensation is necessary with these patterns. I use the matrix system for many situations, but not for waterfalls. Also, I never use hand-held meters. There are simply too many variables to compensate for, and there is no advantage gained; the metering systems built into today's cameras are just as good.

A common problem is the "washing out" of the water into a white mass devoid of detail. Waterfalls with a large flow of water, or those in which a large amount of water passes through a small area, require a fast shutter speed to prevent this. How fast varies from waterfall to waterfall; it is a good idea to keep careful notes until you feel comfortable choosing. I generally avoid speeds slower than $1/30$ of a second on large, powerful falls and a few seconds on cascades with a large amount of white water. Anytime you meter something other than the water itself, it's a good idea to stop down $1/3$ stop from the chosen exposure to prevent the water from "hotspotting."

Another aggravation, particularly on sunny days, is the wide range in the light value between highlights and shadows. If the range is great, there is nothing you can do; the film simply cannot handle the extreme contrast. Take your pictures early in the morning or late in the evening, or come back on an overcast day. If you do take a picture under such unfavorable circumstances and you're using slide film, expose for the highlights and let the shadows go black. With negative film, it is generally better to expose for the shadows.

The aperture/shutter-speed combination you choose will have a definite impact on the photograph. You want an aperture which will give complete depth of field from near to far. I cannot think of any situation in which you would want part of a waterfall scene to be out of focus. Determining the shutter speed is not as simple as just matching a speed with a particular aperture. Fast speeds "freeze" the water, rendering a feeling of power. Slow speeds give the water a silky look, conveying a sense of motion.

Which is preferable is entirely a matter of choice, though there are a few rules to follow. Do not use slow speeds with large, powerful falls or those with a large volume of water. As mentioned previously, this tends to "wash out" the water into a white mass. Likewise, it is generally best to avoid very fast speeds with small, delicate falls. These seem to benefit from the silky look. As a starting point, use speeds of $1/125$ of a second or faster to freeze the motion and $\frac{1}{2}$ second or slower to give a silky look.

To be honest, I usually don't give much thought to whether my shutter speed will freeze the motion or lend a silky look. I'm more concerned with choosing a setting that won't overexpose the water or underexpose the surroundings, while giving me complete depth of field. That's enough to worry about.

Composition

I am always bewildered by photographers who shoot all their photos from one vantage point, never trying different angles of view. Spend some time exploring different shooting locations with different lenses. Don't be afraid to offer a new look to the scene.

There are a few guidelines you should consider when composing your photos. Remember that these are not rules cut in granite; use your own judgement. In fact, the best advice I can give is to make your pictures the way you feel is best, rather than worrying about what anyone else says. However, art directors and editors demand fairly close adherence to accepted standards of composition.

There is one rule that should always be followed: Never include anything that doesn't help the composition. Beginning photographers often try to include too much. Mount your camera on a tripod and carefully scan the scene for anything that isn't necessary, especially distracting leaves and branches jutting in from the sides. The waterfall should be the principal subject, and everything else—trees, rocks, pools, cascades, sky—should be used in moderation to enhance it. An exception comes when shooting from far away, such as photographing Second Falls from the Blue Ridge Parkway. In such a case, you are shooting a mountain scene that includes a waterfall. You are using a waterfall to enhance a landscape, rather than the reverse.

Another rule is to avoid centering horizons. For the

purposes of this discussion, the "horizon" is the horizontal line formed by the bottom of the waterfall. Center this line only if it does not stretch across the frame from edge to edge.

An image's strongest compositional points are at the intersections of lines drawn to divide the frame into horizontal and vertical thirds. In theory, you should place the strongest part of the scene on one of these imaginary intersections. In practice, this is not always possible with something as large as a waterfall, though it will work with foreground matter, such as rocks or small cascades.

A common practice among landscape photographers is using tree branches to frame the scene. This is quite effective with waterfalls, as long as the top and bottom are not completely covered by the branches and there is enough depth of field to keep everything in focus.

One compositional problem you will discover is that very often, the best vantage point is the middle of the stream. If it's summertime, you can simply slip off your shoes and wade in. But if it's winter, the last thing you want to do is get wet. For cold-weather waterfall photography, I use a pair of over-the-boot hip waders available from Leonard Rue Enterprises (see the appendix). These waders are very compact and lightweight. I keep a pair in my pack at all times; I have found them indispensable for crossing streams. Many of the trails in this book require fording streams much too large to rock-hop. A word of warning is in order here: always use extreme caution when wading into streams. Stay away from swift currents, and never cross above dangerous falls or cascades.

You needn't worry about setting up your tripod in the water. It will suffer no ill effects as long as you wash off any mud or sand before retracting the legs. Something you do need to be concerned about is camera shake due to moving water. Try to set up away from swift currents, and make sure the tripod's legs are placed securely in the stream bottom.

Though it should be obvious, it is worth noting that the majority of waterfall photographs should be taken in a vertical composition. A horizontal framing often includes unnecessary elements and may not allow you to include all of the falls. There are many exceptions, however, so be sure to explore all the possibilities.

Lighting

Lighting can make the difference between a good photograph and a great photograph. You should always be aware of the light and how it affects the scene.

A common misconception is that the best time for photography is a bright, sunny day. On the contrary, this is actually one of the worst times to photograph many subjects, especially waterfalls. Sunny days produce dark shadows and bright highlights. This effect is pronounced with waterfalls, as the sun often reflects brightly off the white water, while there may be shadows to the side. Film simply cannot handle this contrast range. The solution on clear days is to shoot early in the morning or late in the evening, when the waterfall is not illuminated by direct light.

Overcast days are excellent for nature photography. The cloud layer acts as a giant diffuser, filling in the shadows to provide even lighting. Overcast days are ideal for shooting waterfalls, as long as you follow an important rule: Don't include the sky in the photo, especially if there is nothing separating it from the top of the falls.

My favorite lighting conditions are during a heavy fog or a light, misty rain. Photos made at these times have a dramatic, ethereal look. Pay close attention to the lighting at the top of the falls when shooting in fog. If it is dark gray, all is well. If it is fairly light, as is often the case, it may be recorded as a washed-out white. Try changing your position so there is something other than sky at the top. Be aware that fog can be highly reflective and that it requires some exposure compensation. I often open up from $^1/_3$ to $^2/_3$ of a stop.

Rainbows, Moonbows, and Sunstars

Rainbows

A common sight at some waterfalls, rainbows are formed when rays from the sun are refracted and reflected by water droplets, which act like tiny prisms. It should be obvious, then, that in order to see one, the sun must be shining. But as stated earlier, this is one of the worst times to photograph waterfalls.

There are very few falls which have all the conditions necessary to produce a good rainbow photo. One which does—not surprisingly, given its name—is Rainbow Falls. This waterfall produces a great amount of spray and thus a large rainbow, and it is viewed from an open area, which reduces the contrast. By changing your position between the base and the upper trail, you should be able to see a rainbow any time of the year when the spray is heavy enough. However, certain times and vantage points are better than others. It's best to photograph the rainbow from the upper trail; the high vantage point improves the chances of seeing a large rainbow, and the rainbow will be in a better compositional position. Look for it between midmorning and early afternoon.

A polarizing filter greatly intensifies the colors in any rainbow. Look through the lens while rotating the filter to the desired intensity. Be careful, though; rotate it too much and you will completely erase the rainbow.

Moonbows

A moonbow is the same phenomenon as a rainbow, with one major difference: light rays from the sun reflect off the moon before being refracted and reflected in the water droplets. As with rainbows, the conditions necessary for the occurrence of moonbows are fairly common, but the conditions necessary to view and photograph them are rare indeed. Moonbows undoubtedly occur at several waterfalls in North Carolina, but to my knowledge, they can only be seen at Rainbow Falls.

To see and photograph a moonbow, a number of requirements must be met: the moon must be at the proper altitude and position in the sky; it must be full, or nearly so; there can be no clouds in the sky; and the waterfall must produce a heavy amount of spray. It is a lucky person indeed who has witnessed a moonbow. To improve your chance of seeing one at Rainbow Falls, visit during September or October, which seem to be when the moon is in the best position, and wait several hours after moonrise to allow the moon to reach the proper altitude. Look for a moonbow from the upper trail, but don't expect to see the colors. It will probably appear white because of the eye's inability to discern subtle colors at night. Film does not have this limitation, so a photograph will display the colors.

I am not certain of the proper approach to take in shooting the moonbow at Rainbow Falls, since I've not been lucky enough to photograph it myself, but photographer Donny Brake has captured the moonbow at Cumberland Falls in Kentucky with a technique he calls "the three fours." Using a wide-angle lens and

ISO 400 film, he sets the aperture to f/4 and opens the shutter for four minutes. I can tell you that an exposure of four minutes at Rainbow Falls would thoroughly drench your camera, but you could probably quickly wipe the lens a few times during the exposure without affecting the image.

If you use an exposure longer than four minutes or a lens longer than 35mm, the moonbow will be recorded as an undefined blob of color. You can open the aperture to f/2.8, but remember that you will have little depth of field, and that it is very difficult to focus in moonlight.

Finally, it's not a good idea to hike alone at night, so invite an adventuresome friend.

Sunstars

There are several waterfalls in this book which you can safely walk behind. When the sun is shining on the water, you have the perfect opportunity to shoot sunstars. Sunstar photographs are photos of the sun with sharply defined rays. Special filters are available for this, though you can easily accomplish the task without one. Besides, these filters create star beams on every highlight in the scene, which seems unnatural to me. All you need is a wide-angle, fixed-focal-length lens (zoom lenses produce horrible flare when pointed at the sun). Stop the lens down as far as it will go to create the longest possible rays.

The idea is to compose a scene which includes the falling water with the sun shining through it. It's a good idea to include a portion of the overhanging ledge to add stability. I especially look for sunstar opportunities in the winter, when there are icicles hanging from the ledges.

The sun's light is consistent, so your exposures should not vary much. For a starting point, try $1/60$ of a second at f/22 using ISO 50 film, and bracket from there (shoot an exposure at a value over and under this setting).

This is one situation in which you should not use a

Sunstar at Bridal Veil Falls
Nikon F3, 24mm lens, f/22 at $1/30$ second, Kodachrome 25.

Bridal Veil Falls provides an excellent opportunity for this type of photo, particularly in very cold weather when there are always icicles hanging from the bluff.

tripod. Because of the potential for eye damage, you want to quickly compose and shoot. You should never look directly at the sun through the viewfinder. A trick I use is to hold the depth-of-field preview button while I'm composing. With the lens at f/22, the sun does not appear as bright, and the strain on my eyes is lessened.

You certainly don't have to be behind a waterfall to shoot a sunstar, but you do need a light-colored object in the scene to lessen the contrast. Snow, ice, sand, and water all work well.

Shooting in Spray and Rain

A real problem at many waterfalls is dealing with the

constant spray. The problem is compounded by the fact that the spray usually comes directly toward the front of the lens, rather than falling from above, as rain does. If the spray is fine enough and the exposure short enough, you can get by with simply wiping the lens between exposures and drying the camera after the session. If the spray is heavy, or if it is raining, you need to take other measures.

During a light rain, I just hold an umbrella over my camera. I carry a diffusion umbrella with me at all times for shooting closeups; I simply sprayed it with silicone to make it waterproof. I also made a special holder for it that has a hole bored in one end for the shaft and a ¼-20 thread in the other to fit a small ball head that attaches to a Bogen Super Clamp. When I clamp this assembly onto the tripod leg, I can keep out the rain and have both hands free. When I'm ready to release the shutter, I loosen a small retaining knob and hold the umbrella in my hand. It is very important not to leave it attached during the actual exposure, because it would act as a sail, transferring vibrations to the camera.

Using an umbrella is rather clumsy and is not adequate in heavy rains or blowing spray. For these situations, you need a camera cover. The simplest arrangement is to wrap the camera in a plastic bag, securing it with rubber bands. This is awkward at best and does not protect the front element. Custom camera covers are available to fit specific camera/lens combinations, but they do not allow you to see the camera's controls or protect the front element. Underwater camera housings completely protect the camera and lens, but they are awkward and expensive, and you still need to continually wipe the lens port.

The best method is to use a combination of all of the above. First, screw a skylight filter on the lens. When it gets wet, you can continually wipe it without fear of scratching the lens. It's no big deal if you have to replace the filter every once in a while. Next, devise some method of protecting the camera. Try using clear vinyl, available at any automobile upholstery shop. Secure it to the lens with tape or rubber bands, or get real fancy and fashion a Velcro closure.

I carried this whole idea a giant step farther by making a rig that fastens to the lens with a Cokin P-Series filter holder, with a quickly removable skylight filter installed. I compose and meter fully protected from moisture, and when I'm ready to release the shutter, I slide the skylight filter out of the way. Thus, I am only exposing the lens during the actual exposure, and I don't have to continually wipe the filter.

The advantage of using clear vinyl is that it is very tough and allows you to easily see all of the camera's controls. Also, some cameras depend on natural light to allow you to read the aperture ring when looking through the viewfinder. When using telephoto lenses that have built-in hoods, wrapping vinyl around the hood is my first choice for moisture protection. The hood protects the front element, so it is not necessary to add a skylight filter.

Finally, when photographing in spray or rain, make sure you have several clean, soft cloths, lens tissue, and a large bulb blower in your pack.

Four Seasons of Waterfall Photography

Winter

There are several reasons to photograph during winter. It is the least popular season, so you are likely to have the waterfall to yourself. And there is less foliage to blow around during long exposures. Of course, the main reason is the opportunity to include snow and ice. Snow is much lighter than medium tone and must be compensated for to prevent it from appearing muddy. For very white snow, take a meter reading and open up two stops. For darker snow, only one stop may be necessary.

During long periods of subfreezing temperatures, many small falls completely freeze over from top to bottom, creating unique photo opportunities. Ice has a lighter tone than medium, though it is difficult to determine the correct compensation. It is best to meter a medium-toned object to get the exposure.

Spring

Spring offers more opportunities than any other season. In mid-April, trees begin showing leaves, and for several weeks, the leaves have that "virgin green" look. This is a perfect time to shoot waterfalls which are surrounded by deciduous trees. Dogwoods are also in bloom at this time, and you should enjoy this show while it lasts. Unless something is done soon, this beautiful harbinger of spring will be eradicated from our forests by acid rain and the dogwood anthracnose fungus.

Many falls have good wildflower displays on the surrounding banks. These make ideal foregrounds; just be sure to arrive early, before the wind picks up.

Perhaps the perfect complements to a waterfall are mountain laurel and rhododendron. Mountain laurel blooms from about mid-May to mid-June, depending on the elevation, and is common at many waterfalls. Rhododendron blooms from about mid-May to mid-July, depending on the species and the elevation, and is abundant at most falls. Throughout this book, I make reference to including rhododendron blooms in your photos.

It is my hope that photographers will not destroy the very subjects they strive to record as alive and beautiful. A few years ago, I was driving along Roaring Fork in the Smokies when I noticed an ideal photo opportunity. A small dogwood in full bloom was growing at the perfect location to frame a small cascade. I slammed on the brakes, grabbed my gear, and ran to the bank, only to discover that someone had cut down the tree and stuck it in the bank to make his photos. Such action is not only unethical and illegal (it was on national-park property), but it gives all photographers a bad reputation as well.

Summer

Summer is the worst season for photographing waterfalls. The leaves are dull, the wildflowers are gone—though there are some good patches of cardinal flowers, jewelweed, and bee balm—and hordes of people congregate at the falls.

It is the best time, though, for recreation photos. If you're trying to sell your work, it's a good idea to include people in some of your images. Some waterfalls, such as Bridal Veil Falls and Sliding Rock, demand a human presence for the best representation.

Summer is also the best season for searching out salamanders in the streams.

Fall

Anyone who has visited North Carolina's waterfalls and experienced an autumn in the southern Appalachians knows what a special situation it is when the two are combined. This is one of the finest photo opportunities to be had. A warming filter will accentuate the yellows, golds, and oranges, while Tiffen's Enhancing Filter will saturate the red hues. A polarizer will cut reflections and saturate colors; it can be stacked on either a warming filter or Tiffen's Enhancing Filter. Do not stack all three at once.

The "peak" varies from year to year but is usually around the third week of October. High-elevation areas like Yellowstone Falls peak one to two weeks earlier than this, while low-elevation areas like Hanging Rock and South Mountains peak one to two weeks later than the average. It is much better to arrive too late than too early, as there will be fallen leaves on the rocks and in the pools.

The
Waterfalls

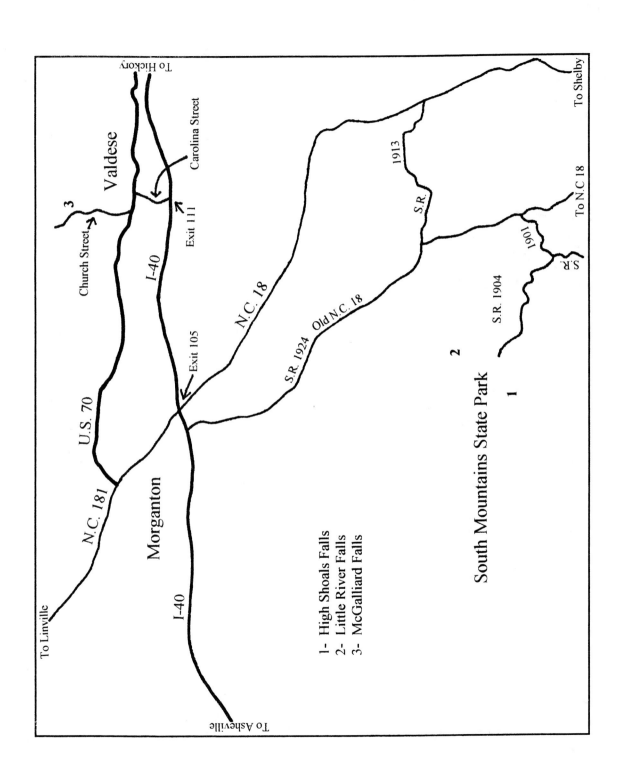

Morganton

Three waterfalls are located in the Morganton area, one near the town of Valdese, just east of Morganton, and two in South Mountains State Park, 18 miles south of Morganton.

South Mountains State Park is little-known except to trout fishermen, something to consider if you are looking for solitude. Though its peaks and waterfalls cannot compare with those farther west, the park is an impressive wilderness area.

High Shoals Falls *

River: Jacob's Fork
County: Burke
USGS quadrangle: Benn Knob
Landowner: South Mountains State Park
Height: About 75 feet
Beauty rating: 7
Trail length and difficulty: 1.25 miles; 4–7

Directions: South Mountains State Park is reached from Interstate 40 by taking Exit 105 onto N.C. 18 South. Drive 10.7 miles to S.R. 1913 (Sugar Loaf Road), on the right, then 4.1 miles on S.R. 1913 to where it ends at S.R. 1924 (old N.C. 18). Turn left and go 2.6 miles to S.R. 1901 (Ward's Gap Road). Turn right onto S.R. 1901 and follow it for 1.3 miles to S.R. 1904. Turn right and drive 3.5 miles to the parking area at the park office.

The trail begins at the park's picnic area, in front of the restrooms, and forks after about 0.4 mile. The right fork takes you to the top. The left fork takes you over a series of steps, bridges, and boardwalks to a viewing platform at the base.

High Shoals Falls
Nikon F3, 24mm lens, f/22 at 2 seconds, Fujichrome Velvia.

The water level was very high, resulting in tremendous spray. Rather than taking a position up front, in the brunt of the spray, I simply set up on the conveniently located viewing deck for this composition. I carefully placed the steps to lead the eye to the falls.

Photo Tips

You can effectively shoot from the observation deck or from a position directly in front, using the boulders as a foreground. Because the park is a unit of the state parks system, it does not open until 8:00 A.M. and closes around sunset. Plan on camping at least one night inside the park to allow yourself a chance to photograph during the morning and evening hours.

The premier attraction in South Mountains State Park, High Shoals Falls is popular among summer visitors as a place to cool off in the constant spray and splash in the pools. Visit in the winter and you will likely have the falls—and possibly the entire park—to yourself.

Jacob's Fork River once supported a large gristmill near the brink. Only a portion of the foundation remains.

Little River Falls

River: Little
County: Burke
USGS quadrangle: Casar
Landowner: South Mountains State Park, though the lower section is private
Height: Initial 20-foot drop, then several hundred feet of cascades to a final 15-foot drop
Beauty rating: 4 at initial drop
Trail length and difficulty: 1.5 miles; 5–9

Directions: From the parking area at South Mountains State Park, drive 0.4 mile back toward the park exit and park on the right. The trail begins on the opposite side of the road and climbs steeply for about 0.5 mile to a fork. Take the right fork and

follow the logging road to a crossing of Little River. Soon afterward, the road bears left at a clearing. Continue straight ahead on a faint trail that soon ends. From this point, it is a steep bushwhack toward the sound of the waterfall.

Do not attempt the climb to the lower falls. It is on private property, and the access is over a thin layer of soil on a steep rockface. One bad step, especially in wet weather, and you will destroy a fragile environment—and very likely go over the falls.

Photo Tip

Pass up the photos on this one and spend extra time on Jacob's Fork River.

Little River Falls is the easternmost major waterfall in North Carolina south of Interstate 40.

McGalliard Falls *

River: McGalliard Creek
County: Burke
USGS quadrangle: Drexel
Landowner: Valdese Parks and Recreation Department
Height: 40 feet
Beauty rating: 6
Trail length and difficulty: 0.1 mile; 2

Directions: McGalliard Falls Park, near Valdese, is reached by driving east from Morganton on Interstate 40 for approximately 6 miles; take Exit 111 and turn right on Carolina Street, heading toward Valdese. Continue 1.1 miles to Main Street

(U.S. 70) and turn left. After 0.5 mile on Main Street, turn right on Church Street and continue 1.35 miles to the park entrance, on the right. Park in the paved parking area.

A paved road leads from the parking area at the park to a crossing of McGalliard Creek near the top of the falls. You can continue a short distance on a moderate path to the base; the path leads by a mill. An overlook of the falls and the mill is located behind the picnic shelter.

McGalliard Falls Park is a popular recreational facility featuring nature trails, tennis courts, softball fields, a picnic shelter, and a playground. Perhaps the biggest attractions are the waterfall and the gristmill. The mill has been completely rebuilt and contains no part of the original structure, although you can still see part of the pipe that was used to sluice water to the wheel. The current mill is operated only during special events. The park is open year-round from 8:00 A.M. to 10:00 P.M., but you can also visit the falls earlier in the morning.

Photo Tips

The falls are photogenic from the base as long as you don't include any of the dirty rocks at the edge of the pool. Use a horizontal composition to include the small falls on the right. The only way to include the mill is to shoot from the viewing platform behind the picnic shelter, but there is a sycamore tree blocking much of the view.

McGalliard Falls
Nikon F3, 28-70mm zoom lens, polarizing filter, f/22 at 4 seconds, Fujichrome Velvia.

I spent several minutes trying compositions that included various foreground elements but settled on this scene that tightly frames the falls. It was easily accomplished by setting up the tripod on the left bank, at the edge of the pool.

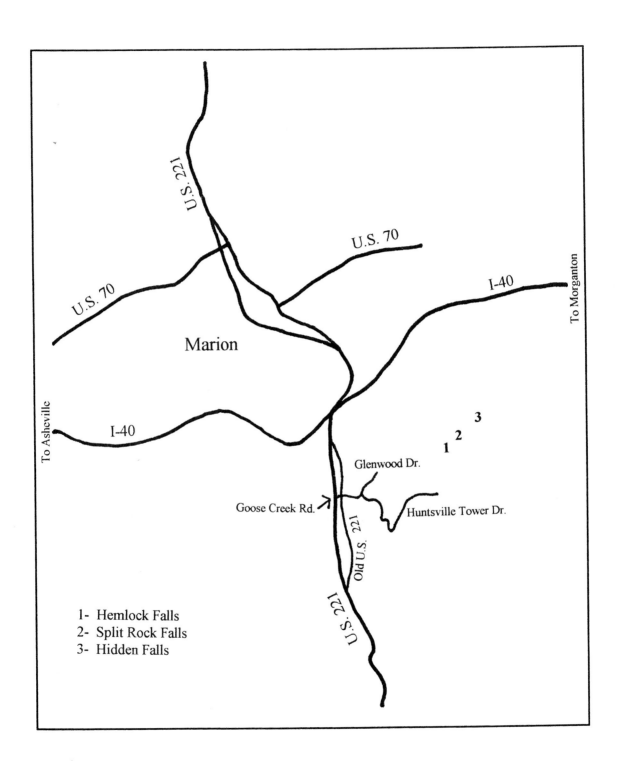

U.S. 221

U.S. 70

U.S. 70

U.S. 70

I-40

To Morganton

Marion

To Asheville

I-40

3

2

1

Glenwood Dr.

Goose Creek Rd.

Old U.S. 221

Huntsville Tower Dr.

U.S. 221

1- Hemlock Falls
2- Split Rock Falls
3- Hidden Falls

Marion

Bob's Creek Pocket Wilderness is located 5 miles south of Marion in McDowell County; the USGS quadrangle is Glenwood. This private wilderness area comprises some 1,067 acres featuring cascading streams, interesting rock formations, and large hemlock trees. A well-designed trail, North Carolina's first National Recreation Trail, winds through the forest and gives hikers the option of either an 8-mile or a 4-mile loop. A primitive campsite is located along the 8-mile loop. Three waterfalls are along the shorter route. Each is small and unphotogenic. With so many significant waterfalls less than an hour's drive from Marion, I do not recommend these unless you are planning to hike the trail anyway.

To get to the wilderness area from Interstate 40, take Exit 85 onto U.S. 221 South. Drive 1.9 miles, turn left on Goose Creek Road (S.R. 1153), and continue 0.2 mile to where it ends at Old U.S. 221 (S.R. 1786). Turn left, drive 200 feet, and turn right on Glenwood Drive (S.R. 1766). Follow Glenwood Drive for 0.4 mile, then turn right on Huntsville Drive (S.R. 1790). Huntsville Drive becomes Huntsville Tower Drive. After 1.8 miles, turn sharply left onto a small gravel road and follow it for 1.4 miles to a gate and a parking area.

The trail begins at the gate on the left-hand side. Follow it through a pine forest to a map board at 0.2 mile and a map box at 0.75 mile. The short loop begins at the map box. For the gentlest route, turn left. After approximately 0.8 mile, you will come to a sharp switchback to the left. Continue straight toward the sound of cascading water; you will reach Hemlock Falls 75 feet from the main trail.

Return to the main trail and continue to a fork 0.2 mile from Hemlock Falls. Turn right, cross the footbridge, and follow the trail 100 feet to Split Rock Falls.

It is about 0.6 mile farther on the main trail to Hidden Falls, so named because you can't see it until you're standing directly in front. Look for a rock bluff on the right and a side trail on the left that leads 50 feet to the falls.

It is approximately 1.1 miles along the loop back to the map box.

Shelf Fungi
Nikon F3, 105mm macro lens, f/22 at 2 seconds, Fujichrome Velvia.

The trail leading through Bob's Creek Pocket Wilderness provides numerous photo opportunities, but not for waterfalls. All three are small and unphotogenic. Concentrate your photography on other areas of the forest, particularly intimate scenes such as this.

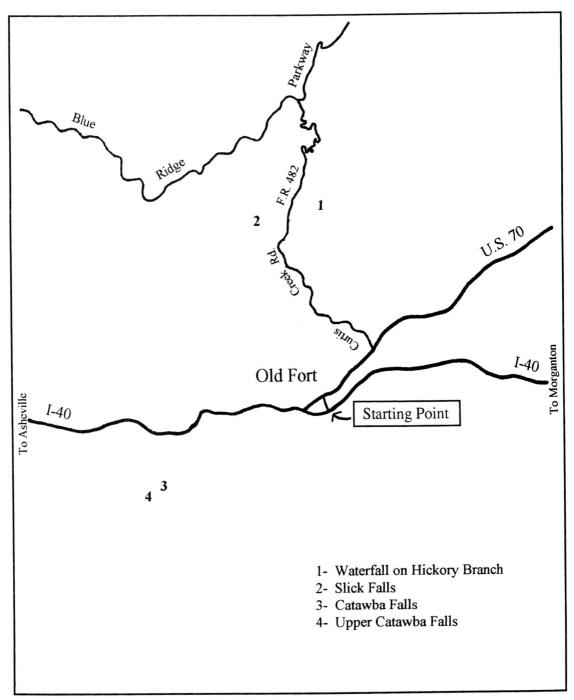

Blue

Ridge

Parkway

F.R. 482

Creek Rd.

Curtis

U.S. 70

I-40

To Morganton

Old Fort

I-40

To Asheville

Starting Point

2

1

3

4

1- Waterfall on Hickory Branch
2- Slick Falls
3- Catawba Falls
4- Upper Catawba Falls

The starting point is the Old Fort exit (Exit 73) on Interstate 40.

Old Fort

To many westbound travelers on Interstate 40, Old Fort is nothing more than the last town before the 5-mile climb up Youngs Ridge at the Blue Ridge escarpment. However, the town has much to offer, including two popular museums. The Mountain Gateway Museum offers pioneer artifacts, old log cabins, and a film depicting the early days of settlement. Grant's Museum displays the second-largest collection of Indian artifacts in western North Carolina, many of which were found near Old Fort.

Waterfall on Hickory Branch

River: Hickory Branch
County: McDowell
USGS quadrangle: Old Fort
Landowner: Pisgah National Forest,
    Grandfather Ranger District
Height: 25 feet
Beauty rating: 3
Trail length and difficulty: 0.8 mile; 4–8

Directions: From the starting point, head into downtown Old Fort on Catawba Avenue. The road ends at U.S. 70 after 0.4 mile. Turn right, drive 1.8 miles, and turn left onto Curtis Creek Road (S.R. 1227). Curtis Creek Road becomes F.R. 482 as it enters the national forest. Drive 5 miles to Curtis Creek Campsite and park on the far side of the creek at the pit toilet.

Begin the hike at the edge of the woods halfway between the pit toilet and Curtis Creek. There is a small concrete pad here. Ascend the ridge and descend the other side to reach Hickory Branch. Cross the branch, continue upstream, cross the stream again, and make a switchback in a drainage area. The waterfall is a short distance farther upstream. A steep climb down the bank is required to reach the base.

> **Photo Tip**
> Fallen trees and branches on and around the waterfall make it impossible to take a good photograph.

Although small and unphotogenic, this waterfall makes an excellent destination for campers at Curtis Creek Campsite. A trail leads directly from the campsite to join the trail described above at its first crossing of Hickory Branch.

Slick Falls

River: Slick Falls Branch
County: McDowell
USGS quadrangle: Old Fort
Landowner: Pisgah National Forest,
    Grandfather Ranger District
Height: Several hundred feet of cascades and slides
Beauty rating: 3
Trail length and difficulty: 0.9 mile; 10

Directions: I do not recommend this waterfall, but if you wish to see it, park on the side of the road 0.1 mile before the parking area for the waterfall on

Hickory Branch. The trail begins on the left directly opposite the camping area and a "No Horses Allowed in Campground" sign. It parallels the road briefly, then turns right and crosses a small branch 0.25 mile from the road. After another 0.1 mile, the roadbed bears left. Turn right and follow the trail upstream. Cross Slick Falls Branch and begin a steep ascent. At the third left-hand switchback, located in an area of small poplar trees, strike out to the right toward the sound of the falls. There is no trail from this point on, and the going is steep and dangerous.

Photo Tip
Save your film.

Hiking to Slick Falls is not recommended. If you do visit, be careful; this waterfall is appropriately named.

Catawba Falls
and Upper Catawba Falls

Conservationists lobbied for years to protect land on the headwaters of the Catawba River, southwest of Old Fort. Their efforts paid off in the late 1980s, when the National Forest Service acquired 1,028 acres, thus protecting two magnificent waterfalls. Unfortunately, the tract did not contain a public access, and there is currently no way to visit the falls without trespassing. The tract does adjoin Interstate 40, but it is illegal to stop along the road except in emergencies. And you wouldn't want to stop, anyway. This stretch winding up the escarpment is one of the most dangerous along the entire highway.

Efforts are under way to acquire trail access, and for this reason, I have included the waterfalls, minus directions. It is possible that by the time you read this, public access will be available. Contact the Grandfather Ranger District of Pisgah National Forest for information.

Catawba Falls *

River: Catawba
County: McDowell
USGS quadrangle: Moffitt Hill
Landowner: Pisgah National Forest,
    Grandfather Ranger District
Height: Multilevel cascade measuring
    over 150 feet
Beauty rating: 7
Trail length and difficulty:
    If public access is acquired, 1.3 miles
    at a rating of 4

Directions: See opening statement

Photo Tips
Catawba Falls is photogenic almost anytime, but especially so in the winter, when the leaves are off and the water level is up. During the summer, the small stream flow gets lost in a jumble of vegetation. Wade into the pool and shoot from directly in front.

The Catawba River divides into numerous rivulets as it tumbles over the escarpment at Catawba Falls. Trees, grasses, shrubs, and wildflowers grow in abundance on the waterfall itself, restricting viewing during the summer but providing a beautiful sight when the wildflowers are in bloom and during the fall color season. However, the waterfall is most attractive during the winter when the water level is high.

Catawba Falls
Nikon F3, 28-70mm zoom lens, warming filter, f/22 at 1 second.

The only way I could get into position for an effective composition, was to wade into the frigid water. A pair of over-the-boot hip waders kept my feet toasty. However, my fingers were nearly frostbitten!

Upper Catawba Falls

River: Catawba
County: McDowell
USGS quadrangle: Moffitt Hill
Landowner: Pisgah National Forest,
   Grandfather Ranger District
Height: 70 feet
Beauty rating: 8
Trail length and difficulty:
   If public access is acquired, 1.5 miles
   at a rating of 10

Directions: See opening statement. If the trail has been opened to the public, hike to Catawba Falls using the directions given at the ranger station. The trail then climbs by the right side of Catawba Falls and leads 0.2 mile to the base of the upper falls. The climb alongside Catawba Falls is a near-vertical ascent that will require you to use both hands to grab roots, trees, rocks, and anything else you can hold onto. This climb is dangerous anytime, but extremely so in muddy conditions. In icy weather, attempting to reach the upper falls would be suicidal.

Photo Tips

Unlike the lower falls, Upper Catawba Falls is at its most photogenic when the water level is low and in the summer. At these times, it is easier and safer to position yourself for the numerous compositions that are available. Possibilities include using the pool or the small cascades downstream in the foreground. To eliminate as much of the sky as possible, position yourself as far to the right as is practical. See photo on page 1.

Upper Catawba Falls is the uppermost attraction on the storied Catawba River, which flows through North Carolina and South Carolina before entering the Atlantic Ocean at Charleston. Along its route are at least eleven lakes, including the popular Lake Norman in North Carolina and the famous Santee Cooper lakes—Marion and Moultrie—in South Carolina. The river's name changes twice along the way. It becomes the Wateree River below Wateree Lake in South Carolina, then the Cooper River below Lake Moultrie just before entering the Atlantic.

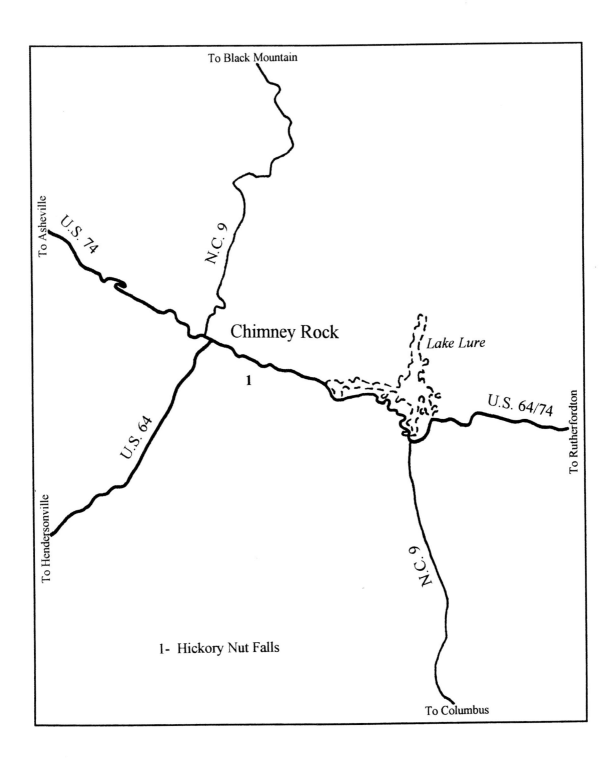

To Black Mountain

To Asheville

U.S. 74

N.C. 9

Chimney Rock

Lake Lure

1

U.S. 64

U.S. 64/74

To Rutherfordton

To Hendersonville

N.C. 9

1- Hickory Nut Falls

To Columbus

Chimney Rock

As with Murphy and Hayesville, there is only one major waterfall listed in this book for Chimney Rock. But unlike those other areas, the reason has nothing to do with geology. Actually, the topography and hard rock (Henderson granite gneiss) of Hickory Nut Gorge, in which Chimney Rock is located, provide the necessary combination for several significant waterfalls. Unfortunately, they are all on private property. Hickory Nut Falls is accessible by paying an entrance fee to Chimney Rock Park.

The 14-mile-long Hickory Nut Gorge contains some of the finest scenery in the southern Appalachians. The steep slopes rise 1,400 feet above the Broad River, popularly called the Rocky Broad. In 1927, the Rocky Broad was dammed to form Lake Lure, which has been described as one of the most beautiful man-made lakes in the world. A few miles upstream from the lake, in the north slope of Bluerock Mountain, is Bat Cave, the largest known fissure cavern in North America. Within its mile of passages live several uncommon salamanders, as well as the expected bats, including the endangered Indiana bat (*Myotis sodalis*). Bat Cave is managed as a private nature preserve by the North Carolina Nature Conservancy.

Without doubt, the greatest attraction in Hickory Nut Gorge is Chimney Rock Park, named after the 315-foot monolith that overlooks the gorge. The park provides numerous photo opportunities year-round but is especially photogenic in the fall. A labyrinth of trails, stairways, and narrow passages gives you and your camera access to these subjects.

Hickory Nut Falls *

River: Fall Creek
County: Rutherford
USGS quadrangle: Bat Cave
Landowner: Chimney Rock Park, a private commercial attraction
Height: Listed at 404 feet by Chimney Rock Park
Beauty rating: 9
Trail length and difficulty: Each of the two trails to the top is 0.75 mile at a rating of 8; the trail to the bottom is 0.7 mile at a rating of 4.
Handicapped Accessible

Directions: The entrance to Chimney Rock Park is on U.S. 64/74. Upon payment of the entrance fee, you will be given park information, including a map of the trails and points of interest.

Photo Tips

There are two excellent views of the falls, one from Inspiration Point and the other from the observation area at the base. From the base, it is best to shoot an isolation shot of the cascades, rather than attempting to include all of the drop, which would clearly flatten the perspective. Inspiration Point provides a dramatic view of the entire waterfall and is especially nice in the fall or early spring.

A big disadvantage of shooting in Chimney Rock Park is the operating schedule. The gates do not open until 8:30 A.M. and close well before sunset, thus taking away any chance of shooting during the best light. Still, by visiting on an overcast day or just before or after a storm, you should be able to create some outstanding images. With so much to shoot, I recommend spending at least one day, preferably more, in the park.

This waterfall is known to everyone who has driven through Hickory Nut Gorge; however, the best views are from inside Chimney Rock Park. The park received national attention in 1992 with the motion-picture release of *The Last of the Mohicans*. Several major scenes were filmed here, including the climactic fight between Chingachgook and Magua at the brink of Hickory Nut Falls.

Nearby waterfalls: Rainbow Falls is on the mountain opposite Chimney Rock Park and is visible from several points along the trails to the top of Hickory Nut Falls. Try shooting it from Inspiration Point with either a wide-angle or a telephoto lens.

To see Camp Minnehaha Falls, drive 2.6 miles west on U.S. 64/74 from the park entrance and turn right on N.C. 9. It is 0.8 mile to a pull-off on the left and a view of the falls.

To see the high waterfall on Turnbreeches Creek, drive 6.1 miles west on U.S. 64 from the park entrance to Hog Rock Road (S.R. 1703). Turn left and drive 1 mile for a view.

The Bottomless Pools, on the east end of the gorge, have on occasion been called a waterfall. They are just small cascades but provide a good lesson in the process of pothole development in mountain streams.

Hickory Nut Falls
Nikon F3, 75-300mm zoom lens, polarizing filter, f/22 at 1 second, Fujichrome Velvia.

This image was made from the viewing area at the base. Using the zoom lens, I was able to get the exact composition I wanted without changing my position.

Stairs leading through Needle's Eye
Nikon F3, 20mm lens, f/22 at 1 second, Fujichrome Velvia.

It took a long time for me to hike the brink of Hickory Nut Falls. I spent all my time photographing along the way. The steps were carefully positioned in the frame to eliminate as many of the tossed soda cans as I could. Near the top of the stairs, I had to take off my pack and carry it in front of me to squeeze through.

View of Chimney Rock and Lake Lure
Nikon F3, 28-70mm zoom lens, polarizing filter, f/22 at ½ second, Fujichrome Velvia.

Hickory Nut Falls is only one of numerous photo opportunities in Chimney Rock Park. This view was made directly from the trail.

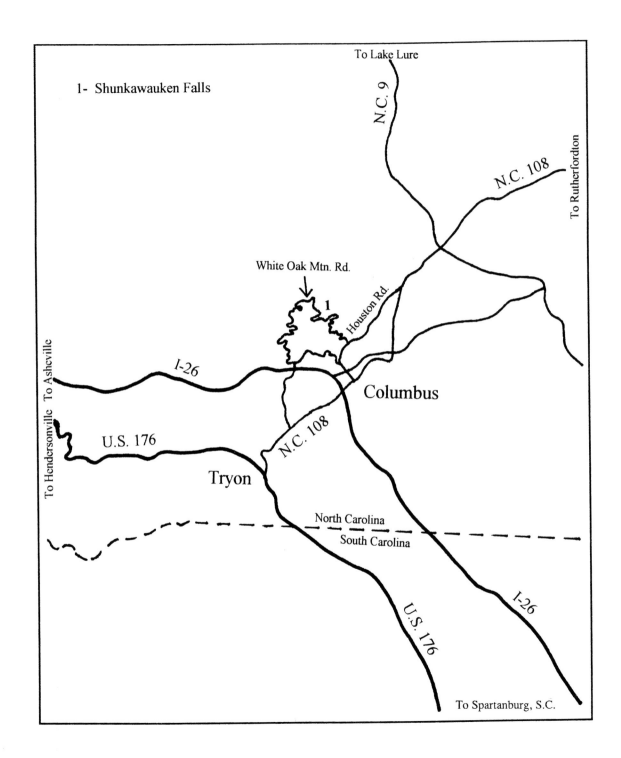

1- Shunkawauken Falls

To Lake Lure

N.C. 9

N.C. 108

To Rutherfordton

White Oak Mtn. Rd.

1

Houston Rd.

I-26

Columbus

To Asheville To Hendersonville

U.S. 176

N.C. 108

Tryon

North Carolina

South Carolina

U.S. 176

I-26

To Spartanburg, S.C.

Columbus

The small town of Columbus, the county seat of Polk County, lies at the foot of White Oak Mountain on the lower edge of the Blue Ridge escarpment. There are excellent views of the mountain from Interstate 26 as it skirts the southwestern portion of Tryon Peak. At 3,235 feet, Tryon Peak is the highest of several summits on the White Oak Mountain massif.

Shunkawauken Falls *

River: Horse Creek
County: Polk
USGS quadrangle: Mill Spring
Landowner: Private
Height: This waterfall is practically one continuous cascade from White Oak's summit to its base; the main upper portion is at least 150 feet high.
Beauty rating: 6
Trail length and difficulty: View roadside
Handicapped Accessible

Directions: From the intersection of Interstate 26 and N.C. 108, drive east on N.C. 108 for 0.4 mile to Houston Road (S.R. 1137). Turn left and drive 0.5 mile to a fork; bear right to continue on Houston Road. After 0.6 mile, turn left onto White Oak Mountain Road (S.R. 1136). It is 2 miles to the upper section of the falls, with a glimpse of the lower cascades at 0.9 mile. A small pull-off is located on the left 0.1 mile beyond the falls.

Shunkawauken Falls
Nikon F3, 28-70mm zoom lens, warming filter, f/22 at 2 seconds, Fujichrome Velvia.

The approach I took here was obvious and straightforward. I backed up as far as I could on the narrow road, set up the tripod on the road's edge, and used a wide-angle lens to include most of the falls and the rail fence.

Photo Tip
A straightforward composition works well here. Shoot from directly in front, using the rail fence to enhance the scene and add scale. During winter, you can photograph the falls with a telephoto lens from the Food Lion parking lot in Columbus.
From the falls, it is 0.7 mile to an overlook of Columbus and the surrounding foothills.

It is unusual for there to be a waterfall of this magnitude so near a mountain's summit; most streams are mere trickles at this point. In this case, a small plateau on the summit containing several small ponds gives Horse Creek its size.

Shunkawauken Falls was known as Horse Creek Falls until 1891, when the name was changed in honor of an Indian chief.

Nearby waterfall: Continue on White Oak Mountain Road approximately 4.6 miles to view a small falls on the left.

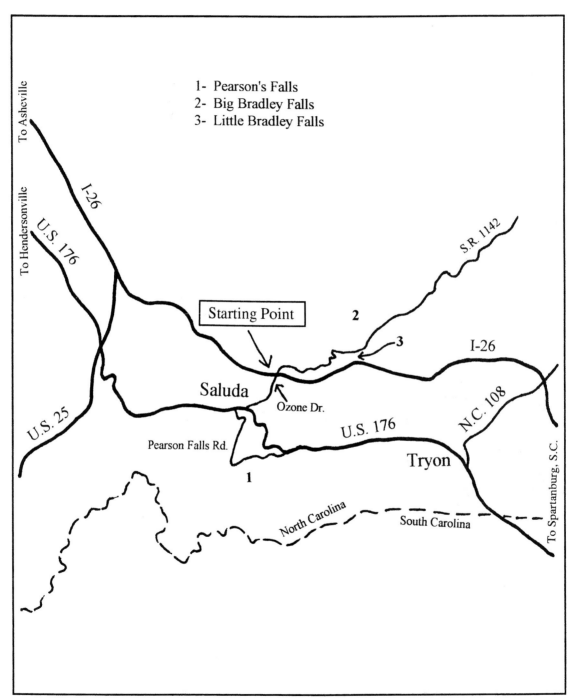

1- Pearson's Falls
2- Big Bradley Falls
3- Little Bradley Falls

To Asheville

To Hendersonville

I-26

U.S. 176

S.R. 1142

Starting Point

2

3

I-26

Saluda

Ozone Dr.

U.S. 25

Pearson Falls Rd.

U.S. 176

N.C. 108

Tryon

To Spartanburg, S.C.

1

North Carolina

South Carolina

The starting point is the intersection of Interstate 26 and Ozone Drive (S.R. 1142) at Exit 28.

Saluda

The once-thriving community of Saluda is enjoying a revitalization since its heyday at the turn of the century. Quaint shops line the streets, and the old train depot has been restored. Saluda is home to the steepest standard-gauge railroad grade in the United States, called the Saluda Grade.

Pearson's Falls *

River: Colt Creek
County: Polk
USGS quadrangle: Saluda
Landowner: Tryon Garden Club

Height: Listed at 90 feet, which is exaggerated
Beauty rating: 7
Trail length and difficulty: 0.3 mile; 3

Directions: From the starting point, drive 1.1 miles south on Ozone Drive (which becomes S.R. 1181) to U.S. 176. Turn left and proceed 2.5 miles to a sign announcing the falls. Turn right on Pearson Falls Road (S.R. 1102) and drive 0.9 mile to the entrance. Stop at the gatehouse and pay the small admission fee, which is well worth it. The gatekeeper will provide all the information you need; the excellent booklet *Pearson's Falls Glen* is available for a nominal fee.

The trail is closed Monday and Tuesday from November 1 to March 1 but is otherwise open every day from 10:00 A.M. to 6:00 P.M.

Pearson's Falls
Canon EOS Elan, 24mm tilt/shift lens, f/22 at 6 seconds, Fujichrome Velvia.

It was raining lightly when I made this image, and a downpour seemed eminent. I had just enough time to fire off a few frames before having to pack it up, but I couldn't make it to the car before getting thoroughly drenched. My wife, Jane, had commandeered the umbrella.

Nature lovers can thank the Tryon Garden Club for having the foresight to purchase Pearson's Falls and the surrounding glen, thus protecting one of the most biologically diverse sites in the area. The glen, now a North Carolina Natural Heritage Area, has been owned and managed by the garden club since the 1931 purchase. The proceeds for admission are used to maintain the property, and all donations are tax-deductible.

The waterfall was named after Charles William Pearson, who discovered the cascade shortly after the Civil War while scouting the Southern Railroad route from Spartanburg, South Carolina, to Asheville.

Nearby waterfalls: From the Pearson's Falls sign on U.S. 176, drive 1.2 miles east to a pull-off on the left. Walk back up the road 0.1 mile for a wintertime view across the gorge of the lower portion of Melrose Falls. This 1.2-mile drive provides views of several wet-weather cascades on the left-hand side of the road.

Big Bradley Falls *

River: Cove Creek
County: Polk
USGS quadrangle: Cliffield Mountain
Landowner: Private, leased as a North Carolina
    Wildlife Resources Commission Game Land
Height: 65 feet
Beauty rating: 9
Trail length and difficulty:
    0.8 mile; 5 at the cliff overlook,
    10 at the base

Directions: From the starting point, drive north on S.R. 1142 for 3.2 miles to a parking area on the right just before the creek. Cross the road, walk past the gate, and enter a field and an abandoned orchard. Pick up the trail at the end of the field. You will reach the creek 0.3 mile from the parking area. Cross the creek—for an adventure, try crossing on the cable/pulley system—and continue about 0.4 mile. At a right turn, you will notice a side trail to the left that leads to the top of the falls. Continue on the main trail 100 feet and take the second side trail (there may be a red blaze on a maple tree). This trail leads to the cliff overlook, the most desirable vantage point. Reaching the base requires a strenuous climb.

It is surprising that a waterfall this spectacular is so little-known—though you might not think so from all the litter left behind. Even with the piles of beer cans, this is a highly recommended hike.

The falls were named for an early settler who had a home and an orchard in the field along the trail.

Big Bradley Falls
Nikon F3, 75-300mm zoom lens, warming filter, f/16 at 1 second, Fujichrome Velvia.

Use of a zoom lens can be a tremendous asset at some waterfalls. Here, I was standing at the edge of a cliff and couldn't reposition myself. With the long-focal-length zoom lens, I was able to shoot several different compositions. Notice the many deciduous trees surrounding the falls. This would be an excellent fall scene. See additional photo in the color section.

Little Bradley Falls

River: Cove Creek
County: Polk
USGS quadrangle: Cliffield Mountain
Landowner: Private, leased as a North Carolina
    Wildlife Resources Commission Game Land
Height: Multilevel cascade measuring
    about 35 feet
Beauty rating: 6
Trail length and difficulty: 0.3 mile; 3–7

Directions: From the parking area for Big Bradley Falls, backtrack 0.5 mile on S.R. 1142 and park at the small pull-off on the left; there is a large rock on the side of the road. Climb down the bank on the footpath and pick up the trail heading upstream. You will pass through an old homeplace in a field of periwinkle and cross a small stream. The falls are a few hundred feet farther upstream.

> ### Photo Tip
> Make sure that your photo does not include any of the clutter at the edge of the pool.

Though not nearly as impressive as its rival downstream, Little Bradley Falls is nonetheless a pretty sight. An excellent day's outing would be to visit Little Bradley, Big Bradley, and nearby Pearson's and Shunkawauken falls.

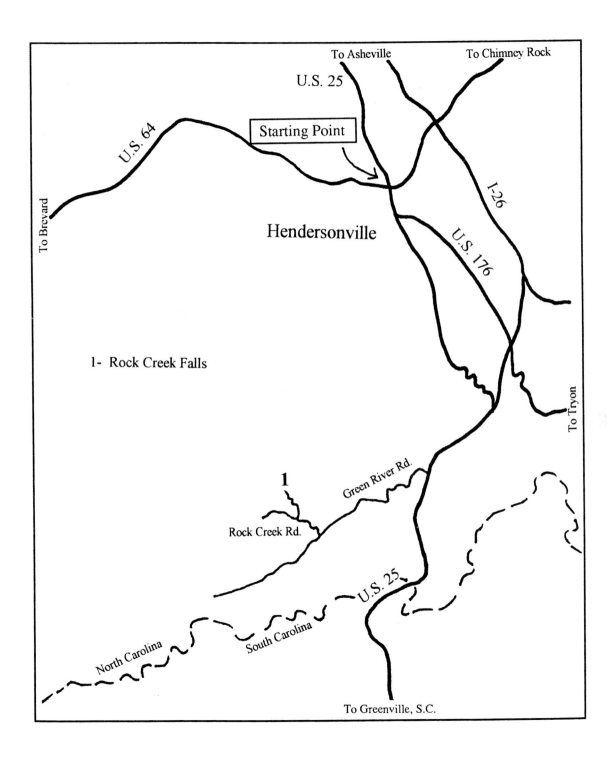

Hendersonville

Hendersonville and the nearby community of Flat Rock have become a summer retreat for the wealthy. The Flat Rock Playhouse, the State Theatre of North Carolina, offers performances throughout the summer. Across the road from the playhouse is Connemara, the Carl Sandburg Home National Historic Site. Perhaps the region's greatest claim to fame is its annual apple crop. Henderson County's 240 orchards produce more apples than any other county in North Carolina, a state that is ranked sixth in the nation among apple producers. The area also contains several nice waterfalls, but all are on private property. The three mentioned here are visible from the road.

Rock Creek Falls

River: Rock Creek
County: Henderson
USGS quadrangle: Standing Stone
Landowner: Private
Height: Cascades measuring over 150 feet
Beauty rating: 3
Trail length and difficulty: View roadside
Handicapped Accessible

Directions: From downtown Hendersonville, drive approximately 9 miles on U.S. 25 South and exit on Green River Road (S.R. 1106). Turn right and drive 2.7 miles to Rock Creek Road (S.R. 1107); turn right again. It is 0.8 mile to a fork, then 0.1 mile on the right fork to the falls.

Of the dozens of waterfalls in this book which have been used to power mills, few contain any significant remains of the structures. At Rock Creek Falls, the main gear shaft and water column, as well as stone columns and rotting debris, are clearly visible.

Nearby waterfalls: Retracing your route on Green River Road from Rock Creek Falls, it is 2.7 miles from Rock Creek Road to S.R. 1109, on the left, then 2.1 miles on S.R. 1109 to a poor view, also on the left, of a cascade on Joe Creek, located on private property.

For a wintertime view of Turley Falls, drive approximately 3.5 miles west on U.S. 64 from downtown Hendersonville and turn left on Turley Falls Road (S.R. 1215). Cross the railroad tracks, bear right, and continue a short distance; the view is across the valley.

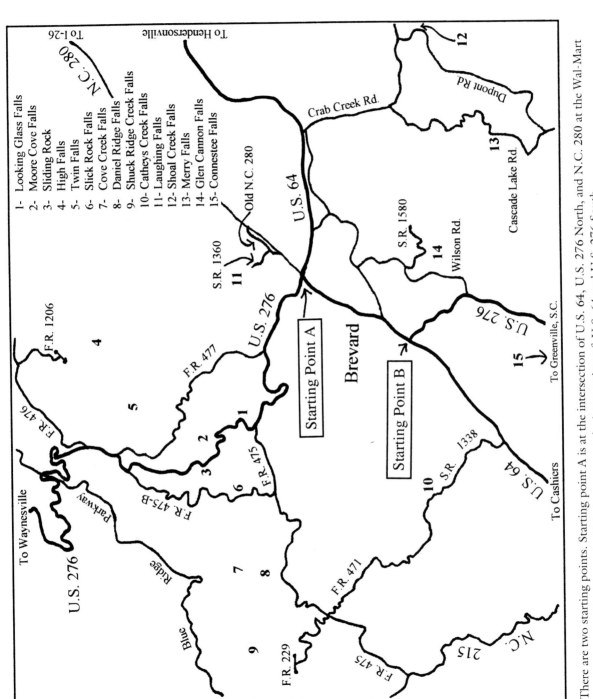

1- Looking Glass Falls
2- Moore Cove Falls
3- Sliding Rock
4- High Falls
5- Twin Falls
6- Slick Rock Falls
7- Cove Creek Falls
8- Daniel Ridge Falls
9- Shuck Ridge Creek Falls
10- Catheys Creek Falls
11- Laughing Falls
12- Shoal Creek Falls
13- Merry Falls
14- Glen Cannon Falls
15- Connestee Falls

There are two starting points. Starting point A is at the intersection of U.S. 64, U.S. 276 North, and N.C. 280 at the Wal-Mart shopping center. Starting point B is downtown at the intersection of U.S. 64 and U.S. 276 South.

Brevard

Brevard is the largest town in Transylvania County, the self-described "Land of Waterfalls." This boasting is not without merit, as Transylvania easily contains more waterfalls than any other county in the state, and very likely the nation. Some estimates suggest as many as five hundred significant falls in the county, though I believe the actual count is less than a third of that. This still far exceeds the next two closest counties, Jackson and Macon.

Why is Transylvania so blessed? Because of its geology and topography. The county lies on the Blue Ridge escarpment, the transition zone between the high mountains and the Piedmont of North and South Carolina. Due to its location, there is a significant variation in elevation, from 6,025 feet on Chestnut Bald to 1,110 feet at Lake Jocassee. In addition, the rocks in this region are very hard and do not wear easily. This is one of the primary reasons that the extreme western part of North Carolina contains few waterfalls; the streams have literally eroded away the soft rock.

Contributing to the size of the cascades in Transylvania County is the high average rainfall. Brevard averages nearly 70 inches annually and Lake Toxaway, in the western part of the county, 80 inches.

Transylvania's waterfalls have long been a major drawing card for tourists, and several brochures, lists, and pamphlets have been printed that describe many of them. You should be aware that many of the falls listed are on private property. In the Brevard area, every waterfall south of U.S. 64 is private, though at least three are visible from the road. It's a safe bet that if you have heard of a waterfall that is not listed here, it is not accessible to the general public.

Looking Glass Falls *

River: Looking Glass Creek
County: Transylvania
USGS quadrangle: Shining Rock
Landowner: Pisgah National Forest, Pisgah Ranger District
Height: This waterfall has been listed at various heights between 60 and 85 feet; it is closer to 60 feet.
Beauty rating: 8
Trail length and difficulty: View roadside. There is a short trail to the base.
Handicapped Accessible

Directions: From starting point A, drive 5.5 miles north on U.S. 276 to a parking area on the right.

Photo Tips
Since this waterfall is so popular, it is also one of the most-photographed in the area. Most people shoot from the trail leading to the base. This is a good vantage point, but why not try something different? The large, angled rock a short distance downstream makes an ideal platform for a horizontal composition. Also, from the parking area, you can walk down the sidewalk a short distance and use the trees to frame the image. See photo in the color section and on the cover.

Looking Glass Falls is one of the most popular waterfalls in the state. It is named after Looking Glass Rock, the towering monolithic dome clearly visible from U.S. 276 and the Blue Ridge Parkway. When frozen, the surface of the cliffs reflects sunlight, thus resembling a looking glass.

This waterfall is highly recommended.

Moore Cove Falls *

River: Moore Creek
County: Transylvania
USGS quadrangle: Shining Rock
Landowner: Pisgah National Forest,
    Pisgah Ranger District
Height: 50 feet
Beauty rating: 7
Trail length and difficulty: 0.7 mile; 5

Directions: From starting point A, drive north on U.S. 276 for 6.5 miles (1 mile beyond Looking Glass Falls) to a parking area on the right. Walk across the bridge and immediately begin the trail on the right at the Moore Cove signpost.

Photo Tips

The best time to visit Moore Cove Falls is probably during the rhododendron bloom. There is a perfectly situated patch of small shrubs a few feet downstream. Be sure to shoot from behind the falls as well, particularly in early spring or fall, when the forest is most interesting. And if you enjoy shooting people, bring along a friend in a colorful swimsuit and have her/him stand under the falls. If handled properly, this could be a highly marketable image.

This is one of my personal favorites, not because it is very large or high—it isn't—but because it offers something in every season: icicles in winter, wildflowers in spring, a cooling shower (standing under the falls) in summer, and brilliant foliage in the deciduous forest in autumn. A large, overhanging ledge allows you to walk behind the 50-foot free fall.

Nearby waterfall: A short distance downstream from Moore Cove Falls is a stream joining Moore Creek from the west. Follow this stream a few hundred feet to an almost identical waterfall about half the size.

Moore Cove Falls
Nikon F3, 24mm lens, f/22 at ¼ second, Kodachrome 25.

It takes time to maneuver into the right position for an effective composition, but it is always worth the effort. For this photo, I was careful to use the rhododendron to enhance the scene without overpowering it.

Sliding Rock *

River: Looking Glass Creek
County: Transylvania
USGS quadrangle: Shining Rock
Landowner: Pisgah National Forest,
   Pisgah Ranger District
Height: 60-foot slide
Beauty rating: 3
Trail length and difficulty:
   Only a very short walk is required.
Handicapped Accessible

Directions: From starting point A, drive north on
U.S. 276 for 7.6 miles to a paved parking lot on the
left.

Photo Tips

Sliding Rock is not worth photographing except when people are sliding on it. Then it becomes an excellent subject. To see the greatest number of people, visit on a hot summer weekend. There is a viewing platform at the base from which to shoot. Leave your tripod in the car; you'll need to hand-hold for maximum flexibility.

Sliding Rock is not really a waterfall, but it is such a popular recreational attraction that its inclusion here seems appropriate. Eleven thousand gallons of water per minute propel adventurous sliders 60 feet into a 6-foot-deep pool. A lifeguard is on duty from Memorial Day to Labor Day.

Sliding Rock

Nikon 8008s, 28-70mm zoom lens, exposure set on aperture-priority automatic, using Matrix metering, Fujichrome 100.

The amount of white water at Sliding Rock is insignificant in an overall scene, so I was able to set the camera on automatic, which allowed me to concentrate on composition instead of exposure. I would not consider photographing at Sliding Rock without the aid of a zoom lens.

High Falls

River: South Fork, Mills River
County: Transylvania
USGS quadrangle: Pisgah Forest
Landowner: Pisgah National Forest,
 Pisgah Ranger District
Height: Small cascade measuring about 20 feet
Beauty rating: 4
Trail length and difficulty: 2 miles; 6

Directions: From starting point A, drive 11.5 miles north on U.S. 276 to F.R. 1206. Turn right and drive 3.3 miles to F.R. 476. Turn right again and drive 1.3 miles to where the road dead-ends at the beginning of the trail.

 Follow the old logging road beside the river for 0.9 mile to a cement bridge. Do not cross the bridge. Instead, bear left and cross a small branch. (A side trail leads up the branch; don't take it.) After 0.8 mile, ford the South Fork of Mills River. The water level can vary from less than 6 inches to over 2 feet; bring waders in cold weather. It is 0.3 mile farther to the falls.

Photo Tips
 There is a large, flat rock just off the trail from which you can shoot, using the pool as a foreground. If the water level is low, wade into the river and try different perspectives.

This cascade does not compare favorably with others in this book in terms of height, but it is scenic and photogenic nonetheless. A large pool at the base provides fine opportunities for wading and fishing.

Nearby waterfall: Glady Branch Waterfall, located some distance downstream from High Falls on Glady Branch, is a tiny cascade and not worth the hike.

Twin Falls

River: Henry Branch and tributary
County: Transylvania
USGS quadrangle: Shining Rock
Landowner: Pisgah National Forest,
 Pisgah Ranger District
Height: Two waterfalls, each approximately
 100 feet
Beauty rating: 8
Trail length and difficulty: 2.2 miles; 5–7

Directions: From starting point A, drive 2.2 miles north on U.S. 276 and turn right on F.R. 477. It is 2.5 miles to a small parking area on the right with a signpost for Avery Creek Trail. Soon after you begin walking the trail, you will pass a side trail on the left leading up the mountain. At 1.2 miles, you will reach a junction with Buckhorn Gap Trail. Follow Buckhorn Gap Trail to the right; you will reach a signpost for Twin Falls Loop after 0.7 mile. It is 0.3 mile to the falls on either the left or right side of the loop.

Photo Tips
 It is difficult to get a decent shot of either of the falls. You can shoot the left one from the right bank a short distance downstream, using ferns or wildflowers in the foreground. But your best bet is to shoot the wildflowers and forest scenes along the trail.

 Twin Falls is unique. Its two high waterfalls are close together and clearly visible from one vantage point, but they are located on different streams. The trail to this twin waterfall is one of the most delightful walks in Pisgah National Forest and is part of the reason for the high beauty rating. If you can, make the hike in early spring, when wildflowers are abundant, or in autumn, when the open deciduous forest changes color. Do not try to climb to the base of the waterfall on the right; there is no trail, and the soil is easily disturbed.

Slick Rock Falls *

River: Slick Rock Creek
County: Transylvania
USGS quadrangle: Shining Rock
Landowner: Pisgah National Forest,
  Pisgah Ranger District
Height: Approximately 35 feet
Beauty rating: 5
Trail length and difficulty:
  This is a roadside waterfall with a 200-foot walk
  to the base.
Handicapped Accessible

Directions: From starting point A, drive 5.2 miles north on U.S. 276 to F.R. 475. Turn left and drive 1.5 miles to F.R. 475-B. Turn right. It is 1.1 miles to a small pull-off on the right by the falls.

Photo Tips
Several moss-covered boulders and a profusion of rhododendron are at the base. Both can easily be incorporated in your photos for additional impact. A good vantage point is the far right side looking back on the falls. You can also shoot from behind the falls. This is an excellent area for spring wildflowers.

The slippery moss which grows at the brink gives Slick Rock Falls its name. It is not uncommon to find the carcasses of deer that have slipped and fallen on this moss on the rocks below.

Cove Creek Falls

River: Cove Creek
County: Transylvania
USGS quadrangle: Shining Rock
Landowner: Pisgah National Forest,
  Pisgah Ranger District
Height: Cascades measuring about 65 feet
Beauty rating: 7
Trail length and difficulty: 1 mile; 6

Directions: From starting point A, drive 5.2 miles north on U.S. 276 to F.R. 475. Turn left and drive 3.2 miles to the parking area for Cove Creek Group Campground, on the left. Park here.
  Follow the road across from the parking area to reach the creek crossing. A footbridge is to the right. Continue 0.3 mile to a large, grassy field with bathrooms on the opposite side. The trail leaves the main road, runs alongside the bathrooms, enters the woods, and forks after 100 yards. Take the right fork for 0.2 mile to a second fork. Take the right fork again, following the sign for Caney Bottom Loop. It is 0.2 mile to a primitive camping area in a hemlock grove beside Cove Creek. An obscure trail follows the creek upstream 0.2 mile to the falls.

Photo Tips
Everything seems to fall in place at Cove Creek Falls to present an ideal photo opportunity. Shoot from the bank using the rocks as a foreground, or wade into the pool for a straight-on composition.

Of the lesser-known waterfalls in the Brevard area, Cove Creek Falls is one of the most scenic. Make plans to visit Slick Rock, Cove Creek, Daniel Ridge, and Catheys Creek waterfalls while in the area. All are attractive and easily accessible.

Cove Creek Falls
Nikon F3, 24mm lens, polarizing filter, f/22 at 3 seconds, Fujichrome Velvia.

Sometimes, the best vantage point for photos is also the easiest to reach. This photo was made right from the trail.

Daniel Ridge Falls *
(Toms Spring Falls, Jackson Falls)

River: Toms Spring Branch
County: Transylvania
USGS quadrangle: Shining Rock
Landowner: Pisgah National Forest,
   Pisgah Ranger District
Height: Over 150 feet
Beauty rating: 6
Trail length and difficulty: 0.3 mile; 3

Directions: Follow the directions to the parking area for Cove Creek Falls, but continue 0.7 mile to a parking area on the right. From the parking area, follow the logging road 0.3 mile to a view of the falls on the left.

Photo Tips
Although this waterfall is impressive, it is not photogenic. Regardless of the vantage point, it is nearly impossible to eliminate all the clutter. Perhaps some of this clutter may prove interesting in the fall.

It is not clear why the Forest Service has adopted the name Daniel Ridge for this waterfall; Daniel Ridge and Daniel Ridge Creek are actually a few miles to the west. Perhaps it is because Daniel Ridge Trail runs just to the left of the falls. Whichever name you call it, Daniel Ridge Falls or Toms Spring Falls, it is well worth the easy hike.

Nearby waterfall: There is a smaller waterfall about 0.75 mile upstream. It can be reached by following Daniel Ridge Trail 0.8 mile to a logging road (the same road that leads to Daniel Ridge Falls). Turn right and follow the road 0.2 mile to the falls, on the left. For a loop, continue 1 mile on this road back to Daniel Ridge Falls.

Shuck Ridge Creek Falls

River: Shuck Ridge Creek
County: Transylvania
USGS quadrangle: Shining Rock
Landowner: Pisgah National Forest,
    Pisgah Ranger District
Height: 25 feet
Beauty rating: 6
Trail length and difficulty: 2.7 miles; 4–9

Directions: From starting point A, drive 5.2 miles north on U.S. 276 to F.R. 475. Turn left and go 6 miles to an intersection at Gloucester Gap. Turn right on F.R. 229 and drive 2.5 miles to where the road dead-ends at a parking area; F.R. 229 may be rough in wet weather.

Walk a short distance on F.R. 229 (do not take the lower, grassy road) and pick up Art Loeb Trail coming in from the left. Follow Art Loeb Trail 0.1 mile to a fork. Turn right and follow the road along the ridge; you will reach Farlow Gap after 1.6 miles. Several trails lead off from the gap. Follow Farlow Gap Trail—located behind a signpost and marked with blue blazes—1.1 miles to the top of the falls. Note: This last 1.1-mile section descends steeply the entire distance.

Photo Tips
If you can negotiate the difficult scramble to the base, you will be rewarded with a very good photo opportunity. A nicely situated rhododendron shrub grows out of the left bank, but you will need a fairly tall tripod to effectively include it. Be sure to eliminate the distracting birch tree on the right bank.

At only 25 feet, Shuck Ridge Creek Falls is one of the smallest waterfalls in this book. But what it lacks in height, it makes up for in beauty. The waterfall is only one of the features along the outstanding Farlow Gap Trail. If you're an avid hiker, consider hiking the entire trail from Farlow Gap to Cove Creek Group Campground near Cove Creek Falls. Complete trail information is available from the Pisgah Ranger Station.

Shuck Ridge Creek Falls
Nikon F3, 24mm lens, polarizing filter, f/22 at ½ second, Fujichrome Velvia.

Although it is not noticeable in this black-and-white photo, the color is what makes the original of this photo appealing to me. The deep, emerald-green of the pool, the forest-green of the rhododendron, and the deep blue of the sky, compliment each other well.

Nearby waterfalls: Approximately 0.75 mile down F.R. 229 from the parking area is a well-graded, gated logging road cutting sharply to the left. This road crosses Laurel Fork and a feeder stream. Each creek has a significant waterfall downstream from the road. Unfortunately, there is no trail to either of them, and the hike is extremely rugged and dangerous; these waterfalls are definitely not recommended.

Catheys Creek Falls *
(High Falls)

River: Catheys Creek
County: Transylvania
USGS quadrangle: Rosman
Landowner: Pisgah National Forest,
　　Pisgah Ranger District
Height: These cascades run several hundred feet,
　　but only 80 feet are visible from the base.
Beauty rating: 5
Trail length and difficulty: 0.1 mile; 7

Directions: If you are in the Davidson River area, follow the directions to Shuck Ridge Creek Falls, but instead of turning right at Gloucester Gap, turn left onto F.R. 471. Drive 4.8 miles to a pull-off on the left.
　　From Brevard and starting point B, drive west 3.3 miles on U.S. 64 to a sign for Kuykendall Group Camp. Turn right and then left onto S.R. 1338, which becomes F.R. 471. Drive 3.1 miles to a pull-off on the right.
　　An obscure trail leads down the bank.

Photo Tip
　Skip this one.

Old photographs show this to have been an impressive waterfall. Now, it is a cluttered mess from fallen trees and branches.
　The waterfall and creek were named after Captain George Cathey, a Revolutionary War veteran.

Nearby waterfall: A few publications list a waterfall on Cedar Rock Creek, which enters Catheys Creek a short distance upstream from Catheys Creek Falls. A few small cascades are located there, but nothing that could be described as a waterfall, so don't waste your time. There isn't a trail, anyway.

Laughing Falls

River: South Prong, Turkey Creek
County: Transylvania
USGS quadrangle: Pisgah Forest
Landowner: Pisgah National Forest,
　　Pisgah Ranger District
Height: 50-foot cascade
Beauty rating: 3
Trail length and difficulty: 0.2 mile; 3

Directions: From starting point A, drive 0.7 mile east on N.C. 280 and turn left onto Old N.C. 280 (S.R. 1361). It is 0.15 mile to S.R. 1360. Turn left and drive 0.7 mile to where the road dead-ends at a parking area. To walk to the falls, take the right fork in the road and immediately rock-hop the South Prong of Turkey Creek. Follow the road on the immediate left upstream to the falls.

Photo Tip
　Save your film.

This cascade was called "Laughing Waters" by the Cherokees, and if you listen carefully, you might just hear the laughter yourself. Of course, you could do this with any other waterfall as well.

Shoal Creek Falls and Merry Falls

These two waterfalls are on private property and are only partially visible from the road. Neither merits a beauty rating over 2. They are given a separate listing here because they are included in several publications on Transylvania County waterfalls. Shoal Creek Falls is actually just across the border in Henderson County.

To get to them from starting point A, drive 3.6 miles east on U.S. 64 to Crab Creek Road (S.R. 1528). Turn right and drive 4.2 miles to Dupont Road (S.R. 1259). Turn right again. Shoal Creek Falls can be viewed on the left after 0.7 mile. Continue on Dupont Road 4.7 miles to where it ends at Cascade Lake Road (S.R. 1536). Turn right and drive 1.8 miles to view Merry Falls on the left.

The two waterfalls can also be reached from starting point B by driving 10.7 miles south on U.S. 276 to Cascade Lake Road. Turn left and drive 2.5 miles to the intersection with Dupont Road. It is 1.8 miles straight ahead to Merry Falls and 4.7 miles on Dupont Road to Shoal Creek Falls.

Glen Cannon Falls

River: Williamson Creek
County: Transylvania
USGS quadrangle: Brevard
Landowner: Private
Height: Small cascade

Beauty rating: If you love to golf, 10; otherwise, 2
Trail length and difficulty: View roadside
Handicapped Accessible

Directions: From starting point B, drive south on U.S. 276 for 2 miles to Wilson Road (S.R. 1540). Turn left and drive 2.2 miles to S.R. 1580; you will see a sign for Glen Cannon. Turn right and proceed 0.7 mile to a view of the falls.

Photo Tips
If you don't want to include golf in your pictures, you might as well save your film. On the other hand, this is a perfect opportunity for recreational photos. Play a round on the Glen Cannon Golf Course with some friends. Arrange them on the green to create an excellent foreground. Remember that other players are there to play golf, not to watch you take pictures; allow them to play through. If you want a picture of them, ask for permission. If you plan on selling these photos, you will need a model release and a property release from the country club.

Glen Cannon Falls is similar to Shoal Creek Falls and Merry Falls in that it is located on private property and is only partly visible from the road. If you could view it from the base, its beauty rating would be much higher. One way to get a closer look without trespassing is to play a round of golf. The cascade creates the backdrop for the second hole.

The waterfall and the glen in which it is located were named for Albert Cannon, who was hired in the mid-1800s to clear the land. Cannon served as North Carolina's commissioner of agriculture for many years.

There is an equally impressive cascade about 100 yards upstream from Glen Cannon Falls, but it is located on private property and is not accessible to the public.

Connestee Falls *

River: Carson Creek
County: Transylvania
USGS quadrangle: Brevard
Landowner: Private
Height: Commonly listed at 110 feet
Beauty rating: 7
Trail length and difficulty: The falls are adjacent to the parking area; a series of steps leads to the base.

Directions: From starting point B, drive 5.7 miles on U.S. 276 South to a paved parking area on the right. The trail leads from the parking area a few feet to the top, then continues to the base.

Photo Tips

If you use your imagination, you can come up with numerous compositions here. A straightforward approach, and a good one, is to shoot from the lower observation point, possibly using people in the foreground. Batson Creek Falls, the twin waterfall of Connestee Falls, can also be shot from this vantage point by spinning the camera 180 degrees.

Be aware that if you visit on summer weekends, you will have to contend with hordes of people.

According to legend, a young Englishman was wounded and captured by Cherokee warriors. His life was spared, and he soon fell in love with Princess Connestee, who nursed him back to health. They often sat beside a cascade during their courtship. Soon after their marriage, the Englishman was persuaded to return to his own people, and the heartbroken Connestee leapt to her death over the falls.

Whether or not this is the waterfall she jumped from is unknown. It seems to have been named by Dr. F. A. Miles, owner of the Caesar's Head Hotel, in 1882. In a letter to a friend, he stated that the cascade reminded him of the legend of the Indian maiden, and that he had "immediately dubed [sic] it Connestee."

Connestee Falls is often referred to as a twin falls because of the adjoining waterfall on Batson Creek. After the two waterfalls meet, the single Carson Creek is forced into a cleft known as the Silver Slip.

In the early 1970s, a private residential resort began to be built, with Connestee Falls as its namesake and drawing card. The waterfall has since become one of the most popular in Transylvania County. Unfortunately, after the first printing of this book, Connestee Falls was sold and the new owners do not allow access.

Connestee Falls
Canon EOS Elan, 24mm tilt/shift lens, polarizing filter, f/22 at 3 seconds, Fujichrome Velvia.

It took me 2 hours to make this photo. That's how long I waited for a cloud to pass in front of the sun, and remove the harsh contrast from the scene. Sometimes, you have to be patient.

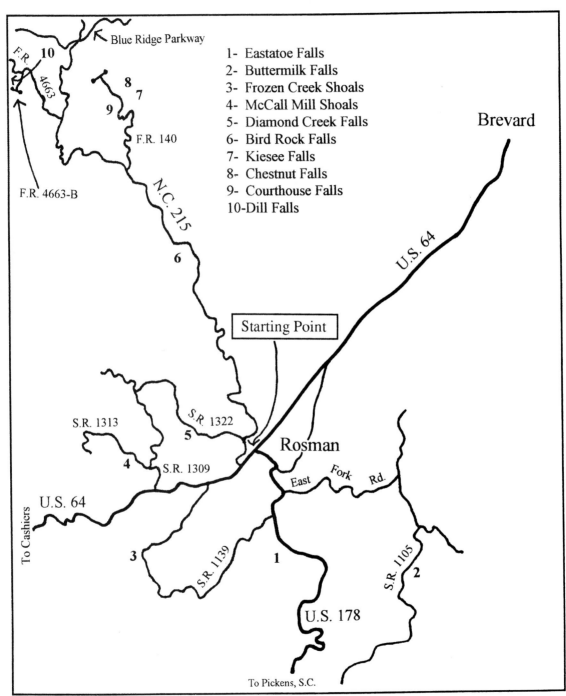

Blue Ridge Parkway

1- Eastatoe Falls
2- Buttermilk Falls
3- Frozen Creek Shoals
4- McCall Mill Shoals
5- Diamond Creek Falls
6- Bird Rock Falls
7- Kiesee Falls
8- Chestnut Falls
9- Courthouse Falls
10-Dill Falls

F.R. 4663

10

8
7

9

F.R. 140

F.R. 4663-B

N.C. 215

6

Brevard

U.S. 64

Starting Point

Rosman

S.R. 1313

S.R. 1322

5

East Fork Rd.

S.R. 1309

4

U.S. 64

To Cashiers

3

S.R. 1139

1

S.R. 1105

2

U.S. 178

To Pickens, S.C.

The starting point is the junction of U.S. 64 and U.S. 178 just north of Rosman.

Rosman

During the early part of the century, Rosman was the most prosperous community in Transylvania County. A local mill sawed 26,000 board feet of lumber daily. Two trains a day hauled logs to the mill along a course that is now N.C. 215 and a portion of the Forest Heritage Scenic Byway, which you will follow to several waterfalls in this hub. You will drive on other portions of the byway when visiting waterfalls in the Waynesville and Brevard areas.

Eastatoe Falls *

River: Shoal Creek
County: Transylvania
USGS quadrangle: Eastatoe Gap
Landowner: Private
Height: 60 feet
Beauty rating: 5
Trail length and difficulty: 0.1 mile; 2

Directions: From the starting point, drive south on U.S. 178 for 3.4 miles to a private drive on the right; you will see a sign for Mountain Meadow Craft Shop. Turn into the drive and park at the craft shop. A trail leads between the craft shop and an old shed.

Photo Tips
There are so many fallen trees and branches at the base that it is difficult to get a satisfactory shot. There is a rhododendron shrub in the creek which makes a good foreground when in bloom.

Eastatoe was the Cherokee name for the Carolina parakeet. The Eastatoe tribe of the Cherokees, known as the "Green Bird People," used the colorful green-and-yellow birds to adorn ceremonial robes.

The Carolina parakeet, once an abundant resident of the Carolinas, has been extinct for at least sixty years.

Buttermilk Falls, Frozen Creek Shoals, McCall Mill Shoals, Diamond Creek Falls

These four waterfalls are all located on private property adjacent to a road. Because of the viewing restrictions, they are not particularly scenic, and none of them makes a good photo subject. As with Shoal Creek Falls and Merry Falls in the Brevard hub, they are given a separate listing here due to their inclusion in several maps, brochures, and books on Transylvania County waterfalls. Remember, if you leave the road right-of-way at any of these falls, you will be trespassing.

Buttermilk Falls

From the starting point, drive 1.6 miles south on U.S. 178 to East Fork Road (S.R. 1107). Turn left and drive 3.5 miles to a stop sign. Turn right, continuing on East Fork Road. After 1.3 miles, turn right on S.R. 1105 at the garbage-collection site. It is 1 mile to a view of the falls on the left.

Frozen Creek Shoals

From the starting point, drive 2.7 miles south on U.S. 178 to S.R. 1139 (Old Toxaway Road) and turn right. Travel 3.7 miles, then turn right to stay on S.R. 1139. Continue 1.25 miles for a view of the falls on the left.

McCall Mill Shoals

From the starting point, drive 4.2 miles west on U.S. 64 to S.R. 1309. Turn right and drive 0.5 mile to S.R. 1313. Turn left. It is 0.3 mile to a view of the falls on the left.

Diamond Creek Falls

From the starting point, drive west on U.S. 64 for 0.5 mile to N.C. 215. Turn right and drive 0.8 mile to S.R. 1322. Turn left. It is 1.3 miles to a view of the falls on the left.

Bird Rock Falls *
(Cathedral Falls)

River: North Fork, French Broad River
County: Transylvania
USGS quadrangle: Rosman
Landowner: Private
Height: Small cascade
Beauty rating: 5
Trail length and difficulty: 0.2 mile; 5

Directions: From the starting point, drive 0.5 mile west on U.S. 64 to N.C. 215. Turn right. It is 7.7 miles to a cluster of buildings on the left. This is Living Waters, the home of There Is More Ministries. Park at the ministry and ask permission to visit the falls. You will be given trail information.

> **Photo Tips**
> Take photos using vertical and horizontal compositions. Both are effective. Use a vertical shot to include more of the cliff face, a horizontal to include more of the river.

The people at Living Waters graciously allow access to their property. In exchange, visitors are asked to check in before visiting the falls, to never go alone (good advice at any waterfall), and to respect the property.

There are actually three small cataracts on the property. Just behind the ministry, at the junction of Shoal Creek and the North Fork of the French Broad River, are two spillovers, one on each stream. The larger of the two is usually referred to as French Broad Falls. Downstream is Bird Rock Falls, where a high cliff looms over the cascade. Hundreds of purple martins used to nest on the cliffs, thus the name Bird Rock. The present owners have renamed the waterfall Cathedral Falls.

Nearby waterfalls: There are several named cascades on the North Fork of the French Broad River where it loosely parallels N.C. 215 through Pisgah National Forest. These cascades are not recommended, as they are all smaller than Bird Rock Falls and much more difficult to get to.

Kiesee Falls

River: Kiesee Creek
County: Transylvania
USGS quadrangle: Sam Knob

Landowner: Pisgah National Forest,
Pisgah Ranger District
Height: 20 feet
Beauty rating: 4
Trail length and difficulty: 0.5 mile; 9

Directions: From the starting point, drive 0.5 mile
west on U.S. 64 to N.C. 215. Turn right and drive
10.2 miles to F.R. 140. Turn right again. It is 2.1
miles to a pull-off on the right, located at a sharp
switchback to the left. Park here.

With so many spectacular waterfalls in the area,
I do not recommend attempting to reach this one.
If you do, you should be an experienced hiker. The
best route is to rock-hop Kiesee Creek and
bushwhack your way upstream to the base. Go in
the summer; the hike will be much easier if you do
not have to worry about getting wet.

Photo Tips

This waterfall is photogenic, but you will do well
to get just your body there, much less a tripod and
camera. If you do take gear, pack as compactly as
possible. One lens, from 24mm to 50mm, will do
nicely.

Kiesee Falls provides a good lesson in geology, as the
creek has carved large potholes and deep chasms out of
solid rock.

The waterfall and creek were named after Chief
Kiesee, a Cherokee who hid out in the area during the
Removal of 1838 and decided to remain rather than
live on the newly established Qualla Indian Reservation. Chief Kiesee was buried under a bluff on the
mountainside overlooking the falls.

Chestnut Falls

River: Chestnut Creek
County: Transylvania
USGS quadrangle: Sam Knob
Landowner: Pisgah National Forest,
Pisgah Ranger District
Height: 25 feet
Beauty rating: 3
Trail length and difficulty: 0.75 mile; 5

Directions: Follow the directions to the Kiesee
Falls trailhead. Continue on F.R. 140 for 0.7 mile
to the gated Kiesee Creek Road, on the right. Park
on the shoulder without blocking the gate. Hike
Kiesee Creek Road approximately 0.7 mile to a
fork at the Chestnut Road sign. Backtrack 150 feet
from the sign and follow the faint trail to the right
(west) into the woods. This trail leads 0.1 mile to
the base of the cascade. Note: If you can't find the
trail, enter the woods at the Chestnut Road sign
and head toward the creek. You will soon intersect
the trail.

Photo Tip

Save your film.

Chestnut Creek flows from the south slope of
Chestnut Bald between Courthouse Ridge and Chestnut Ridge. The creek, the ridge, the mountain, and the
waterfall are all named after the American chestnut
(Castanea dentata). At one time, the chestnut was the
most prominent species in the forest. Its wood was the
main source of tannin and was quite resistant to decay.
Its nuts were an important source of food for man and

wildlife. But in 1904, the fungus *Endothia parasitica* was accidentally introduced in New York City. By the late 1930s, nearly every chestnut in the southern Appalachians had succumbed to the chestnut blight caused by the fungus. Although some small trees remain, they die off before reaching reproductive age. Efforts are under way to reestablish the species using a hybrid that is resistant to the blight.

Courthouse Falls *

River: Courthouse Creek
County: Transylvania
USGS quadrangle: Sam Knob
Landowner: Pisgah National Forest,
    Pisgah Ranger District
Height: 45 feet
Beauty rating: 6
Trail length and difficulty: 0.3 mile; 5

Directions: Follow the directions to the Kiesee Falls trailhead, then continue on F.R. 140 for 0.9 mile to a pull-off on the right just across the creek. A trail leads downstream on the right at the Summey Cove sign. After 0.2 mile, there is a narrow path on the left at the Courthouse Falls sign that leads 0.1 mile to the pool at the base of the falls.

Photo Tip
Be careful about using too long a shutter speed. Because of the large volume of water in such small confines, long exposures will "wash out" the water into a white mass lacking any detail.

The headwaters of Courthouse Creek spring from the west slope of the 5,462-foot summit of Devil's

Courthouse. A cave in the mountain was believed by the Cherokees to be the courtroom where the fearful giant Judaculla held his judgment sessions.

This waterfall is highly recommended.

Nearby waterfall: If you backtrack on F.R. 140 approximately 1.6 miles, there is a small pull-off on the right with a view of a very high waterfall on the opposite mountainside.

Courthouse Falls
Nikon F3, 20mm lens, f/22 at 3 seconds, Fujichrome Velvia.

It took several trips to Courthouse Falls before I could make an acceptable photo. On this occasion, the water level was very low, and the long exposure—necessary in the deep forest setting—did not "wash out" the water too much.

Dill Falls

River: Tanasee Creek
County: Jackson
USGS quadrangle: Sam Knob
Landowner: Nantahala National Forest,
  Highlands Ranger District, Roy Taylor Forest
Height: 50-foot cascade in two levels
Beauty rating: 6
Trail length and difficulty: 0.2 mile; 5

Directions: From the starting point, drive west on U.S. 64 for 0.5 mile to N.C. 215. Turn right and drive approximately 14.1 miles to F.R. 4663, which looks like a driveway leading between old houses. Turn left. Drive 1.9 miles and turn left on F.R. 4663-B, which dead-ends at the trailhead after 0.5 mile. During wet weather, F.R. 4663-B may be too rough for passenger cars.

Hike the center logging road (behind the "Closed to Vehicles" sign) to a crossing of Tanasee Creek a few feet downstream from the falls.

> **Photo Tip**
> Everything comes together here—the waterfall, the rocks, the foliage. An ideal vantage point is the flat area a few feet downstream from the large rocks.

Dill Falls
Nikon F3, 20mm lens, polarizing filter, f/22 at 4 seconds, Fujichrome Velvia.

The 20mm lens is excellent for emphasizing foreground elements such as these boulders. Be careful though; if you are very far back from the waterfall with such a lens, the foreground will be rendered larger than the waterfall.

Tanasee Creek begins on the west side of Mount Hardy Gap, between Herrin Knob and Mount Hardy, and flows along the west side of Tanasee Ridge. Tanasee Ridge is skirted by N.C. 215 as it winds toward the Blue Ridge Parkway.

Mountain residents often corrupt the pronunciation of the name Tanasee (TAN-as-ee) to Tennessee; you will find the latter pronunciation widely used in place of the former.

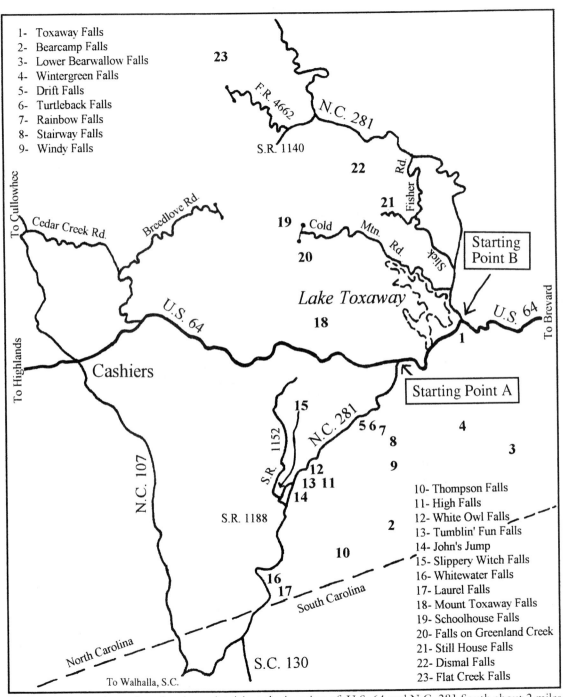

1- Toxaway Falls
2- Bearcamp Falls
3- Lower Bearwallow Falls
4- Wintergreen Falls
5- Drift Falls
6- Turtleback Falls
7- Rainbow Falls
8- Stairway Falls
9- Windy Falls

10- Thompson Falls
11- High Falls
12- White Owl Falls
13- Tumblin' Fun Falls
14- John's Jump
15- Slippery Witch Falls
16- Whitewater Falls
17- Laurel Falls
18- Mount Toxaway Falls
19- Schoolhouse Falls
20- Falls on Greenland Creek
21- Still House Falls
22- Dismal Falls
23- Flat Creek Falls

There are two starting points. Starting point A is at the junction of U.S. 64 and N.C. 281 South about 2 miles west of Toxaway Falls. Starting point B is at the junction of U.S. 64 and N.C. 281 North 0.4 mile east of Toxaway Falls.

Lake Toxaway

The community of Lake Toxaway has more waterfalls within a 15-mile radius than any other point in the state. It is the headwaters of five major river systems. The Toxaway, Horsepasture, Thompson, and Whitewater rivers all flow into Lake Jocassee and create the headwaters of the Keowee River, which joins the Tugaloo River to begin the famous Savannah River. To the north is the Tuckasegee River Gorge, with Tanasee Creek, Wolf Creek, and Flat Creek as major tributaries.

The number of waterfalls on each of these rivers and creeks is remarkable. The Thompson River alone has seven major waterfalls, with the Horsepasture adding another six. The drainage area of the Toxaway River likely contains more than two dozen major waterfalls along its 15-mile run from Cold Mountain Gap to Lake Jocassee.

Toxaway Falls *

River: Toxaway
County: Transylvania
USGS quadrangle: Reid
Landowner: Private
Height: Main drop of 125 feet
Beauty rating: 7
Trail length and difficulty: View roadside
Handicapped Accessible

Directions: U.S. 64 passes over the top of the falls 0.4 mile west of starting point B and about 2 miles east of starting point A.

Photo Tips

At one time, you could walk down the path to the base of Toxaway Falls for an excellent vantage point. Condominiums and a restaurant have since been built on the site and "No Trespassing" signs posted. Now, the only decent view is from the restaurant parking lot, but this is not a good vantage point for photos. One possible approach is to walk down the road and climb out onto the rock, being careful to stay near the road and away from the brink. A horizontal composition works well here, especially during the fall. Many people climb out onto the rock near the top of the falls, but this is very dangerous and is not recommended.

The photos you may have seen taken from a distant, overall view were shot from private property.

Toxaway Falls is situated just below Lake Toxaway and the Lake Toxaway Resort. The development of this area began in the 1890s with the construction of the lake and the famous Lake Toxaway Hotel. Early brochures described the hotel as "a high class resort with the best of service in every particular." That it was, catering to the likes of the Rockefeller, Vanderbilt, Reynolds, and Ford families.

The good times ended in 1916, when a great flood helped bring about the destruction of the earthen dam on Lake Toxaway. All the waters of the lake poured over the falls and through the gorge below. The hotel was closed and the property abandoned. The present lake was created in 1960, when the Lake Toxaway Company built a new dam and began another thriving resort community. The bare-rock expanse at the falls serves as a reminder of the destruction caused by the burst dam.

The waterfall, the lake, the river, a mountain, and a creek are all named after the Cherokee leader Toxaway.

Nearby waterfalls: All of the waterfalls surrounding the Lake Toxaway Resort are on private property.

Toxaway Falls
Pentax K-1000, 28mm lens, polarizing filter, f/22 at ¼ second, Kodachrome 25.

This photo was made before the condominiums were built and the "No trespassing" signs posted. It was also made before I knew anything about lighting and composition. I have included it to let you see how the falls look from the base.

Bearcamp Falls,
Lower Bearwallow Falls,
Wintergreen Falls

These three waterfalls are located on private property and require long, difficult hikes. Access is permitted by the landowner, Crescent Resources, Inc., a subsidiary of Duke Power. You can substantially reduce the trail length by visiting during hunting season, when the road gates are left open. However, road access is allowed only to four-wheel-drive vehicles. Entering the area on foot almost certainly requires overnight backpacking gear. Either way, you should get the Reid topographical map before entering. For more information, contact Crescent Resources (see the appendix).

Bearcamp Falls
(Hilliard Falls)

River: Bearcamp Creek
County: Transylvania
USGS quadrangle: Reid
Landowner: Crescent Resources, Inc.
Height: 60 feet
Beauty rating: 7
Trail length and difficulty:
   Approximately 2.5 miles; 8

Directions: From starting point A, drive 0.7 mile south on N.C. 281 to a dirt road on the left. If there is a gate across the road, you will have to hike from here. If it is open, and if you are in a four-wheel-drive vehicle, turn left and proceed 4.8 miles to a junction with a dirt road. Turn right and drive 3.1 miles to a gate at the Horsepasture River bridge, located approximately 1 mile downstream from Windy Falls. Park here. The trail follows the logging road across the river and ascends Narrow Rock Ridge, with views of Windy Falls. Descend the ridge and take the first road to the left; if you cross a year-round stream, you've gone too far. It is 0.5 mile to a road on the right which crosses Bearcamp Creek and picks up Foothills Trail. Follow this trail upstream 0.3 mile to the sign for Hilliard Falls.

The waterfall can also be reached by hiking Foothills Trail from the Whitewater Falls parking lot. If you are entering the area on foot, this is the preferred route. The outstanding Foothills Trail crosses the four major rivers in the Lake Jocassee watershed—the Whitewater, Thompson, Horsepasture, and Toxaway rivers—as well as Bearcamp Creek, on its route from Table Rock State Park to Oconee State Park, both in South Carolina. For information, contact the Foothills Trail Conference (see the appendix).

> **Photo Tip**
> Wade into the pool and shoot the falls head-on for a nice composition.

The last 10 feet of Bearcamp Falls project over a ledge, creating a semidry area in which exists a spray cliff natural community. The roundleaf sundew (*Drosera rotundifolia*), a common carnivorous plant, grows at the brink.

Nearby waterfall: There is a lower waterfall on Bearcamp Creek just before it empties into Lake Jocassee. Small and very difficult to get to, it is not recommended.

Lower Bearwallow Falls

River: Bearwallow Creek
County: Transylvania
USGS quadrangle: Reid
Landowner: Crescent Resources, Inc.
Height: 30-foot sheer drop
Beauty rating: 8
Trail length and difficulty: 0.2 mile; 10

Directions: Follow the directions to Bearcamp Falls, but instead of turning right at the dirt-road junction, turn left and drive 1.9 miles to the Toxaway River. Turn right into the camping area just before the river. Bearwallow Creek enters the Toxaway River on the other side of the campground. There is no trail to the falls. About the only way to get to it is to wade the creek upstream. The numerous small rapids make this a strenuous trek. Don't attempt this one unless you are an experienced hiker.

> ## Photo Tips
> This is an especially photogenic waterfall. There are numerous possible vantage points. One good choice is from the left a few feet into the creek. Use the grassy area as a foreground.

Few people have seen this waterfall, and most of those who have are anglers. If I were a trout fisherman, I could not think of a place I'd rather be.

A short distance downstream from where Bearwallow Creek empties into the Toxaway River is an area called the Cane Brake. From that point east to the Horsepasture River is prime habitat for the rare Oconee bells (*Shortia galacifolia*), often referred to as shortia. This delicate wildflower, with leaves resembling galax, was discovered in the late 1700s by André Michaux, a French botanist collecting for the Royal Botanical Gardens.

Shortia went unnoticed for another fifty years until Asa Gray, a famous Harvard botanist, stumbled upon the plant in Michaux's collection. Gray spent the next forty years searching for shortia in the "high mountains of Carolina," as described in Michaux's notes. The search ended in 1877, when a seventeen-year-old boy found the plant on the banks of the Catawba River. Two years later, Gray finally had the pleasure of seeing shortia growing in the wild.

Although Lake Jocassee flooded large populations of the plant, shortia can be found in surprising abundance at certain locations in the watershed, where it blooms in late March. *Shortia galacifolia* grows naturally in only six local counties. A closely related species, *Shortia soldanelloides*, grows in Japan.

Nearby waterfalls: There are a few small waterfalls upstream, but they are not worth the effort of getting to them. Upper Bearwallow Falls (also called Kathy Falls) is not accessible to the public despite being listed in nearly every publication on area waterfalls.

Lower Bearwallow Falls
Canon EOS Elan, 24mm tilt/shift lens, warming filter, f/22 at 2 seconds, Fujichrome Velvia.

Very often, the most effective composition is from the middle of the stream. Such is the case at Lower Bearwallow Falls. If you visit during the winter, be sure to bring waders.

Wintergreen Falls
(Winter Falls)

River: Toxaway
County: Transylvania
USGS quadrangle: Reid, at the 1,800-foot contour
   line
Landowner: Crescent Resources, Inc.
Height: About 80 feet
Beauty rating: 7
Trail length and difficulty:
   Approximately 2.5 miles; 9

Directions: Wintergreen Falls joins Dismal Falls and Flat Creek Falls (Jackson County) in a tie for being the most inaccessible waterfalls in the state. Only hard-core, experienced, and foolhardy hikers should attempt any of the three.

Should you decide to visit Wintergreen Falls, follow the directions for Lower Bearwallow Falls to the Toxaway River. If the river is down, you can wade across, or you may be able to ford it in your vehicle. But if the water is up, neither option will be possible.

If you are able to cross, continue on the logging road approximately 0.25 mile to an old road on the left. Follow this road as it parallels the river for 2 miles to a crossing of Panther Branch. At this point, leave the road and bushwhack, snarl, and cuss your way to the falls, about 0.4 mile upstream.

There is another route which can be taken if the river is up or the Crescent Resources access road is closed. From starting point B, drive 5.7 miles east on U.S. 64 to S.R. 1139. Turn right. The road forks left at 0.7 mile. Continue another 2.1 miles to an obscure logging road on the right. Park here. Cross the creek and follow the road 3.4 miles—an excellent ride for mountain bikers—to an old road on the right. This is the road that parallels the river.

> **Photo Tip**
> Lighten your load as much as possible. One lens in the 24mm to 35mm range will work fine.

Wintergreen is a small evergreen wildflower that once grew in profusion around the waterfall. Local residents, not realizing the original intent of the name, have shortened the name to Winter Falls.

The Waterfalls of the Horsepasture River
Drift Falls, Turtleback Falls, Rainbow Falls, Stairway Falls, Windy Falls

The Horsepasture Wild and Scenic River is possibly the most rugged and scenic river in all the southern Appalachians. It has been popular among hikers, swimmers, and trout fishermen for years. In 1984, a 6-mile stretch of the river was very nearly lost. That year, Carrasan Power Company, a California-based hydroelectric concern, received permits from the Federal Energy Regulatory Commission to build a "run of river" power plant on the Horsepasture. This type of plant, which has no reservoir, diverts nearly all of a river's flow through huge turbines to generate electricity—electricity that area power companies said was not needed. The news reached Bill Thomas of nearby Cedar Mountain. Largely through his efforts, a massive grass-roots campaign resulted in a 4.5-mile stretch of the river being designated a State Natural and Scenic River in 1985 and a National Wild and Scenic River the following year.

There are five major waterfalls on the Horsepasture that are accessible to the public.

Drift Falls *
(Driftwood Falls, Bust Your Butt Falls)

River: Horsepasture
County: Transylvania
USGS quadrangle: Reid
Landowner: Nantahala National Forest,
    Highlands Ranger District
Height: 80-foot slide
Beauty rating: 7
Trail length and difficulty: 0.1 mile; 7

Directions: From starting point A, drive 1.8 miles south on N.C. 281 to a pull-off on the left at the guardrail. The falls are reached by scrambling down the riprap and picking up any number of footpaths to the base. You will do well to walk back up N.C. 281 a few hundred feet and begin your descent there. This will eliminate much of the boulder-hopping.

Photo Tips
Drift Falls makes a good snow scene. There is ample surface for the snow to rest upon, and the falls are near the highway. There is an excellent area at the base from which to shoot.

Visit this waterfall on any hot summer weekend and you will see why it is called "Bust Your Butt" by the locals. Thrill seekers chute the falls and climb back up the crude rope to the left. To anyone who has tried it, including the author during his youthful insanity, the slide is appropriately named. A word of warning is in order here: unlike the relatively safe Sliding Rock in the Brevard area, Drift Falls can be extremely dangerous. Several people have drowned in the deep pool after hitting their heads on the way down.

Turtleback Falls *
(Umbrella Falls)

River: Horsepasture
County: Transylvania
USGS quadrangle: Reid
Landowner: Nantahala National Forest,
    Highlands Ranger District
Height: 20 feet
Beauty rating: 7
Trail length and difficulty: 0.4 mile; 3–7

Directions: Follow the directions to Drift Falls, then continue on the trail another 0.3 mile.

Photo Tips
There are three good vantage points for this exceptional cascade. At the first view of the falls from the trail, you can include the brink of Rainbow Falls, a few hundred feet downstream. From head-on, there is a large, flat rock to set up on. And from downstream, you can shoot looking back to the falls, which presents a unique perspective.

Be aware that on summer weekends, the area is crowded with sunbathers and swimmers.

The appropriately named Turtleback Falls glides over a curved rockface, then free-falls 10 feet into what is called the Chug Hole. As with Drift Falls, this area is popular among swimmers. But swimming and sliding are not recommended here either. The Chug Hole possesses strong currents and has been responsible for a number of drownings.

Drift Falls
Pentax K-1000, 24mm lens, f/22 at 1 second, Kodachrome 25.

When I made this photo years ago, my hands were nearly frostbitten. Now for cold-weather photography, I wear wool gloves over polypropylene liners. And if it gets really cold, I'll stuff a chemical hand warmer pack between the two.

Turtleback Falls
Nikon F3, 28-70mm zoom lens, polarizing filter, f/22 at 3 seconds, Fujichrome Velvia.

This is simple, straightforward composition, but an effective one. I arrived early in the morning to avoid contrasty lighting and hoards of people. I knew that later in the day the sunbathing crowd would be out.

Rainbow Falls *
(High Falls)

River: Horsepasture
County: Transylvania
USGS quadrangle: Reid
Landowner: Nantahala National Forest,
    Highlands Ranger District
Height: 150 feet
Beauty rating: 10
Trail length and difficulty: 0.6 mile; 4–7

Directions: Follow the directions to Drift Falls, then continue on the trail past Turtleback Falls to Rainbow Falls.

Photo Tips

This waterfall photographs well in any season, and especially so in winter and fall. Probably the best vantage point is from the trail just before it crosses the open area and enters the woods. A vertical or horizontal composition works well here. You can shoot from the base, but be careful about climbing down the bank, as it is suffering from severe erosion. Photographing from the lower overlook is nearly impossible due to the immense spray. In fact, if the water level is up, you may not be able to avoid the spray from any vantage point.

See the chapter on photographing waterfalls for tips on shooting rainbows and moonbows at Rainbow Falls. See photo in the color section.

One of the most spectacular sights in the mountains, Rainbow Falls greets the onlooker with an immense bombardment of spray. The constant mist creates high-arching rainbows on sunny days, giving the waterfall its name. During winter, this mist freezes on everything it touches, turning the area into an icy spectacle and making the trail treacherous.

Stairway Falls
(Stairstep Falls, Staircase Falls)

River: Horsepasture
County: Transylvania
USGS quadrangle: Reid
Landowner: Nantahala National Forest,
    Highlands Ranger District
Height: Seven steps that average 10 feet
Beauty rating: 7
Trail length and difficulty: 1.6 miles; 4–7

Directions: Follow the directions to Drift Falls, then continue on the trail past Turtleback and Rainbow falls. About 0.5 mile beyond Rainbow Falls, you will cross a good-sized stream and ascend 240 yards to a sharp switchback to the left; this is the second left turn you will come to after crossing the stream. Turn right at this switchback onto a small side trail and descend to the river. Follow the trail downstream to the falls. Continue along the trail a short distance to a high vantage point from which you can view all of the levels.

Photo Tips

A good vantage point is from the rocks a short distance downstream. For a higher vantage point that will include more of the falls, climb onto the hemlock tree that has fallen a short distance downstream.

Windy Falls

River: Horsepasture
County: Transylvania
USGS quadrangle: Reid
Landowner: Crescent Resources, Inc.

Stairway Falls
Nikon F3, 75-300mm zoom lens, warming filter, f/16 at ½ second, Fujichrome Velvia.

Having a zoom lens was a necessity for this photo. I was set up on a fallen hemlock tree and could not change my position by even a few inches without falling off the tree.

Height: Over 700 feet in a series of
   cascades and slides
Beauty rating: 8
Trail length and difficulty:
   Approximately 3.8 miles; 6–10

Directions: Most printed directions for reaching Windy Falls suggest hiking to Stairway Falls and continuing downstream an additional 0.8 mile. You can do this, but unless you are a Green Beret, you will regret it. This is rugged terrain. There is a decent trail, described below, that leads to the falls, but once again, caution is advised; it is long and strenuous.

   Follow the directions to Drift Falls, then continue on the trail past Turtleback and Rainbow falls. About 0.5 mile beyond Rainbow Falls, you will cross a good-sized stream and ascend 240 yards to a sharp switchback to the left; Stairway Falls is to the right on the small side trail. Continue on the main trail approximately 1 mile to a well-graded gravel road. This is the access road described in the directions to Bearcamp, Lower Bearwallow, and Wintergreen falls. Turn right and hike 0.2 mile to a left-hand turn. Take the side trail on the right; there is a large boulder in the trail after 100 feet. This trail descends very steeply about 1 mile to the river just above the falls. Getting a close view requires a considerable amount of rock climbing and root grabbing.

Photo Tips

The only way to get a good view of Windy Falls is from an airplane. If you aren't rich but are inclined to do some strenuous hiking—you shouldn't be here if you're not—there is one good possibility. A short distance downstream from the top is a large, flat area from which you can safely shoot. This vantage point encompasses a portion of the waterfall, with Narrow Rock Ridge looming in the distance. This makes an excellent autumn scene. There is a depression in the rock that may be filled with water. Use this and the green moss as a foreground.

On a list of waterfall superlatives, this one would be in the top ten of nearly every category. The mighty Horsepasture River drops 720 feet in the 0.75-mile stretch that is Windy Falls. At one point, the entire river is squeezed into a narrow cleft only a few feet wide. The thunderous crashing is reminiscent of the California coastline. However, there is no good vantage point from which to view the falls, and all hiking in the vicinity is extremely dangerous.

Allow a full day to see Windy Falls and the others on the Horsepasture River.

Thompson Falls
(Big Falls)

River: Thompson
County: Transylvania
USGS quadrangle: Reid
Landowner: Crescent Resources, Inc.
Height: Over 600 feet in three main
    drops and adjoining cascades
Beauty rating: 8

Trail length and difficulty:
    Approximately 3 miles; 6–10

Directions: From starting point A, drive 3.6 miles south on N.C. 281 to S.R. 1189, on the left. Park at this intersection. There is an old, gated logging road which intersects N.C. 281 and S.R. 1189. Ascend on this road to a fork. Take the right fork. You will enter a previously logged area and come to a second fork at about 0.8 mile. Bear left to reach the Thompson River at about 1 mile. Wade the river and continue on the road approximately 2 miles, passing the sound of two waterfalls that you will think are the main one. Look for a grassy area on the left at a wash beside an open portion of the woods; the area looks as if a tornado has gone through it. Climb down the wash for about 500 feet. At this point, it is a matter of following the sound of the waterfall several hundred feet to the base, a very difficult climb.

Photo Tips

Travel light and in the summer. You will have to get wet to fully explore the possibilities here, and if you are loaded down with gear, you will be too exhausted to concentrate on your photography.

I do not recommend attempting to reach the upper two waterfalls.

The Thompson River drops over 600 feet in a 0.5-mile stretch that ends with Thompson Falls. Two other sizable cascades are in the run; both are practically inaccessible. The main lower section of Thompson Falls is over 100 feet high. A small, deep pool at the base was used by the Cherokees as a place to bathe. Appropriately, the Indians called the falls Seyantooga, which means "bathing in the water."

The Thompson River was named after John Thompson, an early settler.

High Falls

River: Thompson
County: Transylvania
USGS quadrangle: Reid
Landowner: Crescent Resources, Inc.
Height: 70 feet
Beauty rating: 8
Trail length and difficulty: 1.25 miles; 5–7

Directions: Follow the directions to the parking area for Thompson Falls and begin the trail to that waterfall. After approximately 0.8 mile, you will come to a fork. Bear right and continue about 0.4 mile. Look carefully for a very faint side path on the left at a small poplar tree. Climb down the path to the base of the falls. During the summer, the area is heavily overgrown and the side path may not be recognizable.

High Falls
Canon EOS Elan, 24mm tilt/shift lens, polarizing filter, f/22 at 4 seconds, Fujichrome Velvia.

I made both vertical and horizontal compositions of High Falls. I prefer the horizontal format, which includes the boulder and the whirlpool on the left.

Photo Tips
Wade the river to get to the flat, sandy area, from which a vertical or horizontal composition works well. Stay as far to the right as possible to eliminate the spray.

High Falls is probably the least-known of Transylvania's major waterfalls, which is surprising considering its beauty.

The strong fishy smell comes from a trout farm a short distance upstream on a tributary.

White Owl Falls

River: Thompson
County: Transylvania
USGS quadrangle: Reid
Landowner: Crescent Resources, Inc.
Height: 20 feet
Beauty rating: 5
Trail length and difficulty: 0.2 mile; 8

Directions: Park at the same location as for Thompson Falls. Walk down N.C. 281 and enter the woods on the left just before the power-line crossing. Scramble down the riprap and follow the sound of the falls. This area is heavily overgrown during the summer.

Photo Tip
A short distance downstream is a rhododendron shrub growing horizontally out of the right bank. There is an open area in the shrub which perfectly frames the falls. If this rhododendron is in bloom, you will have an outstanding photo opportunity.

Owls once hooted all night long around White Owl Falls, though they almost certainly were not white.

This is a little-known and little-visited waterfall that is well worth the effort for experienced hikers.

Nearby waterfalls: Upstream from White Owl Falls and north of N.C. 281 are two small waterfalls. They are not worth the effort it takes to get to them.

White Owl Falls
Nikon F3, 28-70mm zoom lens, warming filter, f/22 at 3 seconds, Fujichrome Velvia.

There was a nicely situated rhododendron shrub, in full bloom, growing out of the right bank. Unfortunately, it was shaded, while the falls were sunlit. I knew the contrast was too much for the film to handle, so I waded the stream and made this straightforward portrait.

Tumblin' Fun Falls

Just before Mill Creek enters the Thompson River, its waters pour over a high waterfall known as Tumblin' Fun. There is no trail access, and the falls are on private property. However, the owners of the Sweetwater

Trout Farm, just downstream from the falls, are considering constructing a trail to allow access for their customers. Inquire at the farm, which is located on N.C. 281 some 4.1 miles south of U.S. 64. A sign directs you to the left just after you cross the Thompson River.

John's Jump

River: Mill Creek
County: Transylvania
USGS quadrangle: Cashiers
Landowner: Nantahala National Forest,
  Highlands Ranger District
Height: 25 feet
Beauty rating: 4
Trail length and difficulty: 0.1 mile; 6

Directions: From starting point A, drive 4.8 miles on N.C. 281 South and park on the left shoulder. An obscure trail leads down the right side of the creek.

Photo Tip
  Wade into the pool to eliminate the distracting branches.

Believe it or not, this waterfall was named after John Hinkle, who, in the early 1920s, jumped down a large rock to get to the base.

Slippery Witch Falls

River: Mill Creek
County: Transylvania
USGS quadrangle: Cashiers
Landowner: Private
Height: Cascades measuring over 100 feet
Beauty rating: 1
Trail length and difficulty: View roadside
Handicapped Accessible

Directions: From starting point A, drive 4.9 miles on N.C. 281 South and turn right on S.R. 1188 (Whitewater Church Road). After 0.2 mile, turn right on S.R. 1152 (Upper Whitewater Road) and drive 0.4 mile to a pull-off on the right just before the creek. Observe the "No Trespassing" signs and view the falls only from the bridge.

Photo Tip
Save your film.

"Chucky Joe" Huger, an early botanist and traveler, spent considerable time exploring this area. He once described this waterfall as a "slippery bitch" after an incident of unsure footing. His landlady, Mrs. Perry Hinkle, did not approve of his language and cleaned up the description to Slippery Witch. Bitch or witch, the cascade is definitely slippery.

Twin Falls

Approximately 1.1 miles beyond Slippery Witch Falls, S.R. 1152 crosses the Thompson River. Just downstream is Twin Falls. The waterfall is on private property, though it and Slippery Witch Falls have both been listed in some publications as being in Nantahala National Forest. You should be aware that if you leave the roadside at either of the two, you will be trespassing.

Whitewater Falls *
(Upper Falls)

River: Whitewater
County: Transylvania/Jackson
USGS quadrangle: Cashiers
Landowner: Nantahala National Forest, Highlands Ranger District
Height: 411 feet
Beauty rating: 10
Trail length and difficulty: 0.2 mile; 2
Handicapped Accessible

Whitewater Falls
Nikon F3, 75-300mm zoom lens, polarizing filter stacked on warming filter, f/22 at 2 seconds, Fujichrome Velvia.

This photo was made from the same vantage point as most published photographs of Whitewater Falls—the lower overlook described in the text. However, using the long zoom lens, I was able to present a different perspective of the falls by isolating the upper drop. See additional photo in the color section.

Directions: From starting point A, drive 8.6 miles on N.C. 281 South. Turn left at the Whitewater Falls Scenic Area sign and drive 0.2 mile to the parking area. It is 0.2 mile on the paved trail to the upper overlook. Continue to the right down a long series of steps to reach the middle overlook. A lower viewpoint is reached by scrambling down to the projecting rock a few feet in front of the middle overlook. There is no safe way to get to the base.

Photo Tips

You can shoot from any of the three vantage points described above. From the upper overlook, it is difficult to eliminate the foreground clutter. Also, if you shoot from behind the split-rail fence (the safest option), you will cut off the bottom portion of the falls. A better option is the middle overlook, from which you can shoot the scene framed by large evergreen trees. My favorite vantage point is the lower overlook. It offers the closest view, and there are a few trees that can be used to frame the image.

Whitewater Falls looks great with snow or during early spring. During the rhododendron bloom, if you work carefully, you can include a few blossoms in the foreground. In autumn, this is one of the finest photo opportunities in the southern Appalachians.

Whitewater Falls is the most spectacular cascade east of the Rockies, and nearly the highest as well. There are several waterfalls in the southern Appalachians that are listed as being higher, but none of these has the combination of height, water volume, and open expanse that Whitewater Falls does. Even if it isn't technically the highest, it surely ranks as the finest.

The paved trail that leads to the overlook and continues as a path to the left was once a section of the old Bohaynee Road. It is now part of Foothills Trail. You can follow this path to a ford of Whitewater River a short distance upstream from the falls. If you foolishly decide to make an attempt near the brink, remember this: Whitewater Falls claims more lives than any other in the state. In fact, the cascade is so dangerous that permanent mounting posts have been installed for attaching the cables that haul out the bodies. It is nearly as dangerous to hike to the base. Any attempt to do the latter will also threaten the fragile spray cliff natural community which thrives in the moist environment.

Whitewater Falls has been designated a North Carolina Natural Heritage Area.

Nearby waterfalls: From the trail leading to Whitewater Falls, you can hear—as well as see, during the winter—a waterfall across the gorge. This is Laurel Falls, described separately.

A few miles downstream on the Whitewater River is Lower Whitewater Falls, located in South Carolina. At 400 feet, the waterfall is impressive and well worth the hike. From the road leading to the Whitewater Falls parking area, drive south on N.C. 281 for 0.4 mile to the entrance of Duke Power's Bad Creek Pumped Storage Station. The gatekeeper will provide a map and access information.

Laurel Falls
(Corbin Creek Falls)

River: Corbin Creek
County: Transylvania
USGS quadrangle: Cashiers
Landowner: Nantahala National Forest,
　　Highlands Ranger District

Height: Continuous series of cascades
  about 400 feet high
Beauty rating: 3
Trail length and difficulty: 0.8 mile; 8

Directions: Follow the directions to Whitewater
Falls and take the trail to the right at the upper
overlook. The trail leads to the middle overlook,
turns right, and descends steeply to Whitewater
River. Cross on the footbridge. After 0.1 mile, you
will reach Corbin Creek. The lower cascade of
Laurel Falls is reached by working your way up the
right bank. Seeing any more requires strenuous
rock climbing.

 The trail you have been following is part of the
outstanding Foothills Trail. It continues east and
crosses the Thompson, Horsepasture, and Toxaway
rivers on its way to Table Rock State Park in South
Carolina.

> ## Photo Tip
> During the right conditions, you might make a
> decent photo of Laurel Falls, but it's really not
> worth the effort. Pass on this one unless you're
> hiking Foothills Trail anyway.

 If Corbin Creek were a little larger and did not have
the dense overstory that it does, Laurel Falls would be
an impressive waterfall. The creek tumbles over the
same ridge and descends the same distance as
Whitewater Falls. Unfortunately, there is no way to see
all of the falls from one vantage point. And to see all
of the cascades individually would require a difficult
and dangerous climb.

Mount Toxaway Falls

River: Tributary of Little Hogback Creek
County: Jackson
USGS quadrangle: Big Ridge
Landowner: Private
Height: Cascades measuring several hundred feet,
  only a portion of which is visible
Beauty rating: 1
Trail length and difficulty: View roadside
Handicapped Accessible

Directions: From starting point A, drive west on
U.S. 64 for 3.7 miles and turn right on Tower
Road. Take the right fork immediately after you
turn. Drive 1 mile to the overlook at the right-hand
switchback. Note: The last 0.5 mile of this route is
on a very steep gravel surface with hairpin turns.

> ## Photo Tips
> In early spring or autumn, you can make a good
> photo of the mountainside and the expensive
> homes on the ridge. The waterfall will accent this
> image but is not worthy of a photo itself.

 If you continue on Tower Road, you will reach the
4,777-foot summit of Mount Toxaway at the fire
tower. The views from here are much more impressive
than those at Mount Toxaway Falls, which flows on
the west side of the mountain and south from Hogback Mountain.

The Waterfalls of Panthertown Valley

Schoolhouse Falls, Falls on Greenland Creek

Sierra Magazine described Panthertown Valley as "one of the least known, but most magnificent areas in the Southern Appalachians." Others have called it the "Yosemite of the East." Through the eyes of a tourist, the valley might not look any different from any other pretty mountain scene, but to a biologist, it is truly significant. At least eight globally endangered plant species are present, along with eleven natural communities, four of them very rare.

In 1986, the Nature Conservancy began negotiations with the landowner, Liberty Life Insurance, to purchase the tract. Everything seemed to be going well until Duke Power suddenly slipped in and bought the valley for $10 million. The conservation community was shocked. Duke Power eventually sold the property to the Nature Conservancy, which in turn sold it to the United States Forest Service, but not before a 230-kilovolt transmission line had been run across one end.

There are no developed trails in Panthertown Valley, only old logging roads and fishing trails. No motorized traffic is allowed. The Forest Service is walking a fine line between allowing access to the public and protecting this fragile resource. In fact, it is with mixed feelings that I include this section in the book. Part of me wants to keep quiet in hopes that the area won't become another Shining Rock and be loved to death, while another part believes that education is the best policy. In light of the fact that Panthertown Valley is becoming more and more publicized, making human traffic inevitable, I have chosen the latter.

The valley is laced with numerous streams that contain several waterfalls, but only two are included here. The rest require difficult bushwhacking and detailed directions or are insignificant compared to others nearby.

There are two access points for entry into the valley. The western access is used and recommended more often. It provides the finest views, is closer to more of the attractions, and has more parking. To reach it, drive west on U.S. 64 for 8 miles from N.C. 281 South; this location is 1.9 miles east of N.C. 107 in Cashiers. Turn right on Cedar Creek Road (S.R. 1120) and drive 2.2 miles to Breedlove Road (S.R. 1121). Turn right and drive 3.5 miles to where the road dead-ends at the parking area.

The eastern access is closer to the listed waterfalls but provides almost no parking; if you plan on camping or spending a full day in the valley, it is strongly advised that you enter from the western end. To reach the eastern access, drive 0.85 mile north on N.C. 281 from U.S. 64. Turn left on Cold Mountain Road (S.R. 1301) and drive 5.8 miles to the gate. You can park at the gate or in the grassy area just before it, but do not block the road.

Schoolhouse Falls

River: Greenland Creek
County: Jackson
USGS quadrangle: Big Ridge
Landowner: Nantahala National Forest, Highlands Ranger District
Height: About 20 feet
Beauty rating: 7
Trail length and difficulty: From the east end, 0.85 mile; 5. From the west end, approximately 3 miles; 5.

Directions: From the east end, walk down the gravel road about 0.8 mile to a fork just before the creek. Take the side trail on the left, which leads upstream to the falls.

Crabtree Falls
Canon EOS Elan, 24mm tilt/shift lens, polarizing filter, f/22 at 2 seconds, Fujichrome Velvia.

I liked the dense foliage but I was careful to not let it completely cover the falls. The wind created from the falling water caused the foliage to blow almost constantly. It took quite a while before I was able to make a sharp image.

Harper Creek Falls
Canon EOS Elan, 24mm tilt/shift lens, polarizing filter, f/22 at ¼ second, Fujichrome Velvia.

This photo is one of very few in this book that was made on a sunny day, when the waterfall is receiving direct lighting. The reason it works in this situation is that the sun is low in the sky, and the waterfall is in the open, allowing it to be evenly illuminated. Adding to the appeal of the image is the early spring growth and the deep blue sky. This composition would not work with an overcast sky.

Rainbow Falls
Pentax K1000, 28mm lens, polarizing filter, f/8 at ¹/₃₀ second, Kodachrome 25.

When I made this photo years ago, I did not have a system for shooting in spray. The spray was so intense that I could not set up my tripod. Instead, I quickly made a hand-held shot, then turned away from the spray and wiped the lens. By repeating this process over a period of several minutes, I was able to make a couple of satisfactory images. Of course, I got thoroughly drenched in the process.

Second Falls
Nikon F3, 75-300mm zoom lens, Tiffen Enhancing Filter stacked on warming filter, f/22 at ½ second, Fujichrome Velvia.

This image was made a few feet from my truck, beside the Blue Ridge Parkway. The Enhancing Filter emphasizes the red hues while the warming filter adds a warm tone. Some people may argue that this is too much color saturation, but the filters, and the Fujichrome Velvia film, only serve to record the vivid colors as I perceived them in my mind.

Mouse Creek Falls
Nikon F3, 28-70mm zoom lens, polarizing filter, f/22 at 3 seconds, Fujichrome Velvia.

Anyone should be able to make a photo of Mouse Creek Falls as good as this one. The only requirements are a 2-mile hike, an overcast day, and of course, proper equipment. The zoom lens allowed me to get the precise composition that I wanted.

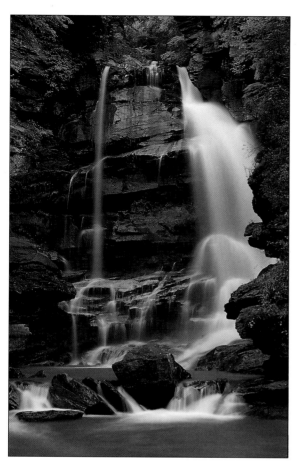

Big Bradley Falls
Nikon F3, 28-70mm zoom lens, f/16 at 1 second, Fujichrome Velvia.

During normal stream flow, the constant spray generated by Big Bradley Falls makes photography aggravating. The setup described on page 21 enabled me to make this photo without harm to my gear, but not without getting myself thoroughly drenched in the process.

Hunt-Fish Falls
Nikon F3, 20mm lens, warming filter, f/22 at 2 seconds, Fujichrome Velvia.

I arrived too late to photograph the falls surrounded by peak autumn color, but I was thrilled to discover these colorful leaves at the edge of the pool. To photograph the falls during the soft light of dawn, I hiked the 0.75 mile trail with a flashlight before the sun rose.

Looking Glass Falls
Nikon F3, 24mm lens, polarizing filter, f/22 at 2 seconds, Fujichrome Velvia.

I walked past several people who were shooting the typical vertical photo of Looking Glass Falls and made this unique image from the large rock just downstream.

Whitewater Falls
Nikon F3, 28-70mm lens, warming filter, f/22 at ½ second, Fujichrome Velvia.

I visited Whitewater Falls over a period of several days to make a photograph at the peak of autumn color. On the last day I was able to photograph the falls, still a couple of days early for the peak, the lighting was horrible. I set up my tripod and waited 3 hours before I could make this image.

Forney Creek Cascade
Nikon F3, 28-70mm zoom lens, f/22 at 4 seconds, Fujichrome Velvia.

Light, misty rain and early spring leaves make an unbeatable combination. This photograph is a favorite of mine.

Midnight Hole
Nikon F3, 20mm lens, polarizing filter, f/22 at
3 seconds, Fujichrome Velvia.

If I find a strong foreground element, such as this moss-
covered rock, I will compose the scene with it in the center
of the frame. The renowned, landscape photographer David
Muench is noted for this. I'm not worried about my
photographs looking like Muench's. I should be so lucky!

Linville Falls
Nikon F3, 75-300mm zoom lens, polarizing filter
stacked on warming filter, f/16 at 2 seconds,
Fujichrome Velvia.

You don't have to travel to remote places to make great
photographs. This image of Linville Falls was photographed from the easily accessible Chimney View overlook.
The key to its success is that I made sure to visit on an
overcast day.

From the west end, walk down the gravel road to an intersection. Continue straight until you meet up with Panthertown Creek, then parallel it for some distance until you reach a crossing. Cross the creek and begin paralleling Greenland Creek. After crossing Greenland Creek, take the side trail on the right that leads to the falls. Note: If you enter from the west, it is recommended that you bring the Big Ridge quadrangle (modified for Forest Service use), available from the ranger station.

Photo Tip
There are two excellent vantage points—directly in front and the left bank.

During the 1920s, when the area was being heavily logged, close to two hundred families lived in the valley. A small schoolhouse was built near the falls, but the Depression dried up all the logging jobs. Classes were never held in the building, though it did serve as a homeplace for a number of years.

The deep-brown color of the water is natural and comes from tannic acid in the soil.

Nearby waterfalls: If you drive to the east entrance, you will pass a small falls beside Cold Mountain Road. It is called Shower Falls, and during the summer, standing under it might not be such a bad idea.

Approximately 0.8 mile farther up the road is a small wet-weather cascade on the right, with a similar cascade another 0.2 mile farther, also on the right.

Schoolhouse Falls
Nikon 8008s, 28-70mm zoom lens, polarizing filter stacked on warming filter, f/22 at 2 seconds, Fujichrome Velvia.

This image again proves how indispensible the 28-70mm zoom lens is for waterfall photography. Changing my position would not have been as effective.

Falls on Greenland Creek
(Holly Falls)

River: Greenland Creek
County: Jackson
USGS quadrangle: Lake Toxaway
Landowner: Nantahala National Forest,
    Highlands Ranger District
Height: 70 feet in two sections
Beauty rating: 7
Trail length and difficulty:
    From the east end, 1.5 miles; 5.
    From the west end, approximately 4 miles; 7.

Directions: From the east-end gate, walk back up the road and cross the small stream on the steel bridge. Take the side trail on the immediate right, which follows a property line to a clearing. Turn left and continue to the gate at a gravel road. From there, follow the old logging road that leads sharply to the right; after about 0.75 mile, you will reach Greenland Creek at a small clearing. Continue upstream on a small path approximately 0.4 mile to the falls.

From the west entrance, use the Big Ridge and Lake Toxaway quadrangles (modified for Forest Service use) to determine the best route. The falls are located at the 3,880-foot elevation of Greenland Creek.

Photo Tip
From a vantage point directly in front, and using a vertical composition, you cannot go wrong.

A landowner on nearby Ravenrock Mountain spent several years trying to track down the name of this waterfall, with no success. When he finally concluded that it probably didn't have a name, his daughter Holly decided to name it after herself. Carlton McNeil, the unofficial guide to Panthertown Valley, says the waterfall is too pretty to be named after Holly, so he calls it Cheyenne Falls, after his dog.

Still House Falls

River: Fork Creek
County: Transylvania
USGS quadrangle: Lake Toxaway,
    at the 3,360-foot contour line
Landowner: Pisgah National Forest,
    Pisgah Ranger District
Height: 30 feet
Beauty rating: 5
Trail length and difficulty: Approximately 0.4
    mile; 9

Directions: Although Still House Falls is located on public property, the only good access is over private land. This route is not described here. A public route is detailed below, but because of its difficulty, you may wish to skip this waterfall. If you do decide to go, you will need the Lake Toxaway quadrangle (modified for Forest Service use) to determine the property lines.

From starting point B, drive 1.35 miles north on N.C. 281 and turn left on Slick Fisher Road (S.R. 1306). Drive 2.1 miles and turn left on McIntosh Road (S.R. 1375). It is 0.55 mile to a small pull-off on the right at the left turn around the ridge. Park here. Using the Lake Toxaway quadrangle, find the property line that begins at the intersection of McIntosh Road and the Tennessee Valley Divide (this is where you are parked) and leads northwest toward the summit of Big Pisgah Mountain. Follow this property line, being sure to stay on the right-hand side, to an obvious trail. Turn right. After 60 feet, turn right onto a faint side trail which leads to the falls.

The entire flow of Fork Creek is forced through a 6-inch cleft in a high bluff. The hydraulic action causes the creek to shoot out over the precipice and form Still House Falls.

Just to the side under the bluff is an abandoned still site.

Dismal Falls

River: Dismal Creek
County: Transylvania
USGS quadrangle: Lake Toxaway
Landowner: Pisgah National Forest,
    Pisgah Ranger District
Height: Over 200 feet
Beauty rating: 7
Trail length and difficulty: 1.75 miles; 10

Directions: There are several requirements for a hike to Dismal Falls. You should have a map, a compass, quality hiking boots, and a temporary loss of sanity. Only Flat Creek Falls is as dangerous as this one. If you go, at least follow this advice: don't go alone, and notify someone of your plans.

From starting point B, drive 1.3 miles north on N.C. 281 and turn left on Slick Fisher Road (S.R. 1306), which provides a smoother route than staying on N.C. 281. Continue 4.4 miles to where Slick Fisher Road ends farther up N.C. 281. Turn left. It is 0.3 mile to a pull-off on the right. Park here. Begin your hike across the road on the gated trail. After 1 mile and several creek crossings, you will walk under a power line and pass a side trail on the left. A few hundred feet beyond the side trail, strike out through the woods on the left. The Lake Toxaway quadrangle shows a trail leading up Dismal Creek to the falls. This trail does not exist; it is strictly off-trail hiking from this point on.

After crossing the West Fork of the French Broad River, continue straight. You will intersect Dismal Creek. You can follow Dismal Creek upstream to the falls, but if you know how to read a topographical map (you should not be hiking to Dismal Falls if you don't), you will do well to ascend the west ridge paralleling the creek. This will considerably reduce the amount of rock climbing. If you choose to follow the ridge, work your way back toward the creek after about 0.5 mile and you should hear, if not see, the waterfall. If you choose to follow the creek, you will come to a small waterfall at about 0.5 mile. Dismal Falls is upstream a few hundred feet.

There are several creeks off Big Pisgah Mountain and Shelton Pisgah Mountain that parallel Dismal Creek, and it is easy to get confused. Study the map.

Dismal Falls is appropriately named. Bluffs, boulders, crevices, and rhododendron thickets combine to create an area that is enjoyed by only a hardy few.

From N.C. 281 near Owens Gap, there is a fair view of the falls with Big Pisgah Mountain and Shelton Pisgah Mountain to the left and right, respectively.

Dismal Falls is a North Carolina Natural Heritage Area.

Nearby waterfalls: Nearly every stream flowing off the north side of Big Pisgah Mountain and Shelton Pisgah Mountain contains small waterfalls. The next stream west of Dismal Creek has a very nice free fall of about 70 feet. There is no trail to this waterfall, but it is much easier to get to than Dismal Falls. Follow the route to Dismal Falls but continue straight on the main trail instead of turning left into the woods. When you reach a small area of white pines after about 0.2 mile, look for red ribbons tied to branches on the left. Follow these ribbons across the West Fork of the French Broad River and on to the waterfall. If the ribbons are no longer there and a trail has not been cut, it is not worth trying to find the waterfall.

There is also a small waterfall to the right of the main trail where it enters the large grassy area.

Flat Creek Falls

River: Flat Creek
County: Jackson
USGS quadrangle: Big Ridge
Landowner: Nantahala National Forest,
    Highlands Ranger District, Roy Taylor Forest
Height: Several hundred feet of cascades and
    slides, along with a sheer drop of 100 feet
Beauty rating: 9
Trail length and difficulty: 2 miles to upper overlook,
    3 miles to base; 10

Directions: Viewing Flat Creek Falls from the base requires the most difficult and dangerous hike of any waterfall listed in this book. There is an upper overlook of the falls that is not as difficult to reach, but the view is not good and is not worth the effort. Also, this area of Roy Taylor Forest is laced with old logging roads and trails, most of which are not shown on the topographical map. These routes traverse private property, further complicating a hike to the falls. My recommendation is not to go. If you do go, the following directions are only meant to be used in conjunction with the Big Ridge quadrangle, modified for Forest Service use.

From starting point B, drive 1.3 miles north on N.C. 281 and turn left on Slick Fisher Road (S.R. 1306), which provides a smoother route than staying on N.C. 281. Continue 4.4 miles to where Slick Fisher Road ends farther up N.C. 281. Turn left. Drive 3.4 miles and turn left on S.R. 1140. It is 1.7 miles to a fork; head right on F.R. 4662. Drive 2.1 miles to where the road dead-ends at a parking area. Park here. Note: The Forest Service has plans to put a gate on F.R. 4662 at Tritt Knob, which will add approximately 0.75 mile to the following hike.

Cross Flat Creek; you will soon come to a camping area. An old logging road leads left from the camping area and, if you take every turn to the right, comes out at Grassy Gap after approximately 2.5 miles. This is by far the easier route, but it passes through 0.5 mile of private property, and not all the roads are shown on the map. It is not recommended that you travel on private property.

Instead, bear right at the camping area; you will reach a small ridge after 0.1 mile. There is a trail intersection at this point. Turn right and follow an extremely overgrown roadbed as far as possible and descend to Flat Creek. After crossing the creek, you will come to a beaver pond. During the summer, the area around the beaver pond is extremely overgrown and difficult to pass through.

It is also prime rattlesnake country. Cross the creek again and work your way to the logging road on the far side. This road, shown as a single dotted line on the topographical map, leads right to Grassy Gap. To the left, it skirts the west end of Isinglass Knob and meets the road shown on the topographical map at a gap; this is the route you would have followed if you had turned left at the camping area.

Once at Grassy Gap, you can follow the ridge to a poor view of the top of the falls. To reach the base, follow the logging road to the private-property boundary (refer to the topographical map) and descend to Flat Creek. Follow the creek upstream to the falls.

Again, this is an extremely difficult and dangerous hike. The only reason I am including this waterfall is because some people will see the falls on the map and attempt the hike without directions.

Photo Tips

No photo opportunity exists from the top. From the base, you can make a photo of the main drop and lower cascades, but positioning yourself will be hazardous to your health. If the water level is up, the immense spray will prevent you from taking any pictures.

Strap all of your gear to your back so you will have both hands free on the hike.

Flat Creek Falls and nearby Dismal Falls are waterfalls that are best left alone. Although both are very scenic, they simply are not worth risking your life over. At Flat Creek Falls, the fragile environment is easily disturbed due to loose soil. This is extra incentive to stay away.

Nearby waterfalls: Upper Flat Creek Falls is about 0.25 mile upstream from the second crossing of Flat Creek. It is small and not worth the difficult hike.

To see Cold Creek Falls, retrace your route to N.C. 281 and turn left. After 2.45 miles, turn right on S.R. 1762 just beyond the lake. It is 1 mile to where S.R. 1760 leads straight ahead and S.R. 1762 continues to the right. Continuing on S.R. 1762, it is 0.5 mile to a view of the falls on the right.

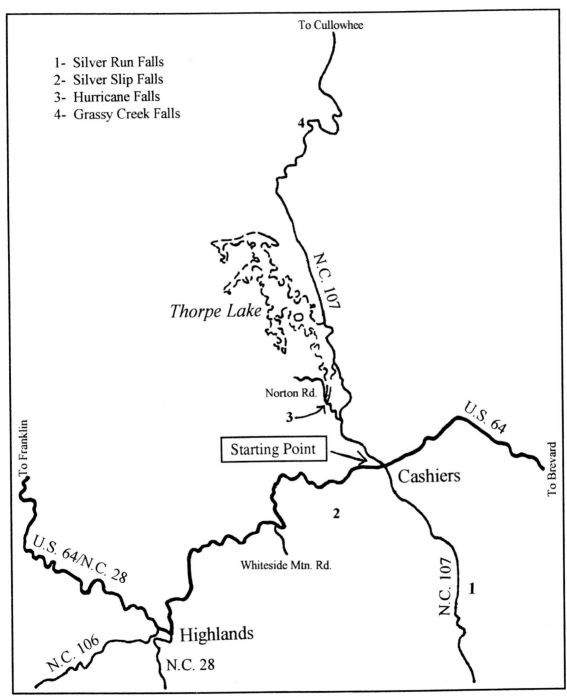

1- Silver Run Falls
2- Silver Slip Falls
3- Hurricane Falls
4- Grassy Creek Falls

To Cullowhee

4

N.C. 107

Thorpe Lake

Norton Rd.

3

U.S. 64

Starting Point

Cashiers

To Franklin

To Brevard

2

U.S. 64/N.C. 28

Whiteside Mtn. Rd.

N.C. 107

1

N.C. 106

Highlands

N.C. 28

The starting point is the intersection of U.S. 64 and N.C. 107.

Cashiers

The popular resort town of Cashiers (pronounced Cash-ers) provides a multitude of outdoor recreational opportunities. Fishing, water-skiing, sailing, golf, and tennis are available, as well as excellent hiking and rock climbing. Four major rivers spring from this 3,486-foot plateau: the Whitewater, the Horsepasture, the West Fork of the Tuckasegee, and the well-known Chattooga of *Deliverance* fame.

Silver Run Falls *

River: Silver Run Creek
County: Jackson
USGS quadrangle: Cashiers
Landowner: Nantahala National Forest, Highlands Ranger District
Height: 25 feet
Beauty rating: 6
Trail length and difficulty: 0.1 mile; 2

Directions: From the starting point, drive 4 miles south on N.C. 107 and park on the left side of the road. There are a utility pole and a holly tree at the pull-off; the well-graded trail begins at the holly tree. Along the way, you will have to either wade the Whitewater River or cross on a tricky footlog.

Photo Tips
    A few years ago, you could hardly make a bad photo here. Now, you have to be careful to eliminate the fallen hemlock trees. A good choice is to shoot from the left bank right at the base. The resulting profile can be very effective. Or you can wade the pool and shoot from the other side. If you are visiting with family or friends and would like a picture of them, you can use the downed trees to your advantage. Position the people on the trunks in the foreground of the scene.

The large, open pool and sandy beach make this a popular destination. The pool provides a safe and easily accessible swimming area.

Silver Slip Falls *

River: Chattooga
County: Jackson
USGS quadrangle: Cashiers
Landowner: Private
Height: Impossible to tell; probably 100 feet
Beauty rating: Waterfall, 1; overall view from the overlook, 10
Trail length and difficulty: 1 mile; 6

Directions: Silver Slip Falls is on private property and is not accessible. However, a view can be had from a trail overlook on Whiteside Mountain.
    From the starting point, drive west on U.S. 64 for 4.6 miles to Whiteside Mountain Road (S.R. 1600). Turn left. It is 1 mile to a large parking area on the left. A 2-mile loop trail traverses the summit of the mountain; the left-hand route offers the more gentle ascent. The view of the falls is from the northeast at the plaque commemorating the Crouch family's generosity in making the lands below available to the Forest Service.

Photo Tips

Once you reach the summit of Whiteside Mountain, you will forget all about the waterfall. The views are spectacular and will be the focus of your photography. Remember that the most pleasing lighting occurs during the early-morning and evening hours. The south side provides a perfect sunrise viewpoint, but this requires a 1-mile hike with a flashlight. Similarly, the rising full moon can be photographed from the south side. If you use a little common sense, bring along a friend, and carry a spare light, either of these excellent opportunities can be safely realized.

Camping is not allowed on the summit.

Directions: From the starting point, drive 1.8 miles north on N.C. 107 and turn left on Norton Road (S.R. 1145). It is 0.6 mile to a pull-off on the right with a view of the waterfall.

Photo Tip

About 100 feet from the pull-off is an opening in the trees which nicely frames the waterfall and works well in the fall or early spring.

Whiteside Mountain provides some of the most outstanding views in all the Appalachian Mountains. The 4,930-foot summit rises 2,100 feet from the valley floor, with sheer rock walls over 700 feet high. The area has long been popular among rock climbers, and the cliffs provide an ideal habitat for the endangered peregrine falcon. The 2-mile Whiteside Mountain Trail, a National Recreation Trail, receives more than 200,000 visitors a year.

Hurricane Falls has the distinction of being able to vary in height. The cascade spills into Thorpe Lake, formerly Lake Glenville, which was renamed in 1951 to honor Nantahala Power and Light Company's first president. When the lake is below capacity, the waterfall is several feet higher than normal.

Nearby waterfalls: Two other small waterfalls spill into Thorpe Lake, one on Norton Creek, the other on Mill Creek. However, the only way to see them is from a boat. The marina, five miles north of Cashiers on N.C. 107, has rental boats and information.

Hurricane Falls

River: Hurricane Creek
County: Jackson
USGS quadrangle: Glenville
Landowner: Private
Height: Cascades measuring about 40 feet
Beauty rating: 4
Trail length and difficulty: View roadside
Handicapped Accessible

Grassy Creek Falls

River: Grassy Creek
County: Jackson
USGS quadrangle: Glenville
Landowner: Private
Height: About 100 feet
Beauty rating: 5
Trail length and difficulty: View roadside
Handicapped Accessible

Directions: From the starting point, drive north on N.C. 107 for 10.4 miles to a pull-off on the left. The pull-off is in a sharp curve; it is much safer to drive past it, turn around, and come back than it is to cut across traffic.

Photo Tip

Walk down to the edge of the West Fork of the Tuckasegee River and use it as a foreground in your photo.

If you look at the Glenville topographical map, you will notice that this waterfall is shown on Little Mill Creek. Grassy Creek is the next stream south. Supposedly, the mapmakers accidentally switched the names, and that is the reason for a Grassy Creek Falls on Little Mill Creek. The river in the foreground is the West Fork of the Tuckasegee River.

Nearby waterfalls: Retrace your route on N.C. 107. After 4.25 miles, turn right on Pine Creek Road (S.R. 1157). Drive 1.4 miles to a crossing of the Thorpe Lake Dam. Look downstream to view the brink of what used to be Onion Falls. The 200-foot slide was lost in 1941 when the dam was built; all the water is diverted to a power plant several miles downstream.

About 0.5 mile farther downstream is High Falls, located on private property. This waterfall was described in the book *Scenic Resources of the Tennessee Valley* as being "among the three or four most beautiful and impressive cataracts in the Tennessee Valley Region." It, too, suffered a loss of water when the dam was built.

Silver Run Falls
Nikon F3, 28-70mm zoom lens, polarizing filter, f/22 at 3 seconds, Fujichrome Velvia.

This portrait was made from the side of the pool, a few feet into the water. From this vantage point I could easily exclude the distracting fallen trees.

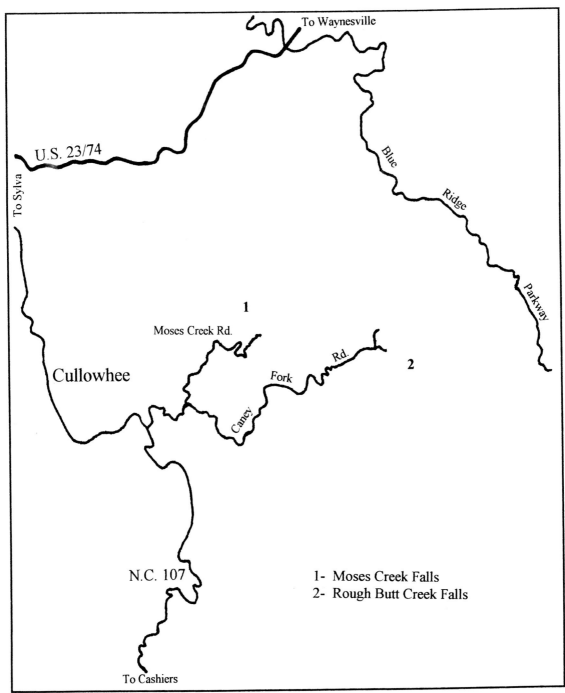

To Waynesville

U.S. 23/74

To Sylva

Blue

Ridge

Parkway

1

Moses Creek Rd.

Cullowhee

Fork

Rd.

Caney

2

N.C. 107

1- Moses Creek Falls
2- Rough Butt Creek Falls

To Cashiers

The starting point is the main entrance to the Western Carolina University campus.

Cullowhee

This cascade is completely enshrouded in rhododendron, requiring you to climb down a steep bank for the best view, which still isn't very good.

Begun in 1889 as a school for local children, Western Carolina University, which encompasses much of the Cullowhee community, is now a major unit of the North Carolina public university system.

Nearby waterfall: From the starting point, drive 1.2 miles south on N.C. 107 to S.R. 1001 and turn right at the sign for Speedwell. After 1 mile, turn left on S.R. 1157, then drive 4.1 miles to a pull-off on the left. Walk across the road for a view of a waterfall on Cullowhee Creek.

Moses Creek Falls

River: West Fork, Moses Creek
County: Jackson
USGS quadrangle: Tuckasegee
Landowner: Nantahala National Forest,
  Highlands Ranger District, Roy Taylor Forest
Height: This is a steep, cascading waterfall several
  hundred feet long; the main upper section is
  about 50 feet.
Beauty rating: 3
Trail length and difficulty: 1.5 miles, open to four-
  wheel-drive vehicles; 5–7

Directions: From the starting point, drive 3.6 miles south on N.C. 107 and turn left on Caney Fork Road (S.R. 1737). Go 1.9 miles to Moses Creek Road (S.R. 1740) and turn left, then proceed 2.7 miles to a sharp switchback to the right. Park here unless you have a four-wheel-drive vehicle. The trail follows Moses Creek upstream (crossing it once) for 1.1 miles to a crossing of the West Fork of Moses Creek. Continue another 0.1 mile along the East Fork of Moses Creek, then cut sharply to the left and begin a 0.3-mile ascent to the falls.

Rough Butt Creek Falls

River: Rough Butt Creek
County: Jackson
USGS quadrangle: Tuckasegee
Landowner: Nantahala National Forest,
  Highlands Ranger District, Roy Taylor Forest
Height: 60 feet, with only about 40 feet visible
  from the base
Beauty rating: 6
Trail length and difficulty: 1.1 miles, with all
  except the last 0.1 mile open to four-wheel-drive
  vehicles; 7

Directions: From the starting point, drive 3.6 miles south on N.C. 107 and turn left on Caney Fork Road (S.R. 1737). It is 9.25 miles to a fork in the road and the trailhead. If you don't have a four-wheel-drive vehicle, find a suitable parking place without blocking any driveways. Take the right fork past a few old houses and gardens, cross Caney Fork, and follow the old logging road upstream 0.8 mile to a crossing of Rough Butt Creek. Cross the creek and follow the trail upstream to the base of the falls. The trail is very faint and may not be recognizable, but it never strays from the creek side. It should be avoided during wet weather due to slippery rocks.

Photo Tips

It is difficult to take a bad photo here. All of the elements are perfectly arranged to complement the waterfall. The best vantage point is the right bank, so you will need to wade the creek. If at all possible, visit this waterfall while the rhododendron is in bloom.

What a pleasant surprise! This is one of those waterfalls that you just sort of stumble upon. Rough Butt Creek is a beautiful mountain stream, perfect for fishing and wading, and the falls make an ideal photo subject.

Rough Butt Creek Falls
Nikon F3, 28-70mm zoom lens, polarizing filter stacked on warming filter, f/22 at 2 seconds, Fujichrome Velvia.

It takes the sun several hours to climb high enough to directly illuminate Rough Butt Creek. Thus, even though the sun was shining brightly, I was able to make this photograph at 11:00 in the morning, without having excessive contrast in the scene.

Cascade on Rough Butt Creek
Nikon F3, 20mm lens, polarizing filter
stacked on warming filter, f/22 at 2
seconds, Fujichrome Velvia.

It is rare for me to hike directly to and from a
waterfall without stopping along the way to make
other photographs. By keeping my senses open to
other opportunities, I can create equally satisfy-
ing images such as this.

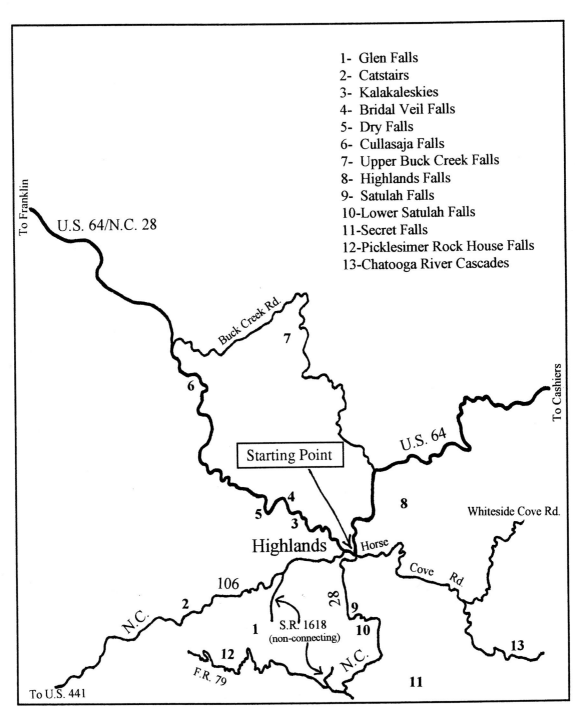

1- Glen Falls
2- Catstairs
3- Kalakaleskies
4- Bridal Veil Falls
5- Dry Falls
6- Cullasaja Falls
7- Upper Buck Creek Falls
8- Highlands Falls
9- Satulah Falls
10-Lower Satulah Falls
11-Secret Falls
12-Picklesimer Rock House Falls
13-Chatooga River Cascades

To Franklin

U.S. 64/N.C. 28

Buck Creek Rd.

To Cashiers

U.S. 64

Starting Point

Whiteside Cove Rd.

Highlands

Horse

Cove Rd.

106

N.C.

28

S.R. 1618
(non-connecting)

N.C.

F.R. 79

To U.S. 441

The starting point is the center of Highlands at the intersection of U.S. 64 and N.C. 28.

Highlands

At 4,118 feet, Highlands was the highest town east of the Mississippi until 1981, when the Watauga County community of Beech Mountain, at 5,005 feet, was incorporated. Highlands has long held a reputation as a desirable resort area with fine inns and quaint shops. The wintertime population of about nine hundred swells to nearly twenty thousand during the summer. Reservations are in order for anyone wishing to spend the night during the tourist season.

The many spectacular waterfalls are part of the appeal of the area. Highlands is literally surrounded by falling water. Most of these waterfalls are on national-forest lands and are accessible to the public.

Glen Falls *

River: East Fork, Overflow Creek
County: Macon
USGS quadrangle: Highlands
Landowner: Nantahala National Forest,
   Highlands Ranger District
Height: Three separate drops
   of about 70 feet, 60 feet, and 15 feet,
   with connecting cascades
Beauty rating: 7
Trail length and difficulty: 0.75 mile; 7

Directions: From the starting point, drive west on U.S. 64 for 0.3 mile to a stoplight. Turn left on N.C. 106 and drive 1.7 miles to a sign for Glen Falls Scenic Area. Turn left, then immediately right onto S.R. 1618. Drive 1.1 miles to where the road dead-ends at a parking area. Park here.

Take the left fork at the trail's beginning. After 0.25 mile, you can follow a side trail to the top of the upper waterfall. The main trail continues to the base of the upper falls, then to the base of the middle falls, then 0.2 mile to a sign directing hikers to the lower falls. Only the upper two cascades are worth the steep hike.

Photo Tips
There are two very good vantage points. The first is from the top of the upper falls, with excellent views of Blue Valley. There, you get the feeling that the waterfall is 1,000 feet high. The second is at the base of the middle falls; use the hemlock tree to frame the image. You can also shoot from the foot of the upper falls, but the constant spray is a real problem. Allow yourself several hours to fully explore the opportunities.

The cascading East Fork of Overflow Creek drops 640 feet in the 0.5-mile stretch that is Glen Falls. This waterfall is easily accessible and highly recommended.

Catstairs *

River: Tributary of Overflow Creek
County: Macon
USGS quadrangle: Scaly Mountain
Landowner: Nantahala National Forest,
   Highlands Ranger District
Height: Over 100 feet
Beauty rating: 4
Trail length and difficulty: View roadside
Handicapped Accessible

Glen Falls
Canon EOS Elan, 24mm tilt/shift lens, warming filter, f/22 at 3 seconds, Fujichrome Velvia.

Even with the use of the tilt/shift lens, I was not able to prevent distorting the image while photographing this close. The waterfall is much higher than it appears in this scene.

Directions: From the starting point, drive 0.3 mile west on U.S. 64 to a stoplight. Turn left on N.C. 106. The waterfall is visible on the right after 5.1 miles; you can park at the Blue Valley Overlook, located at 5 miles, and walk the last 0.1 mile to see the waterfall.

Photo Tip
   This cascade is not photogenic, but the Blue Valley Overlook provides good scenic opportunities.

The Catstairs, namesake of the waterfall, is a steep, rocky ridge on the southeast slope of Scaly Mountain. The ridge and the mountain contain several rare plant species and have been designated a North Carolina Natural Heritage Area.

   The waterfall completely dries up during periods of arid weather.

The Waterfalls of the Cullasaja River Gorge
Kalakaleskies, Bridal Veil Falls, Dry Falls, Cullasaja Falls

   The turbulent Cullasaja River flows westward from Highlands, dropping 1,400 feet in the 7.1-mile stretch from Lake Sequoyah to the bottom of Cullasaja Falls. Along its route are four major waterfalls and numerous smaller cascades. The gorge is host to several rare and endangered plant species. One, the dwarf polypody fern (*Grammitis nimbata*), is found nowhere else in North America.

   The section of U.S. 64 paralleling the river is a National Forest Service Scenic Byway, and the gorge is a North Carolina Natural Heritage Area.

Kalakaleskies

Nearly every publication on area waterfalls states that the Kalakaleskies are a series of eighteen small falls in the 0.25 mile between Lake Sequoyah and Bridal Veil Falls. One publication suggests that there is a trail leading from Bridal Veil Falls. It is obvious that the writers of that information have not hiked this section of the river. You could not count eighteen waterfalls with any stretch of the imagination, and there certainly is no trail.

Though reaching the base is strenuous, there is a picturesque series of three small cascades just below Sequoyah Dam. And some distance downstream, the entire Cullasaja River is forced between rock walls only 2 feet apart and into a deep pool; the river churns and boils for 30 feet before settling down. There also is an abandoned power station in this stretch. If you decide to see for yourself, be advised that it will require an extremely dangerous and difficult hike, using both hands and feet. Enjoy the view from the dam and save your energy for the other waterfalls in the gorge.

To see the cascades below Sequoyah Dam, drive 2.1 miles west from the starting point on U.S. 64 and park on the left.

Bridal Veil Falls *

River: Tributary of the Cullasaja River
County: Macon
USGS quadrangle: Highlands
Landowner: Nantahala National Forest,
   Highlands Ranger District
Height: About 60 feet
Beauty rating: 4
Trail length and difficulty: View roadside
Handicapped Accessible

Directions: From the starting point, drive 2.45 miles west on U.S. 64. Trust me, you can't miss it.

Bridal Veil Falls
Canon EOS Elan, 24mm tilt/shift lens, f/22 at ½ second, Fujichrome Velvia.

The foreground in this scene is not natural; it is part of a highway beautification project. The architect must have been a photographer because the two boulders are perfectly positioned as foreground elements for a photograph. I was hoping for a red convertible driven by a beautiful blonde, but I had to settle for a station wagon. You can't have everything, I guess.

Dry Falls
Nikon F3, 28-70mm zoom lens, warming filter, f/16 at ½ second, Fujichrome Velvia.

Photo Tips

Late-afternoon sunlight produces rainbows at Bridal Veil Falls, but be careful when shooting beside the road.

Seeing all of the waterfall requires shooting from the other side of the road. Don't try to eliminate the highway; the allure of this waterfall is the fact that you can drive underneath it. Shooting cars doing just that will create a more realistic representation and a more marketable image.

Bridal Veil Falls also offers an excellent opportunity for shooting sunstars (see the chapter on photographing waterfalls).

Bridal Veil Falls has the distinction of being the only waterfall in this book that you can drive under. This is quite an experience, especially in the summer with the sunroof open.

In winter, portions of the falls freeze; during the record freeze of 1977, the entire waterfall was a huge block of ice from top to bottom.

Dry Falls *

River: Cullasaja
County: Macon
USGS quadrangle: Highlands
Landowner: Nantahala National Forest,
    Highlands Ranger District
Height: Approximately 80 feet
Beauty rating: 8
Trail length and difficulty: 0.1 mile; 5

Directions: From the starting point, drive 3.25 miles west on U.S. 64 (0.8 mile past Bridal Veil Falls) to a parking area on the left. A paved trail leads behind the falls.

When the water level of the Cullasaja River is low, everyone visiting Dry Falls stops at one point behind the falls and looks out over the gorge. By setting up right on the trail, you can take advantage of this, as I did in this scene. However, this photograph has a "posed" feeling to it that I'm not crazy about.

Photo Tips

You can shoot from either side of the falls or from behind, but there is no way to eliminate the chain-link fence from your photos. You might shoot from behind the falls and include a person in the foreground. If you do this, the only way to have detail in both the background and foreground is to use fill-flash. Lacking this ability, you will either have an overexposed background or a silhouetted person. If you use a point-and-shoot camera, the person will definitely be silhouetted.

Here, the Cullasaja River projects over an overhanging cliff, allowing people to walk behind the waterfall without getting wet, hence the name Dry Falls. If the river is up, you may question the appropriateness of the name; the constant spray will soon have you drenched. This spray nourishes the spray cliff natural community which exists on the cliffs behind the falls.

Nearby waterfalls: Approximately 2.5 miles downstream on U.S. 64 is a small pull-off on the right. Walk across the road and climb down the steep bank to view a very nice cascading waterfall.

Continue downstream an additional 0.6 mile to view Quarry Falls, a popular swimming hole located right beside the road.

Cullasaja Falls *

River: Cullasaja
County: Macon
USGS quadrangle: Scaly Mountain
Landowner: Nantahala National Forest,
   Highlands Ranger District
Height: Cascades measuring about 250 feet
Beauty rating: 9

Trail length and difficulty: View roadside
Handicapped Accessible

Directions: From the starting point, drive 8.75 miles west on U.S. 64 (5.5 miles beyond Dry Falls) to a pull-off on the left with a view of the falls.

With the possible exception of Interstate 40 through the Smokies, this section of U.S. 64 is the most dangerous road in the mountains. The highway literally hangs on the sheer rock cliffs, with barely enough room for two cars, much less trucks. It is strongly advised that you drive beyond the pull-off, turn around at a safe place, and retrace your route. This will allow you to pull off the right side of the road, rather than crossing traffic. Local truckdrivers, well aware of the dangerous pull-off, blow their horns before rounding the curve.

Cullasaja Falls
Nikon F3, 75-300mm zoom lens, warming filter, f/11 at ¼ second, Fujichrome Velvia.

This was one of the easiest photographs I made for this book. I simply set up right beside the road, and zoomed until I got the composition I wanted. The image is framed tighter than I would have preferred, but there was clutter in the scene that I wanted to eliminate.

Photo Tips

A short time ago, the only good vantage point for photographing Cullasaja Falls was the steep bank just at the end of the rock wall. Now, the area has been cleared of trees, and the waterfall is best shot from directly beside the road. Be careful: this is also the most dangerous vantage point.

If you decide to climb to the base, keep in mind that only the bottom portion of the falls will be visible.

The gorge that visitors travel through to get to Cullasaja Falls is part of the route followed by Spanish explorer Hernando De Soto on his 1540 expedition in search of gold. When you think about his men clanking through the gorge in their armor, you can imagine why they quickly left the area.

The name Cullasaja comes from the Cherokee word *Kulsetsiyi*, meaning "honey locust place."

Nearby waterfall: On the opposite side of the Cullasaja Gorge a short distance downstream from Cullasaja Falls is Crow Creek Falls. There is no trail to this waterfall, and the hike is absolutely wicked. You can barely view the waterfall in the winter from U.S. 64, but it is dangerous to look for it while driving. To see it, park and walk as far off the road as possible.

Upper Buck Creek Falls

River: Buck Creek
County: Macon
USGS quadrangle: Glenville
Landowner: Nantahala National Forest,
    Highlands Ranger District
Height: Cascades measuring about 100 feet
Beauty rating: 4

Trail length and difficulty: 0.25 mile; 5–10

Directions: From the starting point, drive 2.6 miles east on U.S. 64 and turn left on Buck Creek Road (S.R. 1538). Proceed 5.5 miles to a sharp right-hand switchback; turn left onto the logging road. Drive a few hundred feet and park at the gate.

Continue on the logging road, hiking to the second right-hand switchback; turn left onto a side logging road. After 200 feet, strike out through the woods on the right and descend toward the sound of the waterfall.

Photo Tip

With so many excellent photo subjects in the Highlands area, you should not waste your time here.

Buck Creek is a beautiful, cascading stream that would certainly be popular were it not for its inaccessibility. Should you decide to visit Upper Buck Creek Falls, you are sure to be alone.

Nearby waterfall: Lower Buck Creek Falls is located a few miles downstream on private property.

Highlands Falls

Two miles east of Highlands is Highlands Falls Country Club, named after a 100-foot drop on the headwaters of the Cullasaja River. The falls are on private property, but you can catch a glimpse from atop Bearpen Mountain.

From the starting point, drive 0.3 mile east on U.S. 64 and turn right on Chestnut Street (S.R. 1602). Drive 0.4 mile and turn left on Big Bearpen Road. It is 1 mile to the beginning of a loop which circles the mountain. Take the left fork; it is 0.1 mile to a view of the waterfall on the left. Note: This view is over a vacant lot. If a house is built here, visitors will not be able to see the falls.

Satulah Falls *

River: Clear Creek
County: Macon
USGS quadrangle: Highlands
Landowner: Private
Height: Slides measuring about 100 feet
Beauty rating: 3
Trail length and difficulty: View roadside
Handicapped Accessible

Directions: From the starting point, drive 2.3 miles south on N.C. 28 and park at the right-hand pull-off. The cascade is on the left.

Photo Tips

This waterfall is on private property, so you should only shoot from the road right-of-way. This may mean having to include some of the roadside clutter.

Do not try to photograph in late fall. The pieces of fence stretched across the creek catch all the fallen leaves to create an unsightly mess.

Much more impressive than the waterfall is the sheer rockface of 4,543-foot Satulah Mountain, clearly visible on the left as you travel on N.C. 28. The mountain, from which the waterfall takes its name, is one of several in the region with such steep slopes that they are nearly devoid of vegetation.

Lower Satulah Falls *
(Clear Creek Falls)

River: Clear Creek
County: Macon
USGS quadrangle: Highlands
Landowner: At the waterfall, the creek forms the boundary line between private property and Nantahala National Forest, Highlands Ranger District.
Height: Over 100 feet
Beauty rating: 6
Trail length and difficulty: View roadside
Handicapped Accessible

Directions: Follow the directions to Satulah Falls. An overlook is located on the right 1.2 miles farther south.

Photo Tips

There is a large oak tree at the overlook which nicely frames Satulah Mountain or the waterfall. To avoid distracting shadows, shoot early in the morning before the sun rises over the mountains. There are few mountain scenes which look better than this one during autumn.

If you're staying in the Highlands area, this easily accessible waterfall is a must-see. To the right are excellent views of Satulah Mountain; to the left is the scenic Blue Valley, with Scaly Mountain looming in the distance.

During the summer, nearly all of the waterfall is hidden behind vegetation.

Secret Falls

As the name implies, few people have heard of Secret Falls, and fewer still have visited it. It is located in Nantahala National Forest, but the only trail access is over private property. You can bushwhack over national-forest lands if you don't mind a long, strenuous hike. For access information, inquire with the Highlands Ranger District (see the appendix). To determine property boundaries, you will need the Highlands topographical map (modified for Forest Service use), available at the ranger station.

The waterfall, recommended for experienced hikers only, is located at the 2,400-foot elevation of Big Creek, south of Highlands.

Picklesimer Rock House Falls

River: Tributary of Abes Creek
County: Macon
USGS quadrangle: Scaly Mountain
Landowner: Nantahala National Forest,
   Highlands Ranger District
Height: 40-foot free fall
Beauty rating: 6
Trail length and difficulty: 0.5 mile; 4

Directions: From the starting point, drive 5.8 miles south on N.C. 28 and turn right on S.R. 1618 at the sign for Blue Valley Campground; S.R. 1618 becomes F.R. 79. Drive 4.2 miles and park at the gated logging road on the right. Hike

Secret Falls
Nikon F3, 20mm lens, f/22 at 4 seconds, Fujichrome Velvia.

By using a very wide-angle lens close to the lower drop, I was able to present an interesting perspective to Secret Falls. The foreground cascade is only about 4 feet high, while the upper drop is nearly 50.

logging road 0.3 mile to a wildlife clearing. Cross the clearing and a small creek. After 50 feet, turn right on a side trail, which may be marked with red blazes. Cross the creek and follow the trail upstream 100 yards.

Photo Tips

You cannot effectively shoot this waterfall on a sunny day because of the extreme contrast range between the water and the recessed bluff. An overcast sky will lessen the contrast but still may not allow you to record everything in detail. Expose for the water and the surrounding vegetation and let the shadows go black. Good compositions can be found in front of, behind, and to the side of the falls.

This waterfall provides a lesson in geology and biology. The stream drops over a high bluff that is deeply undercut, with the rock layers prominently visible. An unfortunate American holly tree has sprouted under this bluff and has no more room to grow. It is interesting to note that all the tree's branches are on one side of the trunk, pointing toward the light.

In earlier times, large bluffs such as this were referred to as "rock houses." And as you might have guessed, a family named Picklesimer lived near this particular rock house.

This wilderness setting is somewhat spoiled by campfire rings under the bluff.

Chattooga River Cascades

The Highlands section of the Chattooga Wild and Scenic River contains a few small cascades and is a popular swimming and sunbathing area. A 2-mile loop trail follows the river upstream. There is no actual waterfall at this location, but because of the area's popularity and its inclusion in Highlands-area publications, it seems appropriate to mention it here.

From the starting point, head east on Main Street (S.R. 1603). Depending on the source, this road may also be called either Horse Cove Road or Bull Pen Road. Follow it for 4.8 miles to a fork where Whiteside Cove Road bears left. Turn right and drive 3 miles to an old iron bridge crossing the river. A parking area for the cascades is on the left.

Nearby waterfall: There is a waterfall on private property on Big Creek. Follow the directions for Chattooga River Cascades, but turn right on Walking-stick Road (S.R. 1608) some 4 miles from the starting point. It is 0.5 mile to a parking area on the right and a view of the falls.

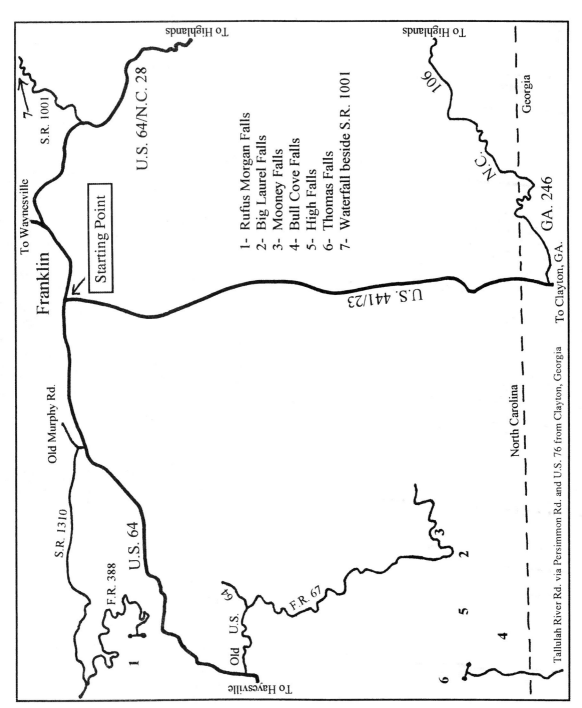

1- Rufus Morgan Falls
2- Big Laurel Falls
3- Mooney Falls
4- Bull Cove Falls
5- High Falls
6- Thomas Falls
7- Waterfall beside S.R. 1001

The starting point is the intersection of U.S. 64 and U.S. 441/23 South.

Franklin

When most people think of Franklin, North Carolina, the first thing that comes to mind is gemstones. Indeed, Macon County is known the world over for its rubies, rhodolite garnets, and sapphires. Collecting these gems and other minerals has become a major tourist attraction for the area.

It may surprise you to learn that Franklin is also blessed with numerous waterfalls, some quite impressive.

Rufus Morgan Falls *

River: Left Prong, Rough Fork
County: Macon
USGS quadrangle: Wayah Bald
Landowner: Nantahala National Forest,
  Wayah Ranger District
Height: Cascades measuring over 70 feet
Beauty rating: 6
Trail length and difficulty: 0.5 mile; 5–6

Directions: From the starting point, drive west on U.S. 64 for 5.8 miles to the Wayah Bald sign and turn right onto Old Murphy Road. After 0.2 mile, turn left onto S.R. 1310 and go 6.3 miles to F.R. 388 (Boardtree Road). Turn left and travel 2 miles to the parking area on the right. The trail is easily followed, but don't be fooled by the first small cascade you come to; the main falls are another 0.1 mile upstream.

Rufus Morgan Falls
Nikon F3, 24mm lens, f/22 at 2 seconds, Fujichrome Velvia.

In all my visits to Rufus Morgan Falls, I have never been able to photograph when the foliage was not blowing. My next visit will be in the winter, when the foliage is not there!

Photo Tips

This waterfall lends itself well to photography. An ideal vantage point is the perfectly placed boulder on the left bank, using the numerous wildflowers in the foreground. You should be aware of wind movement, though. You can also shoot from other points, but not without including much of the clutter at the base.

While photographing in the area, you should visit Wayah Bald. Its historic fire tower provides excellent panoramas and is one of the finest sunrise locations in the mountains. When you get back to S.R. 1310 from Rufus Morgan Falls, go left for approximately 2.5 miles to F.R. 69, then right for about 4.5 miles to the summit.

USGS quadrangle: Rainbow Springs
Landowner: Nantahala National Forest,
 Wayah Ranger District, Southern Nantahala
 Wilderness
Height: 30 feet in two tiers
Beauty rating: 6
Trail length and difficulty: 0.5 mile; 4

Albert Rufus Morgan was a poet, conservationist, and Episcopal priest who loved the mountains and the Appalachian Trail. Called a "modern Moses," he alone maintained 55 miles of the trail for years. In 1950, he founded the Nantahala Hiking Club. Mount LeConte in the Smokies was a favorite peak of his; he climbed it 172 times, the last time at the age of ninety-two. He died on Valentine's Day in 1983 at the age of ninety-seven.

Nearby waterfalls: Berties Falls, listed on the Wayah Bald quadrangle, is not a waterfall, so don't waste you time looking for it.

There is a small cascade on Shot Pouch Creek, reached from the pull-off on S.R. 1310 some 0.9 mile east of F.R. 69.

Big Laurel Falls *

River: Big Laurel Branch
County: Macon

Big Laurel Falls
Nikon F3, 24mm lens, polarizing filter, f/22 at 8 seconds, Fujichrome Velvia.

I made a half-dozen different compositions of Big Laurel Falls, but this one is my favorite. The depth-of-field scales on the lens enabled me to easily keep everything in focus.

Directions: From the starting point, drive west on U.S. 64 approximately 12.1 miles to Old U.S. 64. Turn left and drive 1.8 miles to F.R. 67; you will see a sign for Standing Indian Campground. Turn right. It is 6.8 miles to a pull-off on the right. Park here and begin the trail. After 50 feet, it forks right, crosses Mooney Creek, then forks right again. The falls are another 0.4 mile along the easily followed trail.

Directions: Follow the directions to the Big Laurel Falls trailhead, then continue on F.R. 67 for 0.6 mile to a pull-off on the right. An obvious trail leads to the base.

Photo Tips

In terms of photographic potential, Big Laurel Falls is hard to beat. Rhododendron shrubs perfectly frame the waterfall, and the small cascades, rocks, and pool create ideal foreground material. Lenses from 20mm to 50mm can be used effectively. If the water is up, you may have to wade to get the best shots.

The waterfall also makes a good snow scene; there is plenty of rock surface, both in the foreground and on the falls, for the snow to rest upon.

Photo Tips

The best vantage point is from the trail, where there are numerous rhododendron shrubs to frame the falls. Adventurous photographers may be tempted to crawl out onto the large horizontal birch tree for a different angle, but it is not worth the effort, as I know from experience.

Mooney Falls is a popular destination for tourists, as the trail is short and not too difficult. The falls were likely named after James Mooney, an early ethnologist sent by the government to study the Cherokees' use of plants for food and medicine. Mooney's studies ended up being much more ethnological in nature, and his 1898 report to the Bureau of American Ethnology was largely responsible for our knowledge of the Cherokee cultural heritage.

Though small, this is a delightful waterfall well worth the hike. It makes a nice day-hike for families camping at Standing Indian Campground.

Nearby waterfalls: Both Hurricane Creek and Bearpen Creek, which flow from the north and south sides, respectively, of Yellow Bald, contain small waterfalls. Although there are trails in the vicinity, they do not lead to the falls. I do not recommend the strenuous bushwhack necessary to get to these waterfalls.

Mooney Falls *

River: Mooney Creek
County: Macon
USGS quadrangle: Prentiss
Landowner: Nantahala National Forest, Wayah Ranger District
Height: The main lower drop is about 30 feet.
Beauty rating: 3
Trail length and difficulty: 0.1 mile; 3–4

Southern Nantahala Wilderness Area
Bull Cove Falls, High Falls, Thomas Falls

The following three waterfalls (and the previously listed Big Laurel Falls) are part of the Southern

Nantahala Wilderness Area, created in 1984. They are also part of Standing Indian Basin, a horseshoe-shaped drainage formed by several prominent peaks along the Nantahala and Blue Ridge mountain ranges.

The best-known of these peaks is 5,498-foot Standing Indian Mountain. According to Cherokee legend, a great bird once swooped down and carried off an Indian child to its cave high up on a nearby mountain. The cave was inaccessible to the Cherokees, so they prayed to the Great Spirit for help. The Great Spirit sent a huge bolt of lighting to destroy the beast and its home. A Cherokee warrior posted as a sentry was turned to stone by the lighting as punishment for abandoning his post. Although erosion has taken its toll, you may still be able to make out the "standing Indian" on the mountaintop.

Bull Cove Falls, High Falls, and Thomas Falls are unique in that, although they are accessible by long hikes from the Deep Gap parking area on F.R. 71 in North Carolina, the road access is from Georgia. If you plan on visiting them, I strongly recommend getting the Southern Nantahala Wilderness and Standing Indian Basin map, available from any ranger station.

Bull Cove Falls

River: Bull Cove Creek
County: Clay
USGS quadrangle: Rainbow Springs
Landowner: Nantahala National Forest, Tusquitee
   Ranger District, Southern Nantahala Wilderness
Height: 40 feet
Beauty rating: 6
Trail length and difficulty: 1 mile; 7

Directions: From the starting point, drive 20.7 miles south on U.S. 441/23 to the town of Clayton, Georgia. Turn right on U.S. 76 and go 7.9 miles to Persimmon Road; you will see a sign

Bull Cove Falls
Nikon F3, 24mm lens, polarizing filter, f/22 at 1 second, Fujichrome Velvia.

I was very careful to frame the scene to preserve the diagonal placement of the log. Diagonals make strong compositional elements in a photograph.

for Tallulah River Campground. Turn right. Drive 4.1 miles to Tallulah River Road; this road is initially designated F.R. 70 but changes to F.R. 56 at the North Carolina line. Turn left. It is 7.6 miles to a parking area on the left at a primitive campground.

Begin the trail (F.S. 378) on the opposite side of the road. You will climb steeply for 0.25 mile, cross a gap, and descend to ford Beech Creek. The trail then intersects an old mining road, which leads approximately 0.5 mile upstream to Bull Cove Creek. Cross the creek and pick up the trail which leads upstream to the falls.

Photo Tips

There are numerous possibilities here. The moss-covered rock at the edge of the pool makes a perfect foreground. You can frame the scene so the log lying across the waterfall forms a diagonal running from lower right to upper left. You might also try a few isolation shots of the orange rocks.

Anywhere else, the large tree across the waterfall would be seriously distracting. Here, it seems to enhance this otherwise dull cascade. The deep-orange color of the rocks comes from iron oxide.

High Falls

River: Beech Creek
County: Clay
USGS quadrangle: Rainbow Springs
Landowner: Nantahala National Forest, Tusquitee Ranger District, Southern Nantahala Wilderness
Height: Cascades measuring over 150 feet
Beauty rating: 8
Trail length and difficulty: 2.5 miles; 9

Directions: Follow the road and trail directions to Bull Cove Falls to where the mining road crosses Bull Cove Creek. Continue straight. You will cross Beech Creek after about 0.25 mile. The trail climbs steeply for the next mile. Just before it switches sharply to the left are the rock-wall remains of an old rail support; the rail was used to sluice rocks out of the corundum mine located farther up the mountain until it was shut down in 1906. The trail then begins a very steep ascent. At the next

High Falls
Nikon F3, 24mm lens, polarizing filter, f/22 at 1 second, Fujichrome Velvia.

I did not have a 20mm lens with me when I visited High Falls, but I certainly will if I return. The 24mm lens is just not quite wide enough to include all the falls, and backing up is not an appropriate option.

switchback to the left, look for a faint side trail on the right (straight ahead if you do not make the left turn). There may be an old wooden sign announcing the falls. This side trail leads 0.1 mile to the base of the falls.

Photo Tips

Because you will be so close and the falls are so large, you will need at least a 20mm lens to frame all of it.

When the water is up, this is a perfect waterfall for telephoto isolation shots; you can take your pick from dozens of possible compositions.

Make sure to bring closeup gear; wildflower opportunities abound along the entire trail.

High Falls offers a prime example of rock stratification, with its rock arranged in distinct beds, or layers. The effect is so pronounced that the cascade resembles a large staircase, though this is one staircase you do *not* want to climb. The many nooks and crannies provide ideal habitat for salamanders.

Nearby waterfalls: During very wet weather, you may notice a few small cascades flowing down Scaly Ridge on the way to High Falls. During the dry season, these cascades may be completely dried up.

Thomas Falls

River: Thomas Creek
County: Clay
USGS quadrangle: Rainbow Springs
Landowner: Nantahala National Forest, Tusquitee
    Ranger District, Southern Nantahala Wilderness
Height: 40 feet
Beauty rating: 3
Trail length and difficulty: 0.9 mile; 6–8

Directions: Follow the directions to the Bull Cove Falls trailhead, then continue on F.R. 56 for 1.1 miles to the parking area at the end of the road. The trail is a continuation of F.R. 56. After walking approximately 0.5 mile, you will come to a signpost beside the Tallulah River for Beech Gap Trail #377. Rather than following Beech Gap Trail straight ahead, you should turn left, cross the river, and try to pick up the trail heading upstream; it is poorly marked with blue blazes. This trail leaves the Tallulah River and crosses several small streams before the final steep ascent to the falls.

Photo Tip

There is a fair vantage point from the right bank using the overhanging trees to frame the image, but you will need a 20mm lens to capture the falls in their entirety.

This is one of those waterfalls that certainly would not make the focal point of a trip but is worthwhile if you are already in the area visiting Bull Cove and High falls.

Nearby waterfalls: New Falls, located on Wateroak Creek, which flows into the Tallulah River about 0.3 mile upstream from Thomas Creek, is practically inaccessible. It is not recommended that you try to reach it.

Waterfall beside S.R. 1001 *

River: Tributary of North Prong, Ellijay Creek
County: Macon
USGS quadrangle: Corbin Knob
Landowner: Private

Height: Steep slide of about 50 feet
Beauty rating: 3
Trail length and difficulty: View roadside
Handicapped Accessible

Directions: From the starting point, drive east on U.S. 64 for 2.2 miles to the intersection with N.C. 28. Follow N.C. 28 South/U.S. 64 East toward Highlands. Approximately 3 miles past the intersection, turn left onto S.R. 1001. It is 5.1 miles to a pull-off on the left and a view of the falls.

Photo Tips

This cascade offers little opportunity for creativity. During spring and summer, there is quite a bit of weedy roadside growth at the base. The best times are early spring and just after a snowfall.

This is a small but pretty waterfall. During dry weather, the water flow is substantially reduced. But during periods of wet weather, you will find numerous cascades all along the 3-mile drive through the gorge of the North Prong of Ellijay Creek.

Nearby waterfalls: There are several wet-weather cascades in the gorge, though none is photogenic.

For a faint view of a waterfall on the North Prong of Ellijay Creek, continue on S.R. 1001 for 1.7 miles and pull off the left side of the road.

To see Ellijay Creek Falls, backtrack on S.R. 1001 for 0.8 mile and turn left on S.R. 1528. It is 1 mile to a pull-off on the right with a view of the falls across the road.

Both of these waterfalls are on private property.

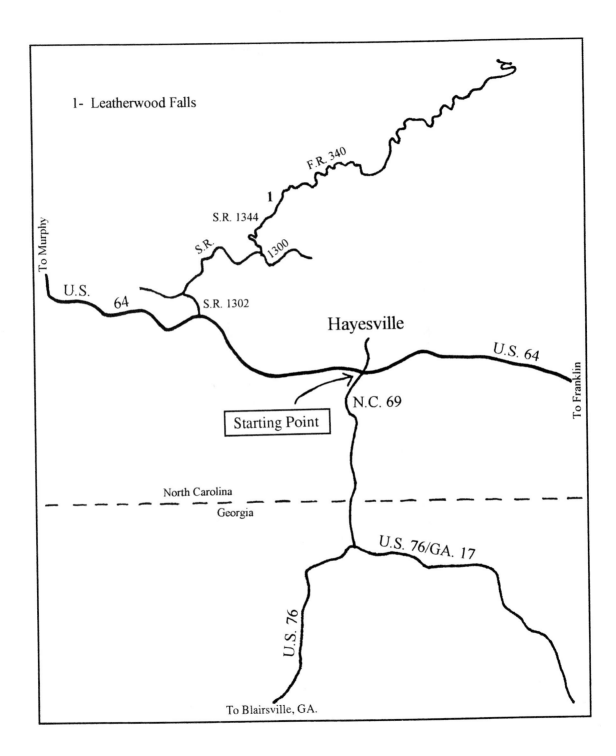

Hayesville

Hayesville is the county seat of Clay County, the least populated county in western North Carolina. A primary reason for its sparse population is that Nantahala National Forest occupies about 50 percent of the entire county. These national-forest lands and nearby Chatuge Lake offer prime opportunities for camping, hiking, swimming, and boating.

Despite the abundance of public property, only one waterfall is accessible in the Hayesville area. Leatherwood Falls is located in the 16,000-acre Fires Creek Wildlife Management Area, which also contains the 5,240-foot summit of Tusquitee Bald. The excellent 25-mile Rim Trail traverses the boundary on an elongated rim. The trail crosses near the top of Leatherwood Falls.

Leatherwood Falls *

River: Leatherwood Branch
County: Clay
USGS quadrangle: Hayesville
Landowner: Nantahala National Forest,
    Tusquitee Ranger District
Height: 25 feet
Beauty rating: 3
Trail length and difficulty: The falls are visible from the parking area, but getting to a good vantage point requires either wading Fires Creek or crossing on the bridge upstream, then bushwhacking to the falls.

Directions: From the junction of N.C. 69 and U.S. 64 just south of Hayesville, drive 4.7 miles west on U.S. 64 to S.R. 1302. Turn right and drive 3.75 miles to S.R. 1344; S.R. 1302 becomes S.R. 1300 en route. Turn left on S.R. 1344, which becomes F.R. 340 as it enters the national forest. It is 1.9 miles to a parking lot and a picnic area at the falls.

Photo Tips

Leatherwood Falls makes a fair photograph, but you need to shoot from right at the base to eliminate the clutter, requiring at least a 24mm lens to frame the entire falls.

Consider taking a few recreational photos of the swimmers or the daredevils jumping off the bridge a few hundred feet upstream.

This cascade is rather unimpressive, but you may wish to visit the area for another reason: Fires Creek, which flows by the base of the falls, provides an ideal swimming hole. The area is often crowded on summer weekends with people picnicking, swimming, and (foolishly) climbing on the falls.

Leatherwood Falls
Nikon F3, 24mm lens, polarizing filter, f/22 at ½ second, Fujichrome Velvia.

To get in position for this photo, I had to wade across Fires Creek and climb to the base of the falls. Considering that it was 90 degrees in the shade, I didn't mind slipping off my shoes and wading in the waist-deep water.

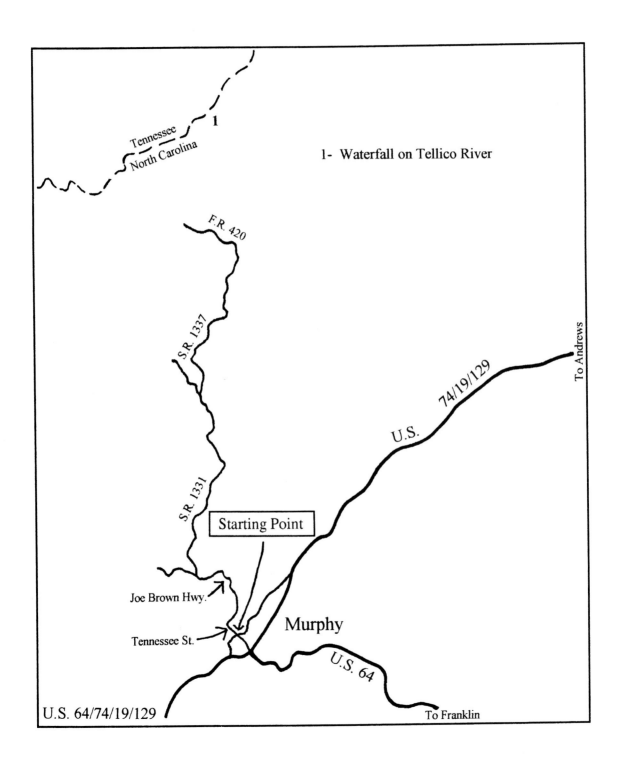

Murphy

This book lists only one waterfall for the Murphy area—the only waterfall listed for all of Cherokee County. In fact, I am aware of only two other significant falls, both on private property. Why is this? The area surrounding Murphy is just as mountainous as any other, and there are plenty of streams. The average annual precipitation in Andrews, just a few miles away, is only 7 inches less than in Brevard, which has a far greater number of waterfalls, so rainfall is not a major factor.

The answer is related to rock type and topography. While Cherokee County is mountainous, it is also true that by the time the streams are large enough to create waterfalls, they have already left the steep mountains for the broad valleys. There aren't any high-elevation plateaus to create an escarpment region as in Macon and Jackson counties. More important, the region is composed predominantly of rocks which do not have the durability necessary to form waterfalls.

Falls on the Tellico River

River: Tellico
County: Cherokee
USGS quadrangle: Big Junction
Landowner: Nantahala National Forest,
   Tusquitee Ranger District
Height: Two small cascades about 200 feet apart
Beauty rating: 4
Trail length and difficulty: If you have a
   four-wheel-drive vehicle, 0.7 mile at a rate of 6;
   if you don't, 3.7 miles at a rate of 7

Directions: From the downtown crossroads in Murphy, head north on Tennessee Street (S.R. 1326) for 2.8 miles; Tennessee Street becomes Joe Brown Highway. Turn right on S.R. 1331 and travel approximately 5.5 miles to S.R. 1337, which becomes F.R. 420. Follow this road for 6.1 miles to the parking area at Allen Gap. You are now entering the Upper Tellico Off-Road Vehicle Area, though you can drive a regular vehicle a couple more miles to the Tipton Creek crossing.

There are numerous possible routes from Allen Gap to the falls, along with several loop options. Only one route is described here. If you visit the area, I strongly recommend purchasing the excellent map available from the Tusquitee Ranger Station.

From Allen Gap, drive 2.45 miles to trail #4, on the right; you must have a four-wheel-drive vehicle from this point on. After 3 miles on trail #4 (the Upper Tellico Off-Road Vehicle Area map incorrectly gives the distance as 3.5 miles), turn left onto trail #5. This is an all-terrain-vehicle trail only, so you'll have to hike from here. It is 0.4 mile to the Tellico River. Walk upstream a few hundred feet along an old logging road and cross the river; you'll have to wade if the water is up. The cascades are another 0.25 mile upstream.

Photo Tips
The lower cascade is the more photogenic, even though a small tree has fallen across the middle.

Take advantage of the opportunities for streamside shots all along the Tellico River.

Although these cascades are scenic, I do not think they are worth a 3.7-mile hike if you don't have four-wheel drive. Even then, I wouldn't recommend them as the focus of a trip. However, they would make a nice addition to an already-planned trip in the Upper Tellico area.

Nearby waterfall: The small stream that you rock-hopped is Peckerwood Creek. Some distance upstream is a high cascade. A brutal bushwhack is required to get to it.

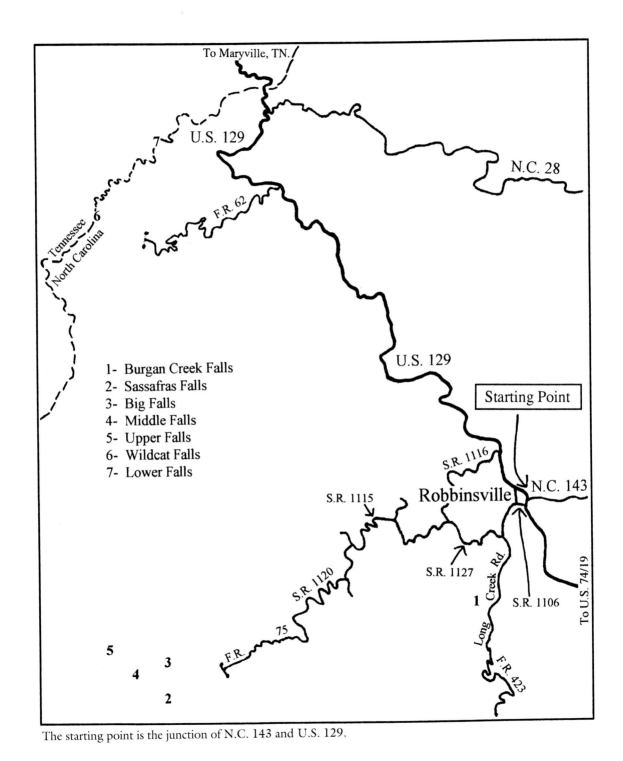

To Maryville, TN.

7

U.S. 129

N.C. 28

F.R. 62

Tennessee
North Carolina

6

1- Burgan Creek Falls
2- Sassafras Falls
3- Big Falls
4- Middle Falls
5- Upper Falls
6- Wildcat Falls
7- Lower Falls

U.S. 129

Starting Point

S.R. 1116

N.C. 143

Robbinsville

S.R. 1115

S.R. 1127

1

Long Creek Rd.

S.R. 1106

To U.S. 74/19

S.R. 1120

F.R. 75

5

3

4

F.R. 423

2

F.R.

The starting point is the junction of N.C. 143 and U.S. 129.

Robbinsville

Historic Robbinsville lies at the foot of the Snowbird Mountains, to the south, and the Cheoah Mountains, to the northeast. To the west are the Unicoi Mountains, containing the popular Joyce Kilmer/Slickrock Wilderness Area. Streams from these mountain ranges flow into Lake Santeetlah, noted for its excellent walleye, largemouth bass, and smallmouth bass fishing.

In downtown Robbinsville are the graves of a famous Cherokee, Chief Junaluska, and his wife, Nicie. In the 1814 Battle of Horseshoe Bend, which took place on the Tallapoosa River in Alabama, Junaluska led a force of Cherokees that defeated the Creek Indians. American troops led by General Andrew Jackson were being held at bay by the Creeks, and Junaluska was credited with saving Jackson's life. Ironically, it was Jackson who as president signed the infamous Indian Removal Act, which proved to be one of the darkest moments in American history. Junaluska was later quoted as saying, "If I had known that Jackson would drive us from our homes, I would have killed him that day at Horseshoe."

Burgan Creek Falls

River: Burgan Creek
County: Graham
USGS quadrangle: Robbinsville
Landowner: Nantahala National Forest,
 Cheoah Ranger District
Height: 40 feet

Beauty rating: 3
Trail length and difficulty: 1.25 miles; 7

Directions: Drive south on U.S. 129 for 0.1 mile from the starting point. Turn right on S.R. 1106. Proceed 0.25 mile to the stop sign and turn left onto S.R. 1127. Follow this road 0.4 mile to a stop sign, turn left to remain on S.R. 1127, then continue 0.6 mile to Long Creek Road (S.R. 1110), which becomes F.R. 423; it is also known as Tatham Gap Road. Turn left and drive 3 miles to a small dirt road on the right beside a large hemlock tree. Park here.

Walk along the side road a short distance to a dam and a small pond. The trail continues on the opposite side of the pond and follows Burgan Creek upstream, crisscrossing it several times before arriving at the base of the falls. The trail is heavily overgrown and completely unrecognizable in places.

I do not think this waterfall is worth the effort required to reach it.

Photo Tip

Burgan Creek Falls is not photogenic, but there are good wildflower opportunities along the trail.

During the Removal of 1838, several outlying stockades were established to hold the Indians until they began their journey westward. One such stockade, Fort Montgomery, was located in present-day Robbinsville. At the time, there was no direct route to present-day Murphy, so General Winfield Scott hired a local resident, James Tatham, to stake out a route over the Snowbird Mountains. F.R. 423 now follows that route from Robbinsville to Andrews. The road is littered with beer cans, and at several spots, it is used as a garbage-dumping site. It is a sad irony that a portion of the Trail of Tears is treated with such disrespect.

Waterfalls in the Snowbird Area
Sassafras Falls, Big Falls, Middle Falls, Upper Falls

Four waterfalls are located in the Snowbird Creek basin, southwest of Robbinsville. The basin has a rich history. It was used by the Cherokees as a hideout during the Removal of 1838, and approximately three hundred direct descendants of those Indians now live in the Little Snowbird community.

In 1908, George Moore established a shooting preserve for the wealthy on the headwaters of Snowbird Creek. By 1912, fenced enclosures were erected and exotic animals imported for guests to shoot. Buffalo, mule deer, brown bear, and wild boars were among the animals hunted. Many of the animals escaped, and one, the wild boar, managed to establish itself in the wild. The boars have since become a destructive nuisance due to their feeding habits. An area foraged by boars looks as if a garden tiller had passed through it.

It is recommended that you obtain the Snowbird Area Trail Map, available at any ranger station, before entering this area.

Sassafras Falls

River: Sassafras Creek
County: Graham
USGS quadrangle: Santeetlah Creek

Landowner: Nantahala National Forest, Cheoah Ranger District
Height: Cascades measuring about 50 feet
Beauty rating: 5
Trail length and difficulty: 3.5 miles; 3–6

Directions: To reach the trailhead from the starting point, drive 1.4 miles north on U.S. 129 and turn left on S.R. 1116 at the sign for the ranger station. Follow S.R. 1116 for 3.3 miles to where it ends at S.R. 1127. Turn right and continue 2.1 miles to a fork where S.R. 1115 bears left. Continue on S.R. 1115 for 2.1 miles, follow a sharp left turn in the road, and drive 1 mile to a bridge across Snowbird Creek. Immediately after crossing the bridge, turn right onto S.R. 1120, which becomes F.R. 75, and follow it 5.9 miles to the parking area at the end.

Take Big Snowbird Trail, which begins at the sign board and follows the left side of Snowbird Creek. After 2.8 miles, cross Sassafras Creek and continue 250 feet to the junction with Sassafras Creek Trail, on the left. Follow Sassafras Creek Trail 0.7 mile to the falls.

Photo Tips
It is difficult to make a good photo here. From a point far enough away to include all the falls, there is a good deal of clutter in the scene. Either use a wide-angle lens up close or back up and shoot isolation photos with a telephoto lens.

Sassafras Creek Trail can be combined with Burntrock Ridge Trail to form a loop into the Snowbird back country. Study the Snowbird Area Trail Map for possibilities.

Big Falls

River: Snowbird Creek
County: Graham
USGS quadrangle: Santeetlah Creek
Landowner: Nantahala National Forest,
    Cheoah Ranger District
Height: Small multilevel cascade
Beauty rating: 6
Trail length and difficulty: 3.9 miles at a rate of 3,
    except for a steep 200-foot climb to the base

Directions: Follow the directions to Sassafras Falls,
but continue straight at the junction of Sassafras
Creek Trail and Big Snowbird Trail. A little over 1
mile from the junction, you will hear the waterfall.
Look for a faint side trail located just before a blue-
blazed poplar tree on the right. This steep side trail
leads to the base.

Photo Tips

An excellent horizontal composition can be had
from the flat, rocky area using the willow shrubs in
the foreground. In late July and August, you might
get lucky and find a few cardinal flowers (*Lobelia
cardinalis*) growing among the grasses.

The person who named this waterfall had a bad sense
of humor. It is scenic and photogenic, but it is
definitely not big.

The shrubs growing along the small island areas of
the creek are silky willows (*Salix sericea*).

Big Falls
Nikon F3, 28-70mm zoom lens, polarizing filter, f/22 at 3 seconds, Fujichrome Velvia.
The wind was calm, allowing me to include the willow shrubs in the foreground and still keep everything sharply focused.

Middle Falls

River: Snowbird Creek
County: Graham
USGS quadrangle: Santeetlah Creek
Landowner: Nantahala National Forest,
   Cheoah Ranger District
Height: 20 feet
Beauty rating: 7
Trail length and difficulty: Approximately 5.1
   miles; 3–7

Directions: Follow the directions to Big Falls and continue a short distance to a fork. Take the trail leading left, which is a rerouted section that will let you avoid dangerous rock scrambling. You will arrive at a campsite after crossing Snowbird Creek on a footbridge. A trail sign marks Big Snowbird Trail straight ahead and Middle Falls Trail to the right. You can follow Big Snowbird Trail upstream to the falls, but you will have to ford Snowbird Creek nearly a dozen times. This might be a good option in the summer, particularly when the cardinal flowers are in bloom, but you should plan on getting wet.

Middle Falls Trail climbs steeply for 0.2 mile and then descends gradually to a trail junction and sign. A connector to Big Snowbird Trail goes to the right. To reach Middle Falls, continue straight over fallen trees and an overgrown trail. You will come to a fork after about 0.2 mile. Turn left. You will reach the falls a short distance downstream. Look for a blue wildlife sign at a side trail leading to the base.

Middle Falls
Canon EOS Elan, 24mm tilt/shift lens, polarizing filter, f/22 at 1 second, Fujichrome Velvia.

I broke my own rule in this image by centering a horizon that stretches across the frame, but as I stated in the section on composition—no rule should be considered absolute. In this image, I feel justified breaking the rule.

Photo Tips

Middle Falls lends itself beautifully to photography. Horizontal compositions work well up close, while a vertical format is more effective farther downstream. Without question, the best time to visit the waterfall is during August, when cardinal flowers are blooming. The numerous sandy islands in Snowbird Creek, especially those in the vicinity of Middle Falls, provide ideal habitat for the brilliant red flowers.

If you are visiting with friends, take a few horizontal photos with them positioned on the right bank. Ask them to leave their backpacks on to create a highly marketable image.

Middle Falls is by far the most attractive of the four waterfalls in the Snowbird area. To make your trip more enjoyable, I recommend visiting during the summer and bringing an old pair of sneakers. This will allow you to safely wade in Snowbird Creek. If you are a photographer, that is exactly what you will want to do.

Upper Falls

River: Snowbird Creek
County: Graham
USGS quadrangle: Santeetlah Creek
Landowner: Nantahala National Forest,
    Cheoah Ranger District
Height: Small sliding cascade
Beauty rating: 4
Trail length and difficulty: 6.3 miles; 3–7

Directions: Follow the directions to Middle Falls. When you reach the campsite at the first crossing of Snowbird Creek, take Middle Falls Trail to the right rather than continuing straight on Big Snowbird Trail. You will ascend steeply for 0.2 mile, then gradually descend to a trail junction. Middle Falls Trail continues straight. Turn right onto the Big Snowbird Trail connector and follow it upstream to the junction with Big Snowbird Trail at the suspension bridge. Continue upstream to the falls. The waterfall is small and hidden; look for a blue wildlife sign. Immediately beyond the falls, the trail becomes narrow and heavily overgrown.

Photo Tips

You must wade the river to get to an appropriate vantage point, which still isn't all that good. You will have better luck shooting river scenes along the way.

Most of the route to Upper Falls follows an old narrow-gauge railroad grade. The Snowbird Creek basin was extensively logged during the 1930s, and the railway was used to haul out the logs. When the Forest Service acquired the land in 1943, the tracks were removed and the land left to slowly heal.

Wildcat Falls

River: Slickrock Creek
County: Graham County, N.C., and Monroe
    County, Tenn.
USGS quadrangle: Tapoco
Landowner: At the falls, Slickrock Creek forms the
    boundary between Cherokee National Forest in
    Tennessee and Nantahala National Forest in
    North Carolina. The North Carolina side is in
    the Joyce Kilmer/Slickrock Wilderness, Cheoah
    Ranger District.

Height: This waterfall has several drops. The lower two are about 8 feet each. The upper section is not visible from the base.
Beauty rating: 6
Trail length and difficulty: 2.6 miles; 8

Directions: From the starting point, drive 13.7 miles north on U.S. 129 and turn left on F.R. 62 (Slickrock Road). Follow this road 7 miles to where it ends at a parking area. A road forks left 0.3 mile from U.S. 129; stay to the right.

Several trails lead from the parking area. Take Big Fat Trail, which begins to the right of the sign board and behind a trail marker. You will descend steeply and reach a junction with Nichols Cove Trail at 1.5 miles. Turn left and continue 100 yards to a junction with Slickrock Creek Trail. Turn right. You will immediately enter a camping area beside Slickrock Creek. Find a suitable place to cross the creek, then continue downstream. You will cross the creek two more times, the latter time at the top of Wildcat Falls. Walk alongside the falls

a short distance and scramble down the riprap to reach the base.

Anyone hiking in the area should purchase the Joyce Kilmer/Slickrock Wilderness and Citico Creek Wilderness map from the ranger station beforehand. The map shows trails and other features, but it is not extremely accurate. Most of the streams, trails, and roads are shifted, and the map lists Big Fat Trail as Big Flat Trail. The Tapoco quadrangle, modified for Forest Service use, corrects these problems but does not cover the entire wilderness area.

Photo Tips

There are a few overhanging hemlock branches to the right that can be incorporated when the wind is calm. Otherwise, try a straightforward composition that isolates the falls.

Don't try to get a shot of the upper section. It is difficult to reach and unphotogenic.

Wildcat Falls
Nikon F3, 28-70mm zoom lens, polarizing filter stacked on warming filter, f/22 at 4 seconds, Fujichrome Velvia.

This is a simple, straightforward image, taken from the edge of the pool. If the wind had not been blowing, I would have incorporated hemlock branches in the foreground.

The trail leading to Wildcat Falls passes through the highly popular Joyce Kilmer/Slickrock Wilderness. Unlike the nearby virgin forests in Joyce Kilmer Memorial Forest, this area was extensively logged, but it has recovered well. Except for encountering numerous other hikers, you will enjoy a memorable wilderness experience. The wilderness is laced with trails that offer everything from cascading mountain streams to panoramic vistas.

Nearby waterfall: Hangover Creek, a major tributary of Slickrock Creek, contains the highest waterfall in the Slickrock basin. Unfortunately, there is no trail, and bushwhacking is strongly discouraged. The Forest Service is planning to construct a trail but has not set a definite completion date. Contact the Cheoah Ranger Station for further information.

Lower Falls

River: Slickrock Creek
County: Graham County, N.C., and Monroe
County, Tenn.
USGS quadrangle: Tapoco
Landowner: At the falls, Slickrock Creek forms the
boundary between Cherokee National Forest in
Tennessee and Nantahala National Forest in
North Carolina. The North Carolina side is in
the Joyce Kilmer/Slickrock Wilderness, Cheoah
Ranger District.
Height: 12 feet
Beauty rating: 4
Trail length and difficulty: 3 miles; 5–8

Directions: From the starting point, drive 15.4
miles north on U.S. 129 and turn left into the
parking area just before crossing Calderwood Lake.
Begin the trail at the end of the parking area. You
will loosely parallel the lake for over 1.5 miles to the
mouth of Slickrock Creek. The trail continues on
the left-hand (North Carolina) side of the creek
over several trees downed by the blizzard of 1993.
At several points, the trail seems to dead-end, but
upon investigation, you will discover that you can
scramble onward. At about 2.7 miles, the trail does
end on the North Carolina side, and you must cross
into Tennessee. There is a pool at this point; the
trail ends at a small rock cliff. There may be a couple
of trees that you can use to help you cross. After
crossing the creek, continue upstream 0.3 mile to
the falls.

You can also get to the waterfall by hiking to
Wildcat Falls and continuing downstream an
additional 3.6 miles, bringing the total distance
hiked to 6.2 miles. This section of trail was severely
damaged by the blizzard, however, so check with
the ranger station before attempting the hike.

Photo Tips
There are numerous downed trees around the
falls that cannot be excluded with a lens wider than
35mm. Shoot a tight composition to eliminate as
much clutter as possible.

Much more interesting than Lower Falls itself is the
trail leading to it. You will encounter numerous
wildflowers and rock walls.

The part of the trail that parallels Slickrock Creek
follows an old railroad grade that was used during
logging operations between 1915 and 1922. Considering how difficult it is to get just your body and a pack
over some stretches of the trail, it's hard to imagine a
railroad hauling out logs. Logging ceased in 1922
when Calderwood Lake was constructed, but not
before 70 percent of the virgin forest in the gorge had
been cut.

Nearby waterfalls: Twentymile Creek Cascade, in
nearby Great Smoky Mountains National Park, is very
small and covered with downed trees. It is definitely
not recommended, but since it is mentioned in a few
publications on waterfalls in the Smokies, I have
included it here. To reach it from the parking area for
Lower Falls, continue on U.S. 129 for 2.1 miles to a
junction with N.C. 28. Turn right and follow N.C. 28
for 2.8 miles to the Twentymile Ranger Station, on the
left. Drive past the buildings to a parking area, then
walk along the road about 0.4 mile to a trail junction.
Continue to the right a few hundred feet to the
cascade.

Other national-park waterfalls are listed in the Bryson
City, Cherokee, and Maggie Valley hubs. The Cherokee hub also contains general information about all
the waterfalls in the park.

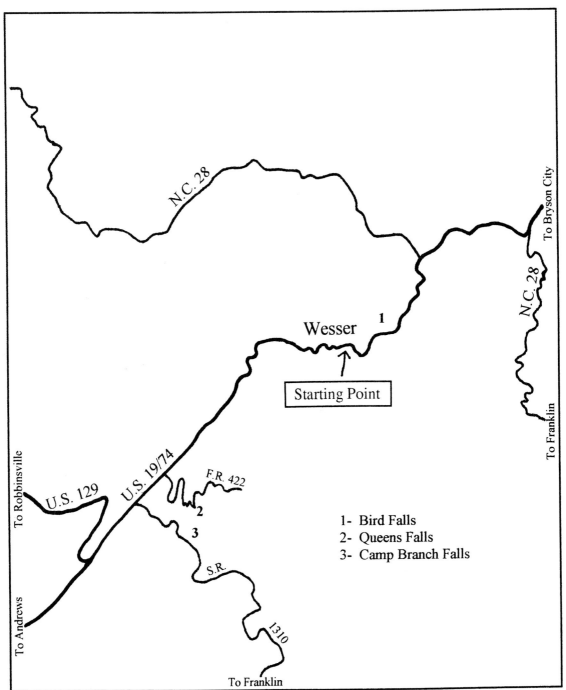

The starting point is the crosswalk on U.S. 19 between the Nantahala Outdoor Center's restaurant and motel.

Wesser

Drive through Wesser at night and you probably won't even know it is there. Drive through on a hot summer day and you'll likely find yourself in bumper-to-bumper traffic along the entire 8-mile stretch of highway that parallels the Nantahala River. Thousands of people come to float the river in canoes, kayaks, rafts, and inner tubes. An entire whitewater industry has sprung up, with the ever-expanding Nantahala Outdoor Center leading the pack.

Bird Falls

River: Bird Falls Branch
County: Swain
USGS quadrangle: Wesser
Landowner: Nantahala National Forest, Wayah Ranger District
Height: Approximately 100 feet
Beauty rating: If the lake is full, 7; if it's not, 4
Trail length and difficulty: The trail is 1.5 miles at a rate of 4, except for a few strenuous boulder crossings; if Fontana Lake is full, visiting by boat is the only option.

Directions: Turn left a few feet north of the crosswalk, cross the Nantahala River, and find a parking place anywhere you can. The trail begins as an old road which closely follows the river downstream for about 0.75 mile. At that point, you will have to walk along the lakeshore. (This is possible only between late fall and early spring, as Fontana Lake is usually full during the summer season. If the lake is full, you will realize it after the first 0.5 mile.) After passing a few boulder piles and making a 90-degree turn to the right, look for a 90-degree turn to the left. The high falls are visible on the right several hundred feet before this turn.

Photo Tips
When the lake is down, the best option is to compose a scene with the Nantahala River in the foreground. Be aware that unless it is overcast, there will be extreme contrast between the light-toned lake bed and the recessed waterfall.

Bird Falls itself is not spectacular. It is the walk and the surroundings which make the trip worthwhile. Walk downstream to the bend in the river for a view of the distant Smoky Mountains; if the lake is full and you have a canoe, this makes an excellent destination.

The lake backs up to the base of the falls, providing an ideal photo opportunity. However, anything large enough to require a boat ramp for launching will have to be put in some distance downstream.

If the lake is full and you don't have a boat, you can still catch a glimpse of the waterfall by taking a ride on the Great Smoky Mountains Railway (see the appendix). The railroad tracks are on private property and should not be used as a trail.

Queens Falls

River: Queens Creek
County: Macon
USGS quadrangle: Hewitt
Landowner: Private
Height: 30 to 35 feet

Beauty rating: 1
Trail length and difficulty: View roadside
Handicapped Accessible

Directions: From the starting point, drive 6.4 miles south on U.S. 19 to F.R. 422. Turn left and drive 3 miles to an overlook of the falls on the right.

Photo Tip
Drive back down to the bridge crossing the Nantahala River and shoot the whitewater rafters as they come by.

Years ago, this was undoubtedly a beautiful waterfall with a heavy water flow. Now, the flow has been severely restricted by Queens Reservoir. The falls are nearly overgrown with vegetation, and a water pipe and a power line are in the view.

Camp Branch Falls *

River: Camp Branch
County: Macon
USGS quadrangle: Hewitt
Landowner: Nantahala National Forest, Wayah Ranger District
Height: This waterfall is over 200 feet, but not all of it is visible from the base.
Beauty rating: 5
Trail length and difficulty: View roadside
Handicapped Accessible

Directions: From the starting point, drive 7.5 miles south on U.S. 19 and turn left on S.R. 1310.

After 2.7 miles, there is a pull-off at the black walnut tree on the left. Walk beyond the pull-off a few hundred feet for the best view.

Photo Tips
You are not going to get a decent photo here unless there is something to divert attention from the visual clutter. Fall colors and snow are a couple of possibilities.
Try a shot with the Nantahala River in the immediate foreground.

Until recently, this waterfall was mostly hidden by trees, but several have been cut to facilitate better viewing. Unfortunately, the trees were left where they fell, creating an unsightly mess along the side of the falls.

A visual plus is the Nantahala River, which flows by the base. Nantahala is a Cherokee word meaning "Land of the Noonday Sun," referring to the lack of sunlight in the steep gorge at any time other than high noon.

The waterfall site is a North Carolina Natural Heritage Area and contains the endangered shrub piratebush (*Buckleya distichophylla*).

Nearby waterfalls: To see a nice wet-weather cascade, continue on S.R. 1310 for 1.35 miles to F.R. 308. A view is on the left.

To see a very pretty 20-foot cascade, turn right on F.R. 308, cross White Oak Creek after less than 0.1 mile, and look upstream.

Rafting on the Nantahala River
Nikon 8008s, 28-70mm zoom lens, exposure set on aperture-priority automatic, using Matrix metering, Fujichrome 100.

Rafting the Nantahala River has nothing to do with waterfalls, but this is probably the finest photo opportunity you will find in the Wesser Hub. It is also amazingly easy. When I finished gathering information on Queens Falls, I drove back down the mountain to the bridge crossing the river. I sat on the bridge and supported the camera on one of the truss supports. The biggest problem was that most of the rafters would wave as they floated by; not something I wanted to record.

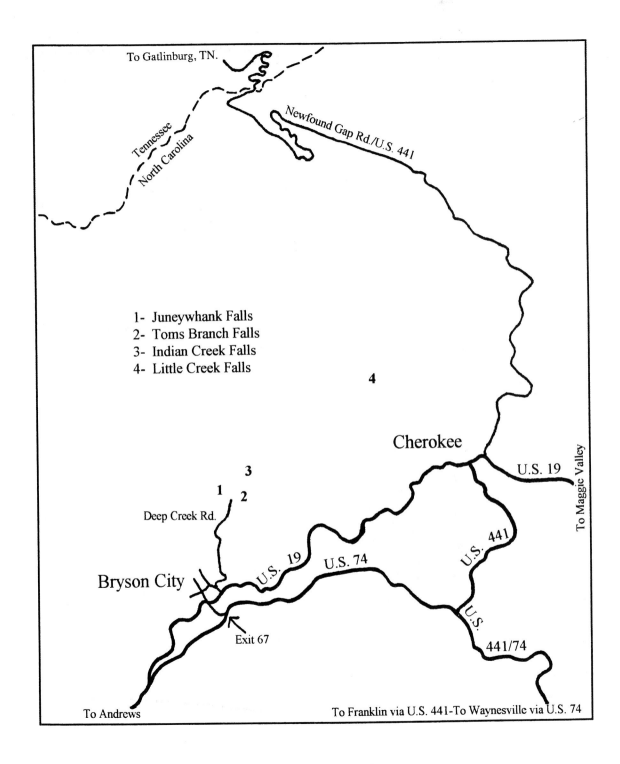

To Gatlinburg, TN.

Tennessee
North Carolina

Newfound Gap Rd./U.S. 441

1- Juneywhank Falls
2- Toms Branch Falls
3- Indian Creek Falls
4- Little Creek Falls

4

Cherokee

U.S. 19

To Maggie Valley

3

1 2

Deep Creek Rd.

U.S. 19   U.S. 74

U.S. 441

Bryson City

U.S.

Exit 67

441/74

To Andrews

To Franklin via U.S. 441-To Waynesville via U.S. 74

Bryson City

In downtown Bryson City, there is a historical marker honoring Horace Kephart, who came to the area in 1904 "to enjoy the thrills of singlehanded adventure in a wild country." He found the wild country he was looking for in the Smoky Mountains just outside Bryson City. By 1913, he had written two books, one of them, *Camping and Woodcraft*, containing practical wilderness information, and the other, *Our Southern Highlanders*, about local folklore. Both of these popular books are still in print.

Kephart was distressed by the destruction of the forests by lumbering. By 1918, logging supported two thousand people along nearby Hazel Creek alone, more than the present-day population of Bryson City. Kephart devoted his time to the formation of a national park. In 1925, he wrote, "When I first came into the Smokies, the whole region was one of superb forest primeval. I lived for several years in the heart of it. My sylvan studio spread over mountain after mountain, seemingly without end, and it was always clean and fragrant. . . . Not long ago I went to that same place again. It was wrecked, ruined, desecrated, turned into a thousand rubbish heaps, utterly vile and mean."

Horace Kephart died in a taxicab accident in 1931, less than a year before the official dedication of 138,843 acres as Great Smoky Mountains National Park.

In recent years, Bryson City has enjoyed a tremendous economic boost from Great Smoky Mountains Railway. The railway began in 1988 as a joint venture between private investors and the state of North Carolina. Since then, over 600,000 people have taken scenic train excursions either from Dillsboro to Bryson City or from Bryson City to the Nantahala Gorge. The Nantahala Gorge excursion provides views of Bird Falls, listed in the Wesser hub. For information on the railway, see the appendix.

The four waterfalls listed here are located in the Deep Creek section of Great Smoky Mountains National Park, near Deep Creek Campground and a picnic area. Other waterfalls in the park are listed in the Robbinsville, Cherokee, and Maggie Valley hubs. The Cherokee hub includes a general discussion of all the park's waterfalls.

Juneywhank Falls *

River: Juneywhank Branch
County: Swain
USGS quadrangle: Bryson City
Landowner: Great Smoky Mountains National Park
Height: The main section of this steep slide is about 30 feet.
Beauty rating: 3
Trail length and difficulty: 0.25 mile; 5

Directions: The trailhead is reached by taking Exit 67 off U.S. 74 as it bypasses Bryson City. Continue straight on this road through two stoplights to a stop sign at 1 mile. Turn right onto Bryson Walk and drive 0.15 mile to where it ends at Everett Street. Turn right, then left onto Depot Street. Follow Depot Street 0.15 mile to Ramseur Street. Turn left; you will immediately round a right-hand curve, where Deep Creek Road begins. Continue on Deep Creek Road 2.2 miles to the park boundary. It is then 0.6 mile to the parking area and the trailhead at the end of the road.

From the parking area, backtrack on the road to a sign on the right marking the trailhead; this is about 100 yards from the picnic area. Begin the

Juneywhank Falls
Nikon 24mm lens, polarizing filter, f/22 at 2 seconds, Fujichrome Velvia.

I normally shoot several different compositions of a scene, in both vertical and horizontal formats. At Juneywhank Falls however, this is the only thing I could decide upon. It worked well; the falls are not nearly as attractive as the photo suggests.

uphill climb. You will soon intersect a horse trail coming in from the left. A side trail soon bears to the right. Continue to the left. You will come to another right-hand side trail that leads to the base of the falls. You can see the waterfall from this point.

> **Photo Tips**
>   Juneywhank Falls does not lend itself very well to photography. From the right bank, you can include the falls and the footbridge using a 20mm to 24mm lens. This is perhaps the most effective composition.
>   After a heavy rain, isolation shots may be effective.

The exact origin of the name Juneywhank hasn't been preserved. Some say that it's Cherokee for "place where the bear passes." It is more likely that the waterfall was named after Junaluska Whank, nicknamed "Juney," who lived in the area. Junaluska Whank was named for Chief Junaluska, mentioned in the Robbinsville hub.

Toms Branch Falls *

River: Toms Branch
County: Swain
USGS quadrangle: Bryson City
Landowner: Great Smoky Mountains
   National Park
Height: Total drop of 80 feet
Beauty rating: 4
Trail length and difficulty: 0.25 mile; 1

Directions: Follow the directions to the parking area for Juneywhank Falls. From the parking area, continue past the gate on the well-graded gravel road. The falls are on the right.

tubes to the Deep Creek launch site, 0.5 mile farther upstream.

Deep Creek Campground operates on a first-come, first-served basis, so get there early if you want to camp.

> **Photo Tips**
>
> This waterfall is most effectively photographed in the winter, when it is least obscured by vegetation. Use the large tree growing by the benches to frame the scene.
>
> During the summer, you will see hundreds of "tubers" floating on Deep Creek, which flows by the base of the waterfall. Take advantage of the situation by shooting recreation photos of them with the falls in the background.

The trail leading by Toms Branch Falls is one of the most popular in the Smokies. During the summer, you will encounter hundreds of fun seekers carrying inner

Indian Creek Falls *

River: Indian Creek
County: Swain
USGS quadrangle: Bryson City
Landowner: Great Smoky Mountains
  National Park
Height: 45-foot slide
Beauty rating: 5
Trail length and difficulty: 0.9 mile; 3

Directions: Follow the directions to the parking area for Juneywhank Falls. From the parking area, walk past the gate on Deep Creek Trail, pass Toms Branch Falls at 0.25 mile, and continue to the junction with Indian Creek Trail at 0.8 mile. Turn right on Indian Creek Trail. You will reach the falls after a few hundred feet. A side trail leads to the base.

> **Photo Tip**
>
> A few years ago, this was a scenic and photogenic waterfall. Now, it is covered with fallen trees and branches that make it unattractive. There is no way to make an acceptable photograph.

Toms Branch Falls
Canon EOS Elan, 24mm tilt/shift lens, polarizing filter, f/22 at 3 seconds, Fujichrome Velvia.

Without tubers in the foreground, Toms Branch Falls needs something to enhance it. The tree in the foreground is an excellent choice. It transforms this dull cascade into a suitable photo subject.

Indian Creek Falls
Nikon F3, 24mm lens, polarizing filter, f/22 at 4 seconds, Fujichrome Velvia.

This photo was made in the summer of 1992, before the falls were covered with fallen trees and branches. It will be some time before nature clears the mess and restores the photographic potential of the falls.

Indian Creek Trail, which passes the falls, is a well-graded gravel road that was originally planned as Indian Creek Motor Nature Trail, similar to Roaring Fork Motor Nature Trail on the Tennessee side of the Smokies. The road would have followed Indian Creek upstream a few miles before turning right and descending Thomas Ridge to Galbraith Creek Road, near Deep Creek Campground. According to rangers at Deep Creek Campground, the motor trail, scheduled to open in 1974, was probably abandoned because of heavy hiker traffic in the area and its inconsistency with a wilderness experience.

Little Creek Falls

River: Little Creek
County: Swain
USGS quadrangle: Smokemont
Landowner: Great Smoky Mountains
   National Park
Height: 75 feet
Beauty rating: 5
Trail length and difficulty: 6.8 miles; 3–7

Directions: At almost 7 miles one-way, this is one of the longest hikes in the book. There is a 1.5-mile access to the falls that is included in some park literature, but it requires parking on private property, and it is unclear whether the National Park Service has a visitor right-of-way through the property. That route is not included here, but you can contact the rangers at the Deep Creek Ranger Station for information.

The trailhead is the same as for the other waterfalls in this hub. Begin on Deep Creek Trail and turn right on Indian Creek Trail at 0.8 mile. You will pass Indian Creek Falls and then cross Georges Branch approximately 2.9 miles from Deep Creek Trail. There is a bench on the left; the road forks here. Take the right fork onto Deeplow Gap Trail, ascend 0.3 mile, and turn left to remain on the trail. (The road that leads to the right is part of the abandoned Indian Creek Motor Nature Trail.) Hike 2 miles to an intersection with Thomas Divide Trail at Deeplow Gap. Continue straight on Deeplow Gap Trail to the base of Little Creek Falls 0.8 mile from Deeplow Gap.

Photo Tips

Two possibilities that will allow you to include all the falls are from directly in front, using the moss-covered logs in the foreground, and from the right bank, using the tree on the left to frame the falls. The spring wildflowers growing along the right bank might be positioned in the foreground.

Telephoto isolation shots work well on this waterfall.

As waterfalls go, Little Creek Falls is not worth a 6.8-mile hike. However, the hike itself is more than worthwhile, especially in early spring and fall. The Great Smoky Mountains Trail Map, available for a nominal fee from the park's visitor center, offers several loop options.

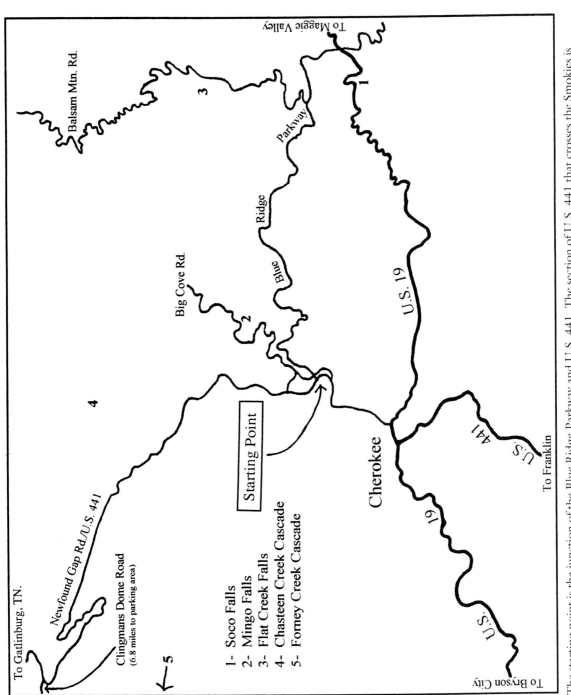

To Gatlinburg, TN.

Balsam Mtn. Rd.

Newfound Gap Rd./U.S. 441

Clingmans Dome Road
(6.8 miles to parking area)

Big Cove Rd.

To Maggie Valley

Parkway

Ridge

Blue

U.S. 19

Cherokee

Starting Point

U.S. 441

To Franklin

19

U.S.

To Bryson City

1- Soco Falls
2- Mingo Falls
3- Flat Creek Falls
4- Chasteen Creek Cascade
5- Forney Creek Cascade

The starting point is the junction of the Blue Ridge Parkway and U.S. 441. The section of U.S. 441 that crosses the Smokies is called Newfound Gap Road.

Cherokee

Located at the foot of Great Smoky Mountains National Park, Cherokee is a popular resort town. The town is located entirely within the boundaries of the Qualla Indian Reservation, home to the Eastern Band of Cherokee Indians. Gift shops line the streets, beckoning tourists, but visitors are encouraged to experience the many cultural and historical attractions as well, such as the Museum of the Cherokee Indian and the Oconaluftee Indian Village. The outdoor drama *Unto These Hills*, a highly dramatized version of the infamous Trail of Tears, is performed every night except Sunday during summer. More than half a million people have seen this stirring drama since the first production in 1950.

Soco Falls

River: Soco Creek and a tributary
County: Jackson
USGS quadrangle: Sylva North
Landowner: Qualla Indian Reservation
Height: About 50 feet
Beauty rating: Viewed from the road, 1; viewed from the base, 5
Trail length and difficulty: During the winter, the falls can be partially viewed from the road. An extremely steep 200-foot climb is required to reach the base.

Directions: From the starting point, drive south on U.S. 441 into downtown Cherokee. After 2.75 miles, turn left on U.S. 19 and follow it north for 10.4 miles. Park at the large pull-off on the right. An obscure path leads to the base.

For another route to the falls, follow the Blue Ridge Parkway north to where it crosses U.S. 19 at Soco Gap. Exit on U.S. 19 South and drive 1.3 miles to the pull-off, on the left.

Photo Tips
From the base, you can probably make a good photograph on an overcast day using a horizontal composition. Numerous wildflowers grow on the bank, but the constant spray and wind will likely prevent you from including them.

Sketchy reports indicate that the Cherokees threw one of Hernando De Soto's men over Soco Falls. Today, the steep bank surrounding the falls is used as a place to throw garbage, much of which ends up in Soco Creek.

Mingo Falls *

River: Mingo Creek
County: Swain
USGS quadrangle: Smokemont
Landowner: Qualla Indian Reservation
Height: Over 150 feet
Beauty rating: 7
Trail length and difficulty: 0.25 mile; 7

Directions: From the starting point, head north on Newfound Gap Road 0.85 mile and turn right at the Jobs Corps Center sign. Follow this road 0.6 mile to where it ends at Big Cove Road, which is unmarked. Turn left and continue 3.3 miles to

Mingo Falls Campground, on the right. Cross the bridge into the campground and park in the designated area. The trail begins to the left of the water station and ascends steeply before leveling off as it approaches the base of the falls.

Photo Tips

Mingo Falls was once an excellent photo subject, but no longer. The blizzard of 1993 left its mark— a jumbled mass of fallen trees and branches. If you make a photo of the entire falls, you will have to frame tightly across the base to eliminate the clutter, using a less-than-ideal composition. A better option is to mount a 200mm or 300mm lens on the tripod and shoot isolation photos. Mingo Falls is one of the best waterfalls I've seen for this type of composition.

Mingo Falls is the most spectacular waterfall in the Smokies and should not be missed.

Mingo Falls
Nikon F3, 75-300mm zoom lens, polarizing filter, f/22 at 2 seconds, Fujichrome Velvia.

This was an extremely easy photograph to make. I simply set up the tripod in a convenient place, and used the zoom lens to find numerous compositions. I did make sure to visit on an overcast day.

Waterfalls in Great Smoky Mountains National Park

Flat Creek Falls, Chasteen Creek Cascade, Forney Creek Cascade

Great Smoky Mountains National Park is America's most popular national park, recording nearly 9 million visits in 1992. Many people come to see waterfalls, but the park is not an ideal location for this. While there are a few scenic waterfalls within the park, most are small and unattractive compared to others in this book. It's true that the Smokies are blessed with rugged topography and hundreds of waterways, but by the time these streams are of significant size, they have already left the steep slopes for the shallow drainage valleys. There are no high plateau regions to allow the streams to attain the size necessary to create major waterfalls, such as those along the southern Blue Ridge escarpment. Abrams Creek, on the Tennessee side of the park, is the only stream in the Smokies that is of significant size when it flows over a major waterfall, in this case Abrams Falls.

This is not meant to discourage you from visiting any of the park's waterfalls. The park is an unparalleled natural wonder, and I strongly recommend that you explore as much of it as you can. Just plan on taking more pictures of cascading mountain streams than of thunderous waterfalls.

Three waterfalls on the North Carolina side of the park are listed next, and other park waterfalls are listed in the Robbinsville, Bryson City, and Maggie Valley hubs. To see other scenic cascades in the park too small or too remote to list here, I recommend hiking the following North Carolina trails: Bradley Fork, Enloe Creek, Hazel Creek, Noland Creek, Richland Mountain, and Sweat Heifer. Trail maps and guidebooks are available at the visitor center.

Flat Creek Falls

River: Flat Creek
County: Swain
USGS quadrangle: Bunches Bald
Landowner: Great Smoky Mountains National Park
Height: 200-foot cascade
Beauty rating: 2
Trail length and difficulty: 1 mile; 6

Directions: From the starting point, drive north on the Blue Ridge Parkway for 10.7 miles and turn left on Balsam Mountain Road. It is 5.1 miles to a pull-off on the left and the trailhead. Hike the trail about 1 mile to a side trail on the left. (To the right, it is approximately 2 miles to Balsam Mountain Campground.) Follow the side trail 0.1 mile to the top of the falls.

> **Photo Tip**
> Save your film.

The walk to Flat Creek Falls is pleasant, but if you are only interested in seeing a waterfall, you'd be better off staying in the car. At the top of the falls, there is a sign warning you to stay on the constructed trail, but there is no trail beyond that point. You can descend to the right of the sign, cross the creek, and view the falls from the bank, but this is dangerous and does not offer a good view. It is extremely dangerous to attempt a descent on the left side of the sign, and the view is no better even if you do.

You can drive back down the road 0.5 mile for a faint view of the falls across the valley.

The Blue Ridge Parkway is closed during periods of snow and ice, and Balsam Mountain Road is always closed during winter.

Chasteen Creek Cascade

River: Chasteen Creek
County: Swain
USGS quadrangle: Smokemont
Landowner: Great Smoky Mountains
   National Park
Height: 30-foot cascade
Beauty rating: 3
Trail length and difficulty: 2 miles; 2–3

Directions: From the starting point, drive 3.8 miles north on Newfound Gap Road and turn right at the sign for Smokemont Campground. Cross the Oconaluftee River and turn left into the campground. Drive to the far end of the campground and park at the gate.

Begin Bradley Fork Trail beyond the gate. After 1.2 miles, turn right onto Chasteen Creek Trail. After 0.75 mile, you will come to a hitching post on the left. Walk past the hitching post and pick up a small trail leading 100 yards to the cascade.

Photo Tips
   You might be able to salvage this scene by wading in the creek to avoid the distracting rhododendron shrubs, but the best photo opportunities are along the trail.

Chasteen Creek Cascade is small and not as scenic as other waterfalls nearby, but the trail leading to it is especially appealing.

Forney Creek Cascade

River: Forney Creek
County: Swain
USGS quadrangle: Silers Bald
Landowner: Great Smoky Mountains
   National Park
Height: Long slide measuring about 200 feet
Beauty rating: 5
Trail length and difficulty: 3 miles; 8

Directions: From the starting point, drive 16 miles north on Newfound Gap Road and turn left on Clingmans Dome Road, which is closed in winter. Follow it to a parking area at 6.8 miles. (Note: On the right at the end of the parking lot, a paved trail leads 0.5 mile to the 6,643-foot summit of Clingmans Dome, the highest peak in the park.)

On the left at the end of the parking lot is Forney Ridge Trail, which begins the route to the waterfall. After 0.1 mile, you will come to a fork; turn left to remain on Forney Ridge Trail. Continue 1 mile to a flat, open area and a junction with Forney Creek Trail, on the right. Forney Creek Trail leads about 2 miles to the cascade. Approximately 1.25 miles along the way, the trail runs down a streambed for a short distance and is difficult to recognize.

Photo Tips
   Don't bother climbing to the base; the best vantage point is from the middle, looking at the upper portion of the slide. Use a vertical composition to eliminate unneeded elements on the sides and to include the overhanging branches.
   This is an especially photogenic waterfall in early spring.

If you don't mind a strenuous hike, Forney Creek Cascade is an excellent destination. The trek passes through a spruce-fir forest before opening into a forest of hemlock, maple, beech, and birch. The first section of the trail is rocky, so wear sturdy hiking shoes.

Notice the streaks of quartz cutting diagonally across the waterfall.

Forney Creek Cascade
Nikon F3, 28-70mm zoom lens, f/22 at 4 seconds, Fujichrome Velvia.

Sometimes, I feel as though I'm being watched over by a photographic God. I hiked the entire 3 miles to this cascade in pouring rain. When I arrived, it subsided just enough to allow me to fire off several rolls. Then it poured again the entire way back. This photo is also included in the color section.

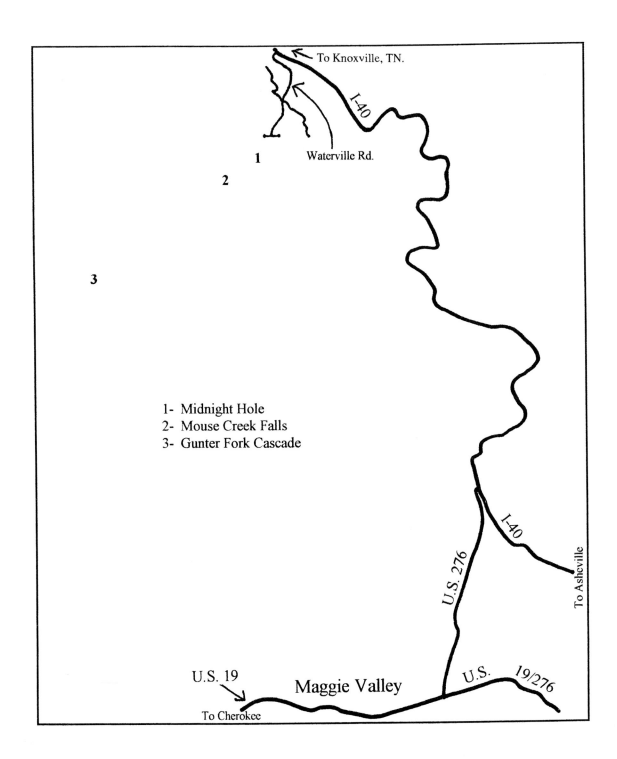

To Knoxville, TN.

I-40

Waterville Rd.

1

2

3

1- Midnight Hole
2- Mouse Creek Falls
3- Gunter Fork Cascade

I-40

U.S. 276

To Asheville

U.S. 19

Maggie Valley

U.S.

19/276

To Cherokee

Maggie Valley

USGS quadrangle: Luftee Knob
Landowner: Great Smoky Mountains
  National Park
Height: 6 feet
Beauty rating: 5
Trail length and difficulty: 1.4 miles; 3

For westbound travelers on Interstate 40, the most direct route to the Smokies—though not always the quickest—is U.S. 19 through Maggie Valley. The tremendous economic boost brought by this route has allowed the community to become a desirable destination in itself.

Motorists winding their way from the valley to Soco Gap are provided with a bit of amusement by a billboard war. Within a few hundred feet of one another are commercial establishments with billboards proclaiming, "One of the most photographed views in the Smokies," "The Smokies most photographed view," "Smokies best view," "Best view in Maggie and Smokies," and my personal favorite, "Most photographed view anywhere." Just down the road is an antique dealer with his own sign proclaiming, "Most photographed junk in Smoky Mountains."

"Maggie" was the daughter of John Sidney Setzer, who became the valley's first postmaster in 1904. The post office is one of only a few named after a woman.

The three waterfalls listed here are located in the Big Creek section of Great Smoky Mountains National Park. Other park waterfalls are listed in the Robbinsville, Bryson City, and Cherokee hubs. The Cherokee hub has a general discussion of all the park's waterfalls.

Directions: Take U.S. 276 north from U.S. 19 for about 5.7 miles to Interstate 40. Head west on Interstate 40 approximately 20 miles and take the Waterville exit, which is just across the border in Tennessee. At the end of the exit ramp, turn left to reach Waterville Road, on the left. (If you are coming from Tennessee, Waterville Road will be on the right at the end of the exit ramp.) Follow Waterville Road 2.1 miles to a crossroads. Continue straight to enter the national park. Park at the end of the road, approximately 0.8 mile from the crossroads.

Big Creek Trail begins a few feet before the parking area. It is a graded Jeep road that parallels Big Creek. Look for a well-worn path leading from the road to the falls.

Midnight Hole

River: Big Creek
County: Haywood

Photo Tips

What this cascade lacks in size, it more than makes up for in photo potential. Use the moss-covered rocks in the foreground of a vertical composition. Use a horizontal format to accentuate the size of the pool. Wade into the creek and try out different perspectives.

At only 6 feet, Midnight Hole can hardly be called a waterfall. It is given a separate listing here because it is such a good photo subject and because it provides one of the most inviting swimming holes I've seen. Also, it is located along the route to two other waterfalls.

The name refers to the deep pool, which is as dark as midnight.

Midnight Hole
Nikon F3, 20mm lens, polarizing filter, f/22 at 3 seconds, Fujichrome Velvia.

This scene is similar to the one in the color section except that it is horizontal. I always shoot both vertical and horizontal formats when I can. In this case, I much prefer the vertical composition.

Mouse Creek Falls

River: Mouse Creek
County: Haywood
USGS quadrangle: Luftee Knob
Landowner: Great Smoky Mountains
    National Park
Height: 35-foot cascade
Beauty rating: 6
Trail length and difficulty: 2 miles; 3

Directions: Mouse Creek Falls is located 0.6 mile beyond Midnight Hole on Big Creek Trail. Walk past the hitching post on the left to view the waterfall pouring into Big Creek.

Mouse Creek Falls
Nikon F3, 28-70mm zoom lens, polarizing filter, f/22 at 3 seconds, Fujichrome Velvia.

This photograph was made from the same location, and using the same lens, as the one in the color section. This easily demonstrates the incredible usefulness of a zoom lens when photographing waterfalls. I prefer the tight composition in the color section over this one, but both are definitely publishable.

Photo Tips

Three effective compositions at this waterfall are a shot from the bank, using the hemlock branches in the foreground; a shot from the edge of Big Creek, using the creek in the foreground; and a tight framing of just the waterfall itself. Be careful about using too long a shutter speed if Big Creek is included. The large flow of water in such a small area will "wash out" much sooner than the waterfall.

The easy 2-mile walk to Mouse Creek Falls provides a perfect day-hike for campers at Big Creek Campground. Nature photographers will find numerous opportunities along the entire trail.

Gunter Fork Cascade

River: Gunter Fork
County: Haywood
USGS quadrangle: Luftee Knob
Landowner: Great Smoky Mountains
  National Park
Height: 20-foot drop, then a steep slide
  of about 200 feet
Beauty rating: 6
Trail length and difficulty: 8.2 miles; 3–6

Directions: Follow the directions to the parking area for Midnight Hole. Begin Big Creek Trail just before the parking area and hike approximately 5.2

miles to the Walnut Bottoms back-country campsite, passing Midnight Hole and Mouse Creek Falls along the way. Just beyond Walnut Bottoms, the Jeep road becomes a foot trail. It continues a short distance to where Gunter Fork Trail turns to the left. Follow Gunter Fork Trail; you will immediately cross Big Creek. Except in the driest of conditions, this is a wet crossing. Continue on Gunter Fork Trail, making numerous stream crossings. You will reach the base of the falls approximately 2.5 miles from Big Creek. There is a small cascade on the right 0.25 mile before the falls.

Photo Tips

It takes a wide-angle lens to include all of the cascade, but due to the nature of the drop, the scene will appear distorted. The upper section is so far away that it will seem tiny compared to the lower slide. There is no way to completely prevent this, even with the perspective-control lenses discussed in the chapter on photographing waterfalls.

The hike to Gunter Fork Cascade is one of my personal favorites. Approximately 5 miles of the route closely parallel the cascading Big Creek on a gently graded Jeep road, providing unequaled opportunities for wading, fishing, photography, and nature study.

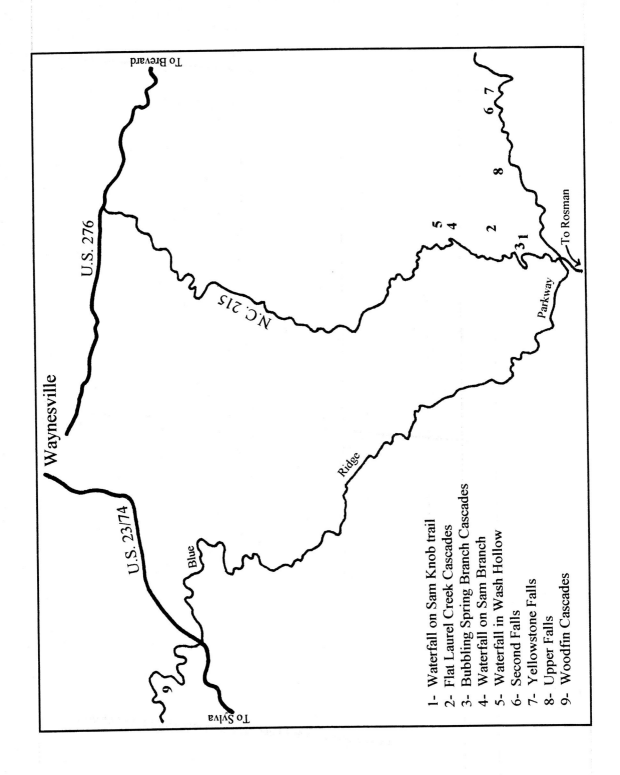

To Brevard

Waynesville

U.S. 276

U.S. 23/74

N.C. 215

To Sylva

To Rosman

Parkway

Blue

Ridge

1- Waterfall on Sam Knob trail
2- Flat Laurel Creek Cascades
3- Bubbling Spring Branch Cascades
4- Waterfall on Sam Branch
5- Waterfall in Wash Hollow
6- Second Falls
7- Yellowstone Falls
8- Upper Falls
9- Woodfin Cascades

Waynesville

The Waynesville area includes the extremely popular Shining Rock Wilderness Area and the less popular but no less appealing Middle Prong Wilderness Area. For nature photography and outdoor recreation, these two areas are hard to beat, yet I have not included waterfalls from either of them. There are two reasons for this. The first and foremost is that there simply aren't any significant falls within their boundaries. The second reason is that they are literally being loved to death. The last thing that is needed is to recommend that people enter these wilderness areas just to see a few minor waterfalls, especially since there are several magnificent ones close by which can be visited without posing as serious an environmental threat.

The Waterfalls of the West Fork of the Pigeon River Gorge
Waterfall on Sam Knob Trail,
Flat Laurel Creek Cascades, Bubbling Spring
Branch Cascades, Waterfall on Sam Branch,
Waterfall in Wash Hollow

The gorge of the West Fork of the Pigeon River might well be called "Little Yosemite," as it contains at least nine cascades worthy of mention, as well as steep mountains that would indeed resemble those in the California park were it not for the trees. No wonder, then, that N.C. 215, which parallels the river, is part of the Forest Heritage Scenic Byway.

Waterfall on Sam Knob Trail

River: Tributary of West Fork, Pigeon River
County: Haywood
USGS quadrangle: Sam Knob
Landowner: Pisgah National Forest,
   Pisgah Ranger District
Height: 125-foot sliding cascade
Beauty rating: 4
Trail length and difficulty: 0.7 mile; 3

Directions: From the junction of N.C. 215 and the Blue Ridge Parkway, it is 0.8 mile north on N.C. 215 to a parking area on the right. Park here. Rock-hop Bubbling Spring Branch and follow the old railroad grade to the cement bridge below the falls.

Photo Tips
If possible, visit this waterfall and the others in the gorge during the fall. During the full-moon phase in September, October, November, and December, the moon rises over the mountains so that it can be positioned in the frame along with the falls. This will only work from a vantage point along N.C. 215 some 1.6 miles from the parkway.

This cascade is not particularly great by itself, but combining it with a hike to Flat Laurel Creek Cascades will make your trip more than worthwhile.

Flat Laurel Creek Cascades

River: Flat Laurel Creek
County: Haywood
USGS quadrangle: Sam Knob
Landowner: Pisgah National Forest,
   Pisgah Ranger District

Height: Practically one continuous cascade along a 0.5-mile stretch of the creek
Beauty rating: 7
Trail length and difficulty: 2 miles; 3

Directions: Follow the directions to the waterfall on Sam Knob Trail, then continue on the trail another 1.3 miles.

Photo Tips
    These cascades are highly photogenic, but the highlight of this trip is the mountain scenery along the way. Hike this trail during autumn and you'll likely forget all about the waterfall. Take some pictures of the creek with Sam Knob in the background. Just be sure to pay attention to the contrast; the creek and the cascades are often in shade while the mountain is in full sun.

You can easily view a portion of these cascades from the trail, but in order to get a closeup view, you must scramble down the steep bank. From that point downstream, there is one cascade after another, though there is no good way to get to them. In fact, your best bet is to walk in the creek bed, rock-hopping your way down.

Bubbling Spring Branch Cascades *

River: Bubbling Spring Branch
County: Haywood
USGS quadrangle: Sam Knob
Landowner: Pisgah National Forest,
    Pisgah Ranger District
Height: Cascades measuring about 200 feet
Beauty rating: 6
Trail length and difficulty: View roadside
Handicapped Accessible

Directions: Follow the directions to the parking area for the waterfall on Sam Knob Trail, but continue 1 mile farther on N.C. 215. The falls are visible on the right at the pull-off.

Photo Tips
    This waterfall needs one of three things—fall colors, spring green, or snow. Note that the sun rises directly over the falls, so you will get the best lighting in late afternoon.

This waterfall is most easily viewed from the road, but you can climb down the bank if you want a closer view. Remember, though, if you do this, you will not be able to view the waterfall in context with its surroundings.

Nearby waterfalls: To glimpse a small waterfall, continue 0.1 mile on N.C. 215 to the next pull-off and walk down the road a short distance.
    For a view of another waterfall, drive 0.1 mile farther to the next pull-off and again walk down the road a short distance.

Waterfall on Sam Branch

River: Sam Branch
County: Haywood
USGS quadrangle: Sam Knob
Landowner: Pisgah National Forest,
    Pisgah Ranger District
Height: 60-foot cascade
Beauty rating: 3
Trail length and difficulty: 0.3 mile; 5

Directions: From the junction of N.C. 215 and the Blue Ridge Parkway, drive 3.9 miles north on N.C. 215 to a sharp left turn in the road and park on the shoulder. (If you cross the river a second time, you've gone too far; turn around and drive back 0.15 mile.) Climb the steep bank and pick up an old, heavily overgrown logging road. This road leads left to the falls.

> **Photo Tip**
> Pass on this one.

This waterfall and the one in Wash Hollow are practically unknown except to local hunters and fishermen.

Note the old logging cables at the base of the falls.

Nearby waterfalls: Some distance upstream is a major waterfall, but reaching it requires rock-climbing skills. During the winter, you can barely make out this waterfall from N.C. 215 some 4.5 miles from the Blue Ridge Parkway.

To see a small cascade, continue down N.C. 215 from the parking area for the waterfall on Sam Branch. It is 0.15 mile to a crossing of the West Fork of the Pigeon River. The cascade is on the left.

Waterfall in Wash Hollow

River: Tributary of Sam Branch
County: Haywood
USGS quadrangle: Sam Knob
Landowner: Pisgah National Forest,
   Pisgah Ranger District; borders Shining Rock
   Wilderness Area
Height: 50 feet
Beauty rating: 4
Trail length and difficulty: 0.4 mile; 5

Directions: Follow the directions to the waterfall

on Sam Branch, then rock-hop the branch and proceed about 100 yards.

> **Photo Tip**
> Bring closeup gear for the wildflowers on the right bank.

The Waterfalls of Graveyard Fields
Second Falls, Yellowstone Falls, Upper Falls

Graveyard Fields is one of the most popular stops along the Blue Ridge Parkway, and for good reason. Graveyard Fields Loop Trail closely parallels Yellowstone Prong in a flat, open valley that lacks the dense forest canopy which prevails over much of the mountains. This open area allows fine views of Graveyard Ridge and is truly a nature photographer's paradise. This is one of my favorite places during the fall. It would be one of my favorites for snow scenes as well, except that the Blue Ridge Parkway is closed during periods of snow and ice.

The area's openness is not natural, but rather the result of an intense fire in 1925 that destroyed over twenty-five thousand acres, much of which had been recently logged. The fire was so hot in the valley that it sterilized the soil, the reason for the unusually slow return to forest.

The area received its name before the fire, when the spruce stumps and trunks—covered in moss and needles—brought to mind a ghostly graveyard.

Second Falls *

River: Yellowstone Prong
County: Haywood
USGS quadrangle: Shining Rock
Landowner: Pisgah National Forest,
   Pisgah Ranger District
Height: Cascades measuring about 60 feet
Beauty rating: 8
Trail length and difficulty: 0.3 mile; 6
Handicapped Accessible

Directions: Graveyard Fields Overlook is located at Milepost 418.8 on the Blue Ridge Parkway. Begin the paved trail at the steps at the north end of the overlook. You will reach Yellowstone Prong after 0.2 mile. Cross the creek and turn right; you will see a sign calling this waterfall Lower Falls. After a short distance, the trail forks right and descends steeply to the base.

Photo Tips

In terms of photography, this waterfall rates a 10. From the base, the falls can be shot with the pool as a foreground, or you can back up and use the rocks, eliminating the pool altogether. An excellent vantage point is from the parkway 0.3 mile north of the overlook. There, you can use a wide-angle lens to frame the falls, with Graveyard Ridge and Black Balsam Knob looming in the distance. In the foreground are azaleas, rhododendron, and serviceberry.

I recommend making a special effort to visit during the fall or early spring. The best lighting occurs from one to two hours after sunrise.

This is a popular waterfall for a few reasons: it can be seen from the Blue Ridge Parkway; it is easily accessible; and its large boulders and deep pool create a tempting spot for sunbathing and swimming. In fact, during the summer, the only way to have it to yourself is to arrive early in the morning.

Second Falls
Nikon F3, 75-300mm zoom lens, warming filter, f/22 at 1 second, Fujichrome Velvia.

Although you can't tell it in this black-and-white photo, I was attracted to this scene by the new spring buds and the blooming serviceberries. I made the photo beside the Blue Ridge Parkway. See additional photo in the color section.

Yellowstone Falls

River: Yellowstone Prong
County: Haywood
USGS quadrangle: Shining Rock
Landowner: Pisgah National Forest,
   Pisgah Ranger District
Height: This waterfall slides 100 feet into a small
   pool, then 25 feet into a larger pool.
Beauty rating: From the cliff overlook, 4; from the
   base, 7
Trail length and difficulty: The trail to the cliff
   overlook is 0.5 mile at a rate of 5; the trail to the
   base is 0.6 mile at a rate of 5–10.

Directions: Follow the directions to Second Falls,
but instead of turning right at the steep descent,
bear left. After 0.25 mile, you will enter a flat, open
area with a campfire ring to the right. You can walk
100 feet past the ring to an overlook of the cascade
from the cliff. Take caution: this is not a developed
overlook and is extremely dangerous.

Reaching the base requires a strenuous, two-
handed climb down the bank at a point several
hundred feet downstream. For environmental
reasons as well as self-preservation, this is not
recommended.

The falls can be glimpsed from the parkway 0.7
mile north of Graveyard Fields Overlook.

Photo Tips

From the cliff overlook, there is really only one
decent shot—looking downstream through the
spruce trees. The ideal vantage points are from the
base and the middle of the falls, but as stated above,
this requires a wicked climb. When deciding
whether to attempt it, remember this: both Second
Falls and Upper Falls provide better photographic
opportunities, and there is a good trail to the base
of each of them.

Yellowstone Falls is similar to Second Falls, except
that it has a small pool in the middle carved out of solid
granite.

The name Yellowstone comes from the yellow li-
chens and minerals on rocks in the valley.

Upper Falls *

River: Yellowstone Prong
County: Haywood
USGS quadrangle: Shining Rock
Landowner: Pisgah National Forest,
   Pisgah Ranger District
Height: The main, steep cascade measures about
   40 feet, with smaller cascades downstream.
Beauty rating: 7
Trail length and difficulty: 1.6 miles; 3–5

Directions: Follow the directions to Second Falls.
After crossing Yellowstone Prong, take an
immediate left onto Graveyard Fields Loop Trail
(F.S. 358). Follow this trail 1.4 miles to the falls.
On the way back, you can make a loop by crossing
the stream at the first wide bend and picking up the
trail to the parking area.

The trail to Upper Falls is one of the most
popular in Pisgah National Forest, and it shows. It
is deeply rutted in places, and there are countless
side paths leading in every direction. You can help
minimize impact by staying on the main trail and
by not visiting the area during rainy weather.

Upper Falls
Nikon F3, 20mm lens, f/22 at ¹/₁₅ second, Fujichrome Velvia.

This is a simple, straightforward composition taken from directly in front of the waterfall. An equally effective composition is from the left bank.

Photo Tips
   One possibility is to cross the creek and shoot from the left bank, using the small cascades in the foreground.
   Looking downstream, there is a good view of the mountains, but if it's sunny and you've timed your visit for the optimal lighting on the falls (one to two hours after sunrise), you probably won't get a decent shot.
   The falls can be glimpsed from the parkway just south of the overlook, but the photo potential is not good.

Dark Prong flows on the north side of Graveyard Ridge. At its confluence with Yellowstone Prong, it becomes the East Fork of the Pigeon River, which flows into the West Fork to become the well-known Pigeon River, which flows through the Champion Paper Mill in Canton. If you have only seen this river downstream from the mill and would like to know what it looks like unpolluted, visit Upper Falls. This is about as far upstream as you can get, and the water is crystal-clear.

Woodfin Cascades *

River: Woodfin Creek
County: Jackson
USGS quadrangle: Hazelwood
Landowner: Private
Height: It is impossible to tell from Mount Lyn Lowry Overlook, but this waterfall is easily 200 feet high.
Beauty rating: 7
Trail length and difficulty: View roadside
Handicapped Accessible

Directions: From the junction of U.S. 23/74 and the Blue Ridge Parkway just west of Waynesville, drive south on the parkway to Mount Lyn Lowry Overlook, located at Milepost 445.1.

Photo Tips

Obviously, you will want to take advantage of Mount Lyn Lowry in the background by shooting a wide-angle landscape, ideally in the fall or early spring. Late-afternoon or evening sun creates shadows around the falls while the surroundings are in full sun; be sure to avoid this.

No doubt, the first question that comes to mind here concerns the cross on the summit of Mount Lyn Lowry. General Sumter L. Lowry, a distinguished veteran of two world wars, had the cross erected in memory of his daughter, Lyn, who died just after her fifteenth birthday. "We . . . felt that she must have been put on this earth for some particular purpose because she was such a wonderful girl. We wanted to do something which would perpetuate her memory and spread joy throughout the land," General Lowry wrote in his memoirs. The date the lighted cross was first turned on was August 6, 1964.

During the summer, Woodfin Cascades is almost completely hidden by foliage.

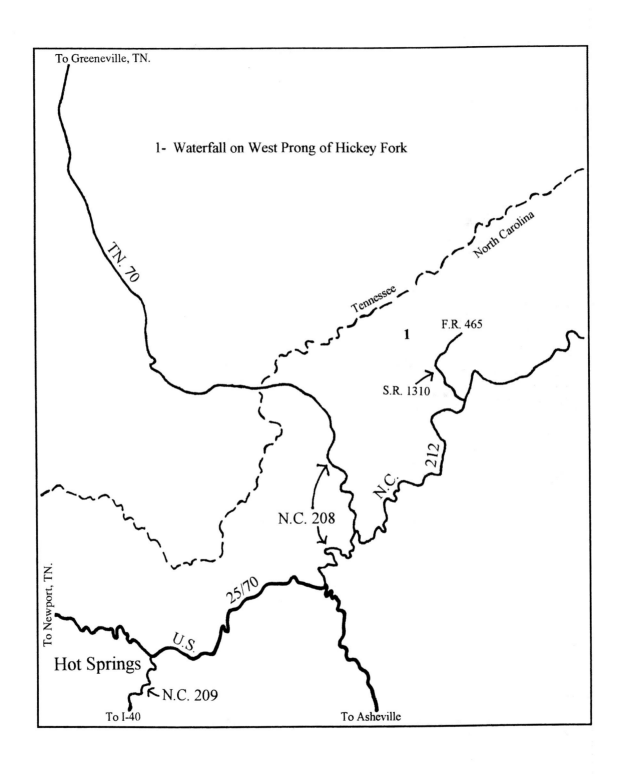

Hot Springs

During the latter half of the nineteenth century, Hot Springs, originally known as Warm Springs, was a resort town with "no superior in any State." Warm Springs Hotel, a 250-foot-long, two-story building built in 1838, could accommodate 500 guests and had a dining room that seated 240. Guests came to enjoy the reputed benefits of the hot springs, which vary in temperature from 98 to 117 degrees. The structure burned in 1884 and was sold to a group of New York investors, who changed the name of the town to Hot Springs and rebuilt the hotel, adding steam heat and electricity. The property also boasted the Southeast's first golf course.

The hotel burned again in 1920, and the town has never regained its former grandeur, though that may change. In 1990, a Virginia couple opened the Hot Springs Resort, featuring hot-springs baths and other services. Long-range plans include a nine-hole golf course and resort cabins.

Other visitors to Hot Springs enjoy hiking in nearby Pisgah National Forest and whitewater rafting on the French Broad River.

Waterfall on the West Prong of Hickey Fork

River: West Prong, Hickey Fork
County: Madison
USGS quadrangle: White Rock

Landowner: Pisgah National Forest, French Broad Ranger District
Height: 25 feet
Beauty rating: 4
Trail length and difficulty: 1.1 miles; 6

Directions: From the junction of N.C. 208 and U.S. 25/70 approximately 5.5 miles east of Hot Springs, head north on N.C. 208. After 3.35 miles, turn right on N.C. 212 and proceed 6.8 miles to S.R. 1310 (Hickey Fork Road). Turn left and drive 1.1 miles to the parking area, on the right.

The trail begins 200 feet farther up the road, on the left-hand side. After hiking for about 1 mile, you will come to a long, sliding cascade on the right. Continue on the trail another 0.1 mile to the main waterfall. The trail passes a few hundred feet from the falls, and there is currently no path leading to the base. You will have to bushwhack to get a closer look.

Photo Tips
This waterfall lends itself well for isolation photos. The rock about 15 feet from the base provides a perfect seat while you explore different compositions.

Notice the thick mosses growing abundantly on the falls, as well as the small grottos behind the waterfall that provide habitat for a spray cliff natural community.

The Pisgah National Forest map incorrectly labels Hickey Fork as Hickory Fork.

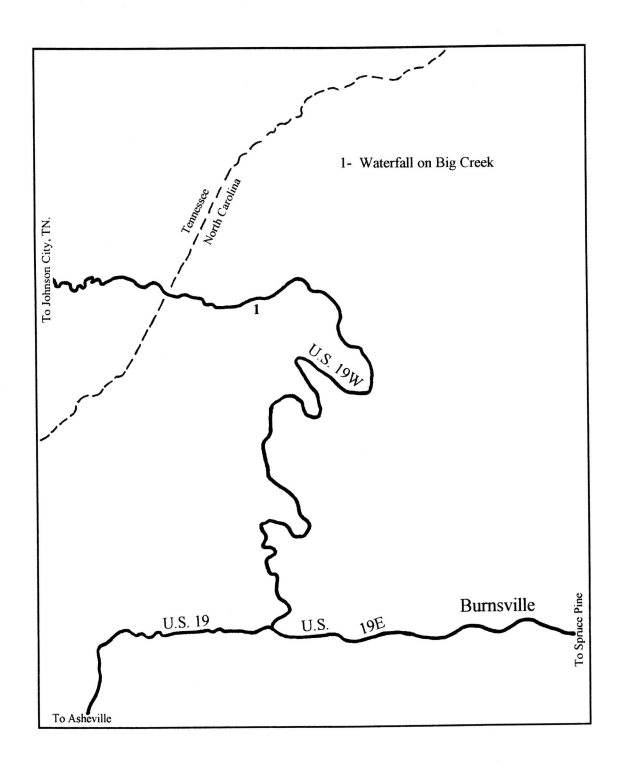

1- Waterfall on Big Creek

To Johnson City, TN.

Tennessee

North Carolina

1

U.S. 19W

Burnsville

To Spruce Pine

U.S. 19

U.S.

19E

To Asheville

Burnsville

Burnsville, the county seat of Yancey County, has changed little since its early days—except that it is no longer the scene of regular fighting, drinking, and murdering, as it was in the late 1800s. It enjoys the reputation of a quaint community situated at the foot of the magnificent Black Mountains.

The historic Nu-Wray Inn, constructed in 1833 on the town square, originally served as a tavern. The popular inn still contains portions of the original structure.

Also at the town square is a statue of Otway Burns, for whom the town is named. Burns built one of the fastest sailing ships of his time, the *Snap Dragon*. He gained fame in the War of 1812 by seeking out and destroying numerous English ships.

Waterfall on Big Creek *

River: Big Creek
County: Yancey
USGS quadrangle: Chestoa
Landowner: Pisgah National Forest,
   Toecane Ranger District
Height: 25 feet
Beauty rating: 6
Trail length and difficulty: View roadside
Handicapped Accessible

Directions: Take U.S. 19E west from Burnsville and turn right on U.S. 19W approximately 5 miles from town. Continue on U.S. 19W for 17.5 miles and park at a left-hand pull-off. The falls are on the left.

The route to this waterfall passes through the scenic Cane River Valley. It parallels the Cane until that river turns northeast to join the North Toe River to become the popular Nolichucky River, of whitewater-rafting fame.

Waterfall on Big Creek
Canon EOS Elan, 24mm tilt/shift lens, polarizing filter, f/22 at 3 seconds, Fujichrome Velvia.

I didn't think this would be a good photograph because it came too easily. I just climbed down a few feet from the road, set up in a comfortable spot, and started shooting. I was pleasantly surprised when the film came back.

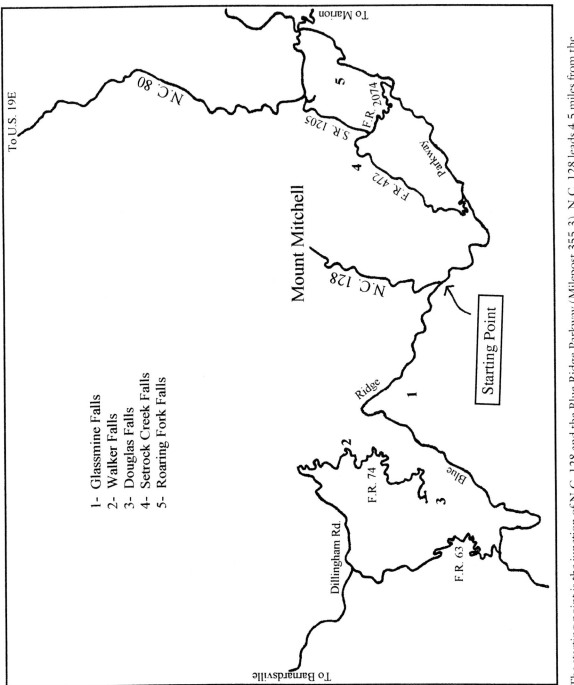

1- Glassmine Falls
2- Walker Falls
3- Douglas Falls
4- Setrock Creek Falls
5- Roaring Fork Falls

To Marion
To U.S. 19E
N.C. 80
F.R. 2074
S.R. 1205
F.R. 472
Parkway
Mount Mitchell
N.C. 128
Ridge
Starting Point
Blue
F.R. 74
Dillingham Rd.
F.R. 63
To Barnardsville

The starting point is the junction of N.C. 128 and the Blue Ridge Parkway (Milepost 355.3). N.C. 128 leads 4.5 miles from the parkway to a parking area on the summit of Mount Mitchell.

Mount Mitchell

At 6,684 feet, Mount Mitchell is the highest mountain in the eastern United States. The high elevation gives it a cooler climate than the surrounding lowlands, a climate more typical of the boreal forests that dominate Canada and Alaska. Thus, flora and fauna associated with the mountain's ecosystem are atypical of the southern Appalachians. At least eight rare plant species and fifteen uncommon animal species live in the spruce-fir forest that blankets the summit. The spruce-fir forest itself is among the rarest, and possibly the most endangered, of the natural communities in North Carolina.

Mount Mitchell State Park, North Carolina's first state park, was created in 1916 by individuals concerned with the destruction of the virgin forests by logging. Today, the forest is being devastated in other ways. The balsam woolly adelgid, an aphid introduced on nursery stock around 1900, established itself in the park in the 1950s. The aphid feeds on the sap of the Fraser fir (*Abies fraseri*), killing the tree in three to seven years. The pest does not effect the red spruce (*Picea rubens*), yet those trees are dying as well. Although certain interests continue to debate the issue, studies have proven that air pollution has severely affected the ecosystem. It is believed that once the forest is weakened by pollution, it becomes vulnerable to other threats, such as the adelgid and the severe winds common on the summit.

Mount Mitchell was named for Dr. Elisha Mitchell, the first person to take measurements of the Black Mountains, in which Mount Mitchell is located. In 1857, Dr. Mitchell fell to his death over the waterfall that also bears his name. Mitchell Falls lies just outside the park boundary on private property. Dr. Mitchell is buried on the summit of Mount Mitchell at the base of the observation tower.

Glassmine Falls *

River: Glassmine Branch
County: Buncombe
USGS quadrangle: Montreat
Landowner: Private
Height: This is a very high, steep slide.
Beauty rating: 7
Trail length and difficulty: View roadside
Handicapped Accessible

Directions: From the starting point, drive south on the Blue Ridge Parkway for 5.7 miles to Glassmine Falls Overlook, on the left at Milepost 361.1. You can view the falls from the overlook or walk a short distance to an upper viewing area.

Photo Tips
This waterfall can be framed tightly using a telephoto lens, but the best treatment is to use the falls as part of an overall scene that includes the surrounding mountains. This is particularly effective in early spring and fall.

You can't help noticing the National Park Service sign at the overlook listing Glassmine Falls as being over 800 feet high. If this were the case, it would be by far the highest single fall of water in the state, and one of the highest in the United States. It's impossible to

Glassmine Falls
Nikon F3, 75-300mm zoom lens, f/22 at $^1/_8$ second, Fujichrome Velvia.

Yes, this is a photo of a waterfall! Except during very wet conditions, this is about all you see of Glassmine Falls. Glassmine Branch begins only a short distance upstream; thus, the low water flow. It's not unusual for the stream to completely dry up. The dead trees are red spruce (*Picea rubens*) which have succumbed to air pollution.

determine the height from the overlook, but I believe this figure is exaggerated, and even if it's not, it can be argued that this is not a true waterfall. During dry periods, it is nothing more than a trickle, and it may even dry up completely at times.

Near the base of the falls are the remains of the Abernathy Mine, where mica was mined. This transparent mineral was often called "isinglass" or simply "glass." Thus, mica mines were often referred to as glass mines.

Walker Falls *

River: Walker Branch
County: Buncombe
USGS quadrangle: Mount Mitchell
Landowner: Pisgah National Forest,
    Toecane Ranger District
Height: 50 feet
Beauty rating: 3
Trail length and difficulty: View roadside
Handicapped Accessible

Directions: From the starting point, drive south on the Blue Ridge Parkway for 12 miles and turn right at the sign for Craggy Gardens Picnic Ground. After 0.3 mile, F.R. 63 bears to the left. Follow it for 6.3 miles to where it ends at Dillingham Road (S.R. 2173). Turn right and drive 5.2 miles to a view of the falls on the left. Dillingham Road becomes F.R. 74 before it reaches the waterfall.

Photo Tip
Walker Falls itself is not very photogenic, but you might get lucky and discover a few wildflowers growing on the grassy banks that can be positioned in the foreground.

The route to Walker Falls is long and bumpy. Make the best of the trip by also visiting Douglas Falls, which is about 5 miles farther up the road.

Douglas Falls *
(Carter Creek Falls)

River: Tributary of Waterfall Creek
County: Buncombe
USGS quadrangle: Montreat
Landowner: Pisgah National Forest,
    Toecane Ranger District
Height: 70-foot sheer drop
Beauty rating: 5
Trail length and difficulty: 0.5 mile; 2–4

Directions: Follow the directions to Walker Falls and continue 4.6 miles on F.R. 74 to where it ends at the parking area. Two trails lead from the far end of the road. The right-hand trail leads to Douglas Falls and continues to the Blue Ridge Parkway near Craggy Gardens.

Photo Tips
The jumble of fallen trees near the base will prove distracting in a photo. You can eliminate them altogether by getting very close with a 20mm lens, or you can shoot from a distance to minimize their effect. If you choose the latter, there are two hemlock trees on the left bank that are well-positioned to frame the falls.

A tiny stream flows over a huge, overhanging bluff to form Douglas Falls. The trail is short and easy, making it ideal for families.

There are several other trails nearby that drape the northern slope of Craggy Gardens. Unfortunately, many of them are obscure and overgrown, and there isn't any accurate information available on them. Trails leading from the Blue Ridge Parkway at Craggy Gardens have been rerouted due to impact on rare plant species and the passing of Mountains-to-Sea Trail. A trail sheet is available from the Craggy Gardens Visitor Center that calls this waterfall Carter Creek Falls and gives directions from the center, but you will be lucky to find the falls using it. Also, a trail guide to the entire area is available from the Toecane Ranger Station, but it is hopelessly outdated. If you plan on doing any hiking in the area, arm yourself with a topographical map and a compass.

Nearby waterfall: At Douglas Falls, the trail steeply ascends the left bank and continues to an eventual intersection with Mountains-to-Sea Trail, which leads to the Blue Ridge Parkway. Located along this trail about 1.3 miles from Douglas Falls is a long, sliding cascade called Cascades Waterfall. The trail is rough in places and heavily overgrown. I don't recommend this waterfall.

Setrock Creek Falls *

River: Setrock Creek
County: Yancey
USGS quadrangle: Old Fort
Landowner: Pisgah National Forest,
    Toecane Ranger District
Height: 75-foot cascade
Beauty rating: 5
Trail length and difficulty: 0.3 mile; 1–3

Directions: From the starting point, drive

approximately 3.3 miles north on the Blue Ridge Parkway and turn left on F.R. 472. Proceed 4.7 miles and park on the right just across from Black Mountain Campground.

Enter the campground and follow the signs for the Briar Bottom group camping area. Before reaching the group camp, you will see a sign on the right for the waterfall. Enter the woods and turn right at the fork.

Photo Tips

The area at the base of the waterfall is easy to walk around, allowing you to safely explore the numerous possible compositions.

As with most forest scenes, this waterfall photographs horribly when the sun is shining.

If you're camping at Black Mountain Campground, this easily accessible waterfall is a must-see.

Experienced hikers are encouraged to explore the spectacular but strenuous Mount Mitchell Trail, which leads from the campground to the summit of Mount Mitchell.

Roaring Fork Falls *

River: Roaring Fork
County: Yancey
USGS quadrangle: Celo
Landowner: Pisgah National Forest,
   Toecane Ranger District
Height: 100-foot cascade
Beauty rating: 6
Trail length and difficulty: 0.5 mile; 3

Roaring Fork Falls
Canon EOS Elan, 24mm tilt/shift lens, polarizing filter, f/22 at 6 seconds, Fujichrome Velvia.

Even with the tilt/shift lens I was not able to completely prevent a distorted image. The waterfall is much higher than it appears in this photograph.

Directions: From the starting point, drive approximately 3.3 miles north on the Blue Ridge Parkway and turn left on F.R. 472. Proceed approximately 7.2 miles, passing the trailhead for Setrock Creek Falls. Note: F.R. 472 becomes S.R. 1205 where the pavement begins. Turn right at the sign for Busic Work Center. Follow this road 0.2 mile and park at the gate.

There is also a route to the falls that does not require driving on gravel roads. Follow the parkway north from the starting point for 11 miles and exit on N.C. 80. Continue north on N.C. 80. At 2.2 miles, turn left on S.R. 1205; there is a small sign for F.R. 472. After turning, cross Still Fork Creek and turn left at the Busic Work Center sign. Follow this road 0.2 mile and park at the gate.

The trail begins to the right of the gate and follows an old logging road to a crossing of Roaring Fork. Just before the crossing, turn right and follow the path 100 feet to the falls.

Roaring Fork flows into Still Fork Creek, which flows into the South Toe River, which parallels N.C. 80 a few miles before joining the North Toe River. The North Toe River flows several miles before being joined by the Cane River to begin the Nolichucky River, one of the premier whitewater-rafting rivers in the Southeast.

Carolina Hemlocks Recreation Area, a popular tubing site, is located along the South Toe River beside N.C. 80.

Photo Tips

Because of the nature of Roaring Fork Falls, using a wide-angle lens will distort the image, causing the waterfall to appear much shorter than it actually is. The perspective-control lenses discussed in the chapter on photographing waterfalls will minimize this distortion.

Telephoto isolation photos work well on this waterfall.

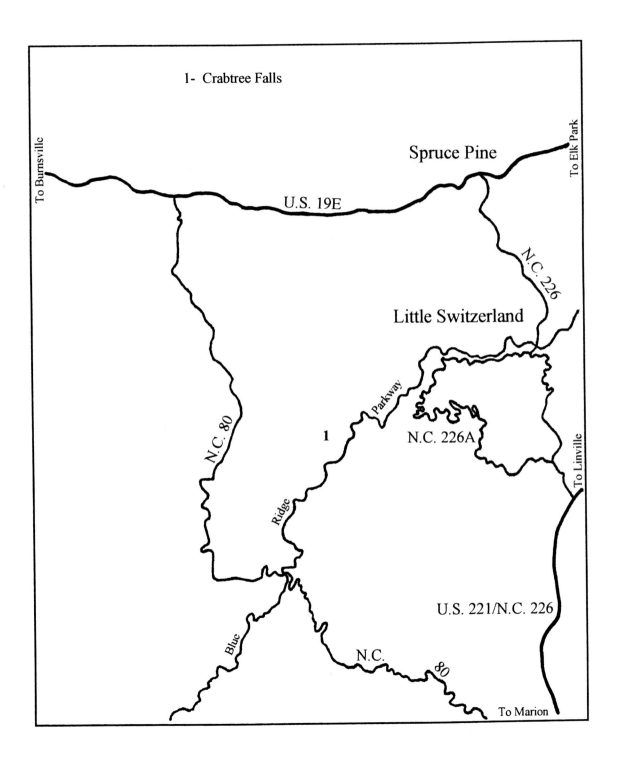

1- Crabtree Falls

Spruce Pine

To Burnsville

To Elk Park

U.S. 19E

N.C. 226

Little Switzerland

N.C. 80

Parkway

1

N.C. 226A

Ridge

To Linville

U.S. 221/N.C. 226

Blue

N.C.

80

To Marion

Little Switzerland

Lying on the crest of the Blue Ridge Mountains, Little Switzerland is a community well-deserving of its name.

While some come to enjoy the spectacular scenery, others come to dig in rock piles. The famous Spruce Pine Mining District is located nearby. Commercial mines from the district account for over 35 percent of the total production of feldspar in the United States, along with 95 percent of the ultrapure quartz that is used in such products as semiconductors. The 200-inch mirror in the Mount Palomar telescope was made with quartz from local Chestnut Flat Mine. In all, fifty-seven minerals have been discovered here, including many that occur in gem grade. A few mines are open to the public, and the annual Mineral and Gem Festival draws rock hounds from around the world.

Begin your visit by stopping at the Minerals Museum, located at the junction of N.C. 226 and the Blue Ridge Parkway.

Crabtree Falls *
(Upper Falls)

River: Big Crabtree Creek
County: Yancey
USGS quadrangle: Celo
Landowner: National Park Service,
  within the Blue Ridge Parkway boundary
Height: 70 feet
Beauty rating: 8
Trail length and difficulty: 0.9 mile; 6

Directions: From the junction of N.C. 226 and the Blue Ridge Parkway, drive 8.4 miles south on the parkway to Crabtree Meadows Recreation Area, located at Milepost 339.5. Turn right and enter the campground. Just beyond the gatehouse, turn right into the large parking area for the falls. The campground is closed during winter, so if you visit then, you will have to walk the 0.25 mile from the gate to the parking area.

A trail leads from the parking lot to a fork that marks the beginning of a loop. The shortest route is to the right. If you continue the loop on your return, you will come to a couple of spur trails on the right that lead to the campground. Stay to the left to reach the junction with the original trail, making a total distance of about 2.5 miles. The distances given on the trail markers are inconsistent.

Photo Tips

Crabtree Falls is among the top ten photogenic waterfalls in North Carolina. For a wide-angle shot, cross the creek and climb the right bank. You can take your pick of numerous compositions that include rocks or foliage in the foreground. There are several trees that work well to frame the falls.

Early spring is the best time to photograph the waterfall, but isolation photos work well at any time of year. See photo in the color section.

Crabtree Falls is the main attraction at Crabtree Meadows Recreation Area and is a popular day-hike for campers and tourists. The trail provides an excellent opportunity for viewing wildflowers, with over forty species present.

The Celo quadrangle lists this waterfall as Upper Falls. It shows a Murphy Falls downstream and has Crabtree Falls listed on Long Branch in nearby Mitchell County. The waterfalls shown on the quadrangle as Murphy Falls and Crabtree Falls are both on private property.

Before the Blue Ridge Parkway was built, the meadows upstream from Crabtree Falls supported several crabtree orchards. The crabapples were used as livestock feed, as well as for human consumption. A few trees still grow in isolated areas of the meadows.

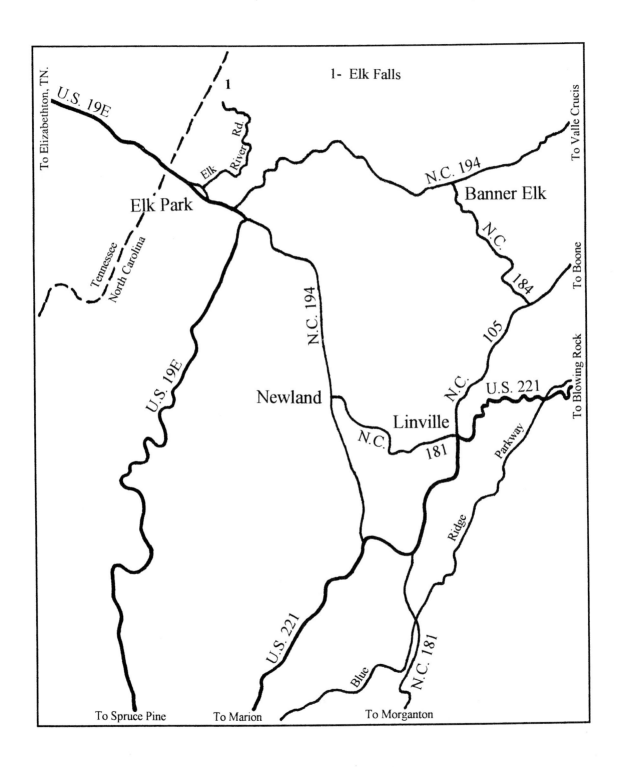

Elk Park

The small town of Elk Park is located in the northwestern section of the state a few miles from the Tennessee border. The name seems to have originated with a park built by a couple of settlers in 1885. The elk (*Cervus elaphus*) was once widespread throughout North America, but by the mid-1800s, it had been nearly extirpated from North Carolina. It is not known whether there were any elk in the settlers' park, but the name suggests that there might have been.

Elk Falls *
(Big Falls)

River: Elk
County: Avery
USGS quadrangle: Elk Park
Landowner: Pisgah National Forest,
   Toecane Ranger District
Height: Approximately 65 feet
Beauty rating: 10
Trail length and difficulty: 0.2 mile; 5

Directions: From the junction of N.C. 194 and U.S. 19E, head north on U.S. 19E toward the town of Elk Park. After 0.7 mile, turn right, then immediately left onto Main Street (S.R. 1303). Continue 0.35 mile and turn right on Elk River Road (S.R. 1305). Follow Elk River Road 4 miles to a parking area on the right beside the river. The trail begins at the parking area and leads downstream to the brink and on to the base of the falls.

Photo Tips

As you might guess from its beauty rating, Elk Falls is an exceptional photo subject. Only Linville Falls offers more possible compositions. You can shoot from the large, angled rock that the trail comes out on, but this is not ideal. Consider wading into the river on the little shoal at the edge of the pool and using the large rocks in the foreground. Shooting from a point downstream will allow you to include the small cascades.

My favorite vantage point, and the only one that will eliminate a washed-out sky, is from the top of the huge rock on the opposite side of the river. Wade the river and climb through the woods, then out onto the rock. From there, you can shoot vertical and horizontal compositions, both of which are extremely effective. The high vantage point allows you to include a small strip of foliage at the top, rather than sky. This is necessary on overcast days.

The sun rises directly in front of the falls, so the optimal lighting on a sunny day occurs either very early or about two to three hours after sunrise. During the summer, about the only way to make a photo that doesn't have someone swimming in the pool is to arrive early in the morning. See photo on page 9.

Elk Falls has one of the largest and deepest plunge pools of any waterfall in the state, and there are numerous flat rocks around the base. It's not surprising, then, that it is often crowded with swimmers, sunbathers, and picnickers. This is a favorite hangout of students from Appalachian State University and Lees McRae College. If you are only interested in taking pictures or finding solitude, visit Elk Falls in the winter or very early in the morning.

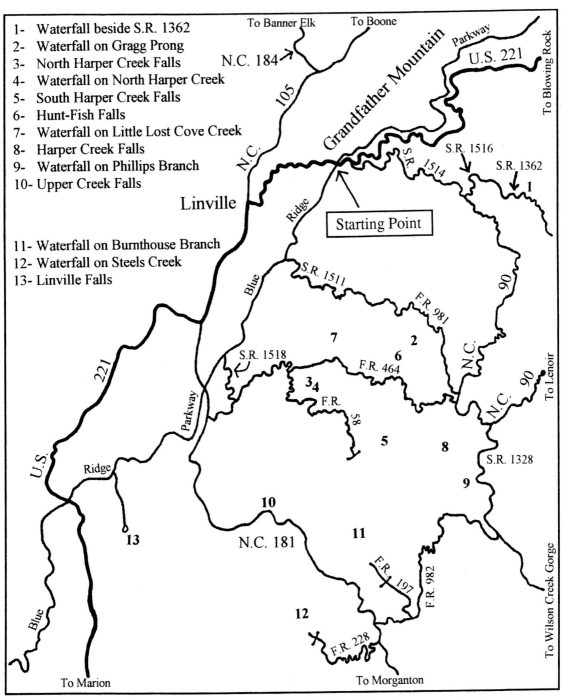

1- Waterfall beside S.R. 1362
2- Waterfall on Gragg Prong
3- North Harper Creek Falls
4- Waterfall on North Harper Creek
5- South Harper Creek Falls
6- Hunt-Fish Falls
7- Waterfall on Little Lost Cove Creek
8- Harper Creek Falls
9- Waterfall on Phillips Branch
10- Upper Creek Falls

11- Waterfall on Burnthouse Branch
12- Waterfall on Steels Creek
13- Linville Falls

Starting Point

The starting point is the northern junction of U.S. 221 and the Blue Ridge Parkway, 3 miles from the town of Linville. Don't confuse this with the southern junction of these two roads at the community of Linville Falls.

Grandfather Mountain

There are few people in the South who are not familiar with Grandfather Mountain's Mile-High Swinging Bridge or the late Mildred the Bear. The privately owned mountain attracts over a quarter-million people to its jagged peaks annually. The southern side of Grandfather is skirted by the Blue Ridge Parkway, which provides excellent views of the ridge as it winds toward the Linn Cove Viaduct.

Although the mountain bears heavy human traffic, it is home to a surprising number of rare plants and animals, more than any other mountain east of the Rockies. Among the federally listed endangered species are the northern flying squirrel (*Glaucomys sabrinus coloatus*), the Virginia big-eared bat (*Plecotus townsendii virginianus*), and the peregrine falcon (*Falco peregrinus*). The diverse flora and fauna and the wilderness character of the mountain have resulted in its being designated an International Biosphere Reserve, the only privately owned one in the world.

The entrance to the mountain is located about 1 mile from the Blue Ridge Parkway on U.S. 221 South. An admission fee is charged.

Streams that flow off the northern side of the mountain quickly leave the steep slopes and enter the lazy Watauga River, which drains the valley. They do not gain enough size to create waterfalls before leaving the steep slopes. Thus, there are no waterfalls listed for that side of the mountain.

In contrast, streams flowing off the southern side have a much greater opportunity to gain size before leveling off. In fact, by the time they quit falling several miles downstream, they have completely left the mountains and entered the flatlands of the Catawba River Valley. The Blue Ridge escarpment is long and gradual at this point, but it provides the necessary steepness for the presence of numerous waterfalls. Indeed, the elevation difference between Calloway Peak, on Grandfather's summit, and the flatlands of the valley is nearly 5,000 feet, the greatest drainage relief found anywhere along the Blue Ridge escarpment.

Every waterfall listed in this hub can be attributed directly or indirectly to the southern drainage of Grandfather Mountain. In each case, I have given the shortest or easiest route from the starting point. I recommend that everyone entering the area stop by the Grandfather Ranger Station and purchase the map of Pisgah National Forest, the Wilson Creek Area Trail Map, and the map of Linville Gorge Wilderness; with these maps, you can plan other routes and loop options. The Wilson Creek area in particular is laced with trails that can be combined with the routes I have given.

Waterfall beside S.R. 1362 *

River: Tributary of Anthony Creek
County: Caldwell
USGS quadrangle: Grandfather Mountain
Landowner: Pisgah National Forest,
   Grandfather Ranger District
Height: Steep 50-foot slide
Beauty rating: 4
Trail length and difficulty: View roadside
Handicapped Accessible

Directions: From the starting point, drive 0.5 mile north on U.S. 221 and turn right on S.R. 1514. Drive 5.3 miles and turn left on S.R. 1516, which becomes S.R. 1362 at the Caldwell County line. Continue 3.3 miles to a view of the waterfall on the left.

Photo Tips

You can shoot this waterfall from the road, and if the rhododendron shrubs are in bloom, that might be the best vantage point. Otherwise, climb down the bank and shoot from the edge of the pool. If the road is dusty, keep a towel handy to cover your camera in case a car passes.

Nearby waterfalls: Some 2.5 miles before the waterfall beside S.R. 1362, the road makes a sharp right turn as it crosses Anthony Creek. Look upstream for a view of a high waterfall on private property.

Continue down the road after seeing the waterfall beside S.R. 1362. You will cross Woodruff Branch after 1.25 miles. Look upstream to see a small cascade.

Waterfall on Gragg Prong

River: Gragg Prong
County: Avery
USGS quadrangle: Grandfather Mountain
Landowner: Pisgah National Forest,
   Grandfather Ranger District
Height: Over 100 feet
Beauty rating: 5
Trail length and difficulty: 1.5 miles; 3

Directions: From the starting point, drive 2.7 miles south on the Blue Ridge Parkway and turn

left on S.R. 1511, which becomes F.R. 981. Proceed 4.8 miles and park on the right just after crossing Gragg Prong.

Walk back across the creek and turn left onto the Jeep road. Follow it a few feet and turn left on the trail. After a second ford of Gragg Prong, a side trail leads to the right. Stay to the left and make a third creek crossing. You will arrive at a small cascade. After walking around the rock at the top of the cascade and crossing two small streams, you will reach the brink of the waterfall. Carefully walk out near the top and view the falls dropping into the gorge.

There is no route to the base.

Photo Tips

Shooting from the base isn't an option, and the top is not an ideal vantage point. You will have better luck making images of the creek along the way.

This waterfall is within the proposed Lost Cove Wilderness Area.

North Harper Creek Falls

River: North Harper Creek
County: Avery
USGS quadrangle: Grandfather Mountain
Landowner: Pisgah National Forest,
   Grandfather Ranger District
Height: Several hundred feet of slides, ending with
   a 40-foot drop
Beauty rating: 8
Trail length and difficulty: 1.1 mile; 8

Directions: From the starting point, drive 5.9

North Harper Creek Falls
Nikon F3, 20mm lens, polarizing filter, f/22 at 4
seconds, Fujichrome Velvia.

To eliminate the overcast sky from the top of the falls, I had to shoot
as close as I could get on the left side. I could not eliminate the stick
jutting from the pool, so I carefully framed the scene to let it point
toward the falls.

miles south on the Blue Ridge Parkway and turn
left on S.R. 1518. Continue 1.75 miles to a fork,
then turn left on F.R. 464. After 2.55 miles, turn
right on F.R. 58 and drive 0.2 mile to a small pull-
off on the left. This is the upper terminus of North
Harper Creek Trail (#266).

Begin North Harper Creek Trail and descend to
cross North Harper Creek. Continue on the trail
and cross the creek two more times. Just beyond
the third crossing, you will arrive at the top of the
waterfall. An extremely steep path leads close by
the falls to the base, but this route is not
recommended. Instead, pick up the trail leading to
the left, away from the creek, and cross a small
branch. About 200 yards from the top of the falls,
an obscure side trail leads to the right; there is a 12-
inch red oak tree at the junction. Take this side trail
and descend steeply to North Harper Creek at the
top of another waterfall (the "waterfall on North
Harper Creek," listed next). Turn right, cross the
creek after 50 yards, and continue 75 yards to the
base of the falls.

Photo Tips

An excellent fall scene can be shot from the top.
Walk out onto the rock and photograph the distant
mountains with the cascades in the foreground.

There are several possibilities at the base; use
your imagination. On overcast days, you will need
to exclude the sky from the photo. To do this,
shoot from the left of the pool and frame tightly
across the top of the falls.

It almost seems as if there are two waterfalls here
instead of one, since you can't see the upper cascades
from the bottom or the bottom drop from the upper
cascades, and since there's a 0.25-mile hike between
the two.

North Harper Creek is an excellent trout stream. The first section of the trail has good wildflower displays, including several uncommon species. The trail and waterfall are within the proposed Harper Creek Wilderness Area.

Waterfall on North Harper Creek

River: North Harper Creek
County: Avery
USGS quadrangle: Grandfather Mountain
Landowner: Pisgah National Forest,
   Grandfather Ranger District
Height: 175-foot slide
Beauty rating: 4
Trail length and difficulty: 1 mile; 8

Directions: Follow the directions to the base of North Harper Creek Falls. You will arrive at the top of this waterfall where the side trail comes out at North Harper Creek.

North Harper Creek Trail closely follows its namesake creek downstream and joins Harper Creek Trail at the junction of Harper and North Harper creeks. There are few streams in the mountains as scenic as these two.

South Harper Creek Falls *

River: Harper Creek
County: Avery
USGS quadrangle: Chestnut Mountain
Landowner: Pisgah National Forest,
   Grandfather Ranger District
Height: Over 200 feet
Beauty rating: 10
Trail length and difficulty: 1.4 miles to the upper
   overlook; 3–6

South Harper Creek Falls
Nikon F3, 20mm lens, polarizing filter, f/22 at 2 seconds, Fujichrome Velvia.

Most visitors will not see South Harper Creek Falls from this vantage point. It requires a strenuous scramble to the base of the falls. If you choose to follow the directions to the lower vantage point, this is what you can expect to see.

Directions: Drive to the trailhead for North Harper Creek Falls, then continue on F.R. 58 an additional 3.9 miles to the trailhead for Harper Creek Trail (#260). A small pull-off is on the right.

Walk across the road and begin Harper Creek Trail. After 1.1 miles, you will come to Harper Creek near the top of the falls. You have two options at this point. You can turn left, still following Harper Creek Trail, pass the top of the falls, and descend steeply to a point near the creek. From there, you can scramble down the bank and follow the creek upstream to the base. This is a very strenuous trek. The recommended option is to turn right on Raider Camp Trail and cross Harper Creek. Proceed past a series of switchbacks, taking everything to the left. You will reach an overlook of the falls 300 feet above Harper Creek.

Photo Tips

Excellent images can be made from the upper overlook or the base. From the base, a wide-angle horizontal composition will record the uniqueness of the U-shaped cliff, with the bottom portion of the falls on the right. A 20mm or even an 18mm lens will be most effective for this type of shot.

From the upper overlook—standing on the edge of a cliff overlooking the falls, with mountains in the background—there is potential for an outstanding photo. On a clear day, shooting during the time period from just before to just after noon will allow the sun to illuminate the bottom of the gorge. Otherwise, there will be harsh shadows to contend with.

This is one of the finest autumn scenes in the southern Appalachians.

The name of this waterfall is presumably meant to distinguish it from North Harper Creek Falls on North Harper Creek, even though the creek here is Harper Creek, not South Harper Creek. At any rate, it is a spectacular two-level cascade.

Harper Creek Trail continues past the falls and follows the creek downstream to S.R. 1328. Numerous trail connections and loop options are along the route.

South Harper Creek Falls lies within the proposed Harper Creek Wilderness Area.

Hunt-Fish Falls *

River: Lost Cove Creek
County: Avery
USGS quadrangle: Grandfather Mountain
Landowner: Pisgah National Forest, Grandfather Ranger District
Height: Two drops of 8 feet, with connecting pools and cascades
Beauty rating: 8
Trail length and difficulty: 0.75 mile; 7

Directions: From the starting point, drive 5.9 miles south on the Blue Ridge Parkway and turn left on S.R. 1518. Proceed 1.75 miles to a fork, then turn left on F.R. 464. Drive 6.25 miles to a parking area on the left. Note: After 2.55 miles on F.R. 464, you will pass F.R. 58, which leads to the trailheads for North Harper Creek, Waterfall on North Harper Creek, and South Harper Creek waterfalls.

Begin Hunt-Fish Falls Trail (#263) at the parking area. You will descend on switchbacks to Lost Cove Creek. Turn right to arrive at the middle of the falls. There is a high cascade to the right. Continue for a short distance and take one of the side paths leading to the base.

Hunt-Fish Falls

Nikon F3, 75-300mm zoom lens, polarizing filter stacked on warming filter, f/22 at 4 seconds, Fujichrome Velvia.

I made this photo while standing at the edge of the pool. The zoom lens allowed me to get the exact composition that I wanted, without having to get wet. Notice the deciduous trees hanging over the falls. I'll definitely return in the fall. See additional photo in the color section.

Photo Tips

A horizontal or verticle framing works well from either the middle section or the base.

This waterfall makes an outstanding snow scene; there is plenty of rock surface for the snow to rest upon.

Visit the waterfall on a summer day and the pictures you take will no doubt include people. That is something to remember if you want outdoor recreation photos.

The high waterfall that drops into Lost Cove Creek at Hunt-Fish Falls makes a fair photo subject itself.

The flat rocks, deep pools, gentle cascades, and relatively safe jumping platforms make Hunt-Fish Falls a popular swimming and sunning area. The site also receives heavy use from primitive campers. It is within the proposed Lost Cove Wilderness Area.

Waterfall on Little Lost Cove Creek

River: Little Lost Cove Creek
County: Avery
USGS quadrangle: Grandfather Mountain
Landowner: Pisgah National Forest,
 Grandfather Ranger District
Height: 80 feet
Beauty rating: 7
Trail length and difficulty: 2 miles; 7

Directions: Follow the directions to Hunt-Fish Falls. At the point where Hunt-Fish Falls Trail first meets Lost Cove Creek, cross the creek and proceed upstream. Cross the creek again; you will soon arrive at a third crossing. After this crossing, the trail becomes easy to lose. What you need to do is follow the stream closely for a short distance and then make a very long, diagonal crossing back to the left-hand side. The creek flows around a number of small islands that you can use to help you cross. This crossing, like the previous ones, is difficult to rock-hop. Plan on wading. From this point, the trail remains on the left-hand side all the way to Little Lost Cove Creek. Rock-hop the creek. The waterfall will be visible on the left. Continue a few hundred feet and take the path that leads to the base.

Photo Tips

It's difficult to make a good photo here, but that's okay. The scenes along the way are outstanding. Wildflowers abound, particularly in the vicinity of the waterfall. Brilliant cardinal flowers (*Lobelia cardinalis*) are common on the sandy islands in Lost Cove Creek.

There are several possible loop combinations through the proposed Lost Cove Wilderness Area that make excellent day-hikes.

If you are interested in primitive camping, the Lost Cove Creek area is ideal, but remember that it is also very crowded.

Harper Creek Falls

River: Harper Creek
County: Caldwell
USGS quadrangle: Chestnut Mountain
Landowner: Pisgah National Forest,
 Grandfather Ranger District
Height: There are three distinct levels; the upper two total about 50 feet, while the lower level is about 12 feet.
Beauty rating: 9
Trail length and difficulty: 1.6 miles, with a difficulty of 4 to the upper overlook and 8 to the base

Directions: As with every waterfall in the Grandfather Mountain hub, there are numerous possible routes to the trailhead. Only one is described here.

From the starting point, drive 2.7 miles south on the Blue Ridge Parkway and turn left on S.R. 1511, which becomes F.R. 981. Follow it 8.8 miles—passing the trailhead for the waterfall on Gragg Prong—to where it ends at N.C. 90 in the community of Edgemont; to the left is the authentic Coffey's General Store. Turn right and drive 2 miles to S.R. 1328, on the right. It is 1.2 miles on S.R. 1328 to a small pull-off on the right at the southern terminus of Harper Creek Trail (#266).

The first 0.4 mile of the trail ascends to a ridge and a junction with a trail coming in from the left. Stay to the right; you will immediately pass Yellow Buck Trail, which turns right and follows the ridge.

Continue on Harper Creek Trail to a fork at a wildlife sign posted on a maple tree. Stay to the right. At 1.3 miles, you will come to a second fork at another wildlife sign, this time on a pine tree. Stay to the right again. After 0.2 mile, Harper Creek Trail leads to the right, while the left trail continues 0.1 mile to Harper Creek Falls. You must climb down a steep bank to get to the base.

Photo Tips

The only good vantage point is from the base. Any other vantage point will either include fallen trees or will not allow all the falls to be seen. A horizontal composition that includes the falls and the large rockface works well.

Because of the open nature of the scene, it photographs well on sunny days. Late-afternoon sun provides the most pleasing lighting.

Pay careful attention if you include much of the sky. It is in the fly zone of Asheville Regional Airport, and exhaust trails are regular occurrences. See photo in the color section.

As with Hunt-Fish Falls and Upper Creek Falls, this waterfall is normally crowded in the summer with swimmers and sunbathers. Trout are often seen trying to jump the lower drop.

Harper Creek Falls is within the proposed Harper Creek Wilderness Area.

Waterfall on Phillips Branch

River: Phillips Branch
County: Caldwell
USGS quadrangle: Chestnut Mountain
Landowner: Pisgah National Forest,
    Grandfather Ranger District

Height: 45 feet
Beauty rating: 3
Trail length and difficulty: 0.4 mile; 8

Directions: Follow the directions to the trailhead for Harper Creek Falls, then continue on S.R. 1328 approximately 0.75 mile. Park on the side of the road just before Phillips Branch. There is a wooden privacy fence on the right. Enter the woods a few hundred feet to the right of the fence. (Do not enter the woods farther than 100 yards to the right of the fence; that area is private property.) Climb the steep bank to pick up an old railroad grade. Turn left and follow it to the falls.

There is no path to the base.

Photo Tip
Save your film.

This waterfall is not photogenic, has no path leading to the base, requires a steep climb to reach the trail, and has no road pull-off. In other words, don't waste your time.

Upper Creek Falls *

River: Upper Creek
County: Burke
USGS quadrangle: Chestnut Mountain
Landowner: Pisgah National Forest,
    Grandfather Ranger District
Height: Main drop of about 100 feet
Beauty rating: 8
Trail length and difficulty: 0.8 mile; 7

Directions: From the starting point, drive 6.75 miles south on the Blue Ridge Parkway and exit onto N.C. 181. (Note: The Chestnut Mountain quadrangle, modified for Forest Service use, incorrectly labels N.C. 181 as N.C. 131.) Drive south on N.C. 181 for 5.65 miles and turn into the parking area on the left.

The trail enters the woods behind the short section of fence and descends on switchbacks to Upper Creek. Cross the creek and descend steeply to the pool at the base. There is a point before reaching the pool where you can walk out to the base of the main drop.

Photo Tips

You can shoot from the base of the main drop or from the very bottom, farther downstream. The lower point is more photogenic, although it lessens the impact of the main drop. Climb out onto the rocks at the edge of the pool and either shoot from the middle of the pool or from the far left side.

This easily accessible waterfall is popular among sunbathers, swimmers, and fishermen, so plan on having company unless you arrive early in the morning.

On the left a few miles farther down N.C. 181 is Brown Mountain Overlook. The overlook is a popular spot for viewing the mysterious Brown Mountain Lights.

Waterfall on Burnthouse Branch

River: Burnthouse Branch
County: Burke
USGS quadrangle: Chestnut Mountain
Landowner: Pisgah National Forest,
  Grandfather Ranger District
Height: About 60 feet

Beauty rating: 4
Trail length and difficulty: 2.4 miles; 8

Directions: From the starting point, drive 6.75 miles south on the Blue Ridge Parkway and exit on N.C. 181. (Note: The Chestnut Mountain quadrangle, modified for Forest Service use, incorrectly labels N.C. 181 as N.C. 131.) Drive south on N.C. 181 for 10.7 miles, passing the trailhead for Upper Creek Falls, and turn left on F.R. 982. Drive 1.3 miles, turn left on F.R. 197, and follow it 1.4 miles to a parking area on the right just before a gate.

Walk along F.R. 197 about 1.2 miles to its end at Upper Creek and the beginning of Greentown Short-cut Trail. Follow the trail 1.2 miles to a crossing of Burnthouse Branch. The waterfall is a short distance upstream.

Photo Tip

The waterfall itself is not photogenic, but you will find numerous subjects along the trail.

Greentown Short-cut Trail is a scenic and challenging route that connects Greentown Trail with F.R. 197. The waterfall adds beauty to the trek, but I do not think it alone is worth a 2.4-mile hike.

Nearby waterfall: The Wilson Creek Area Trail Map notes a waterfall on Upper Creek about 0.5 mile from where F.R. 197 ends. This waterfall is called Lower Upper Creek Falls. It is small, and there is no good access to it.

Waterfall on Steels Creek

River: Steels Creek
County: Burke
USGS quadrangle: Chestnut Mountain
Landowner: Pisgah National Forest,
   Grandfather Ranger District
Height: Large multilevel cascade
Beauty rating: 6
Trail length and difficulty: 0.7 mile; 7

Directions: From the starting point, drive 6.75 miles south on the Blue Ridge Parkway and exit on N.C. 181. (Note: The Chestnut Mountain quadrangle, modified for Forest Service use, incorrectly labels N.C. 181 as N.C. 131.) Drive 11 miles south on N.C. 181, passing the trailhead for Upper Creek Falls and the road leading to the waterfall on Burnthouse Branch, and turn right on F.R. 228. Follow this road 3.8 miles to a parking area at its end.

The road continues as a hiking trail for 0.2 mile to Steels Creek. Cross the creek to pick up Upper Steels Creek Trail, then follow it upstream to the falls. The trail has been severely altered by fallen trees, making it difficult to pass in spots and hard to follow in others. Also, there is no safe way to get to a good vantage point for photos.

> Photo Tip
> The waterfall is picturesque from the base of the upper section, but reaching this vantage point requires a difficult and dangerous climb that I do not recommend.

This is a scenic and interesting waterfall with enormous potholes and deep, emerald-green pools. It's a shame that there isn't a safe access to the base.

Nearby waterfall: Another waterfall is located upstream on Steels Creek a few hundred feet below where F.R. 496 crosses the creek. To reach it, retrace your route to N.C. 181, turn left, and head back up the mountain. After about 4 miles, turn left on F.R. 496. Drive 0.8 mile to a small pull-off on the left and follow the path to the top of the falls. This waterfall is not very big, and it's ugly.

Linville Falls *

River: Linville
County: Burke
USGS quadrangle: Linville Falls
Landowner: National Park Service, within the Blue Ridge Parkway boundary
Height: The upper section is 12 feet and the lower section 60 feet.
Beauty rating: 10
Trail length and difficulty: There are five viewpoints from which to see the falls, with trail lengths ranging from 0.5 to 0.8 mile and difficulty ratings from 3 to 7.

Directions: From the starting point, drive 11.1 miles south on the Blue Ridge Parkway, turn left at Milepost 316.3, and follow the paved road 1.4 miles to the Linville Falls Visitor Center. A sign board at the center gives complete trail details, although the 0.8-mile hike to Erwins View is incorrectly listed as 1 mile. All the trails are well-marked and easily followed.

Linville Falls
Nikon F3, 75-300mm zoom lens, polarizing filter
stacked on warming filter, f/16 at 2 seconds,
Fujichrome Velvia.

This image was made minutes apart from the previous image.
I was at the same overlook and was using the same equipment.
This clearly demonstrates the usefulness of zoom lenses. See
additional photo in the color section.

Linville Falls
Nikon F3, 75-300mm zoom lens, polarizing filter stacked on
warming filter, f/16 at 2 seconds, Fujichrome Velvia.

This view of Linville Falls was made from Chimney View. I shot tighter
compositions of the lower drop while I was waiting for people to walk out
onto the Upper Falls Overlook, so I could make this image. See additional
photo in the color section.

Photo Tips

I could write an entire book on photographing Linville Falls. I'll try to simplify the matter by taking each overlook and discussing its photo potential.

The first viewpoint on the west side of the river is Upper Falls Overlook. From here, you can look upstream to see the 12-foot Upper Falls and its large pool. The falls are photogenic from this viewpoint only if you disregard the sign warning you to stay behind the rock wall, which obviously cannot be recommended. Looking downstream offers a unique perspective of the river as it enters the chasm and heads for the final plunge, but it's hard to make a good photo from behind the rock wall. If you foolishly decide to climb over the wall at this point, at least have the courtesy to notify the rangers so they can have a dive team and body bag waiting.

The next viewpoint is Chimney View, which provides an ideal vantage point for isolation photos. Mount your camera and a 75mm to 300mm–type zoom lens on the tripod and shoot everything, from a wide-angle perspective that includes both drops to a tight framing of just the lower drop. Overcast days provide the best lighting.

Continue on the trail to the final overlook on the west side, Erwins View. From here, you can see both drops, much of the gorge, and the distant mountains. The lighting and the time of year will determine the approach to take. By noon, the sun is high enough to penetrate the gorge and provide fairly even lighting. This is a good time to include the distant mountains and the blue sky with a wide-angle shot. Do not include the sky on an overcast day, and don't shoot a wide-angle composition if there are distracting shadows. The potential for isolation shots from Erwins View is equal to or better than that from the Chimney View overlook. During a snowstorm or at the peak of autumn color, a better waterfall photograph cannot be made.

On the east side of the river, the first viewpoint is Plunge Basin Overlook, which is excellent for viewing but not for pictures, as there are distracting evergreens in the way.

The last viewpoint is from the very bottom. Follow the Linville Gorge trail markers. The trail ends some distance downstream, so you will have to climb around on the rocks to reach the base. Once there, you will have several options. You can tightly frame the falls or shoot a wide-angle shot that includes the sky. To accentuate the huge pool, use a horizontal composition and position the waterfall on the right of the frame. To accentuate the rock wall, use a horizontal composition and position the waterfall on the left of the frame. For a unique perspective, get as close as you can to the rock wall and shoot a profile of the falls. Rainbows are often visible in the heavy spray.

Linville Falls is perhaps the best-known waterfall in the entire Appalachian Mountains, and certainly one of the most scenic. The waterfall marks the beginning of Linville Gorge, one of the deepest canyons in the East, with walls rising nearly 2,000 feet in places. In 1987, peregrine falcons (*Falco peregrinus*) successfully nested in the gorge after being absent from the mountains for over thirty years. Numerous other rare plants and animals are associated with the gorge, including mountain golden heather (*Hudsonia montana*), found nowhere else in the world.

The geology of the gorge is of special interest. According to the theory of plate tectonics, when the Appalachians were being formed millions of years ago, tremendous pressure from continental collisions caused an upheaval in the earth's surface that thrust older rock strata westward, over younger rock. This upheaval formed a precipice of hard, erosion-resistant rock overlying softer rock. The Linville River flowed over this precipice, forming a waterfall that is believed to have been 12 miles downstream from the present Linville Falls. As the river cut into the softer underlying rock, it undermined the harder "cap." Without support from the underlying rock, the cap broke off, causing the falls to migrate upstream. Linville Gorge was cut as this process was repeated over millions of years. Geologists call Linville Falls a "window," because erosion has carved through the older metamorphic gneiss and exposed the younger rocks that form the plunge pool.

The waterfall has experienced geologic changes even in modern times. Around the turn of this century, the upper and lower falls were close to the same height. Floodwaters caused a ledge on Upper Falls to give way, reducing its height. The ledge lodged at the top of the lower section, increasing its height.

The Linville River is similar to the rivers associated with the southern Blue Ridge escarpment in that it begins high on a mountain, in this case Grandfather Mountain, and runs a long course over a plateau before tumbling over the escarpment. In fact, the Linville is the only major river along the northern section of the escarpment that doesn't spring from the escarpment itself. That explains why Linville Falls has the largest volume of any waterfall along the northern Blue Ridge front.

Linville Falls
Nikon F3, 75-300mm zoom lens, polarizing filter stacked on warming filter, f/16 at 2 seconds, Fujichrome Velvia.

This view of Linville Falls is from Erwins View, and it, along with the previous two, illustrates the incredible photographic opportunities of the waterfall. See additional photo in the color section.

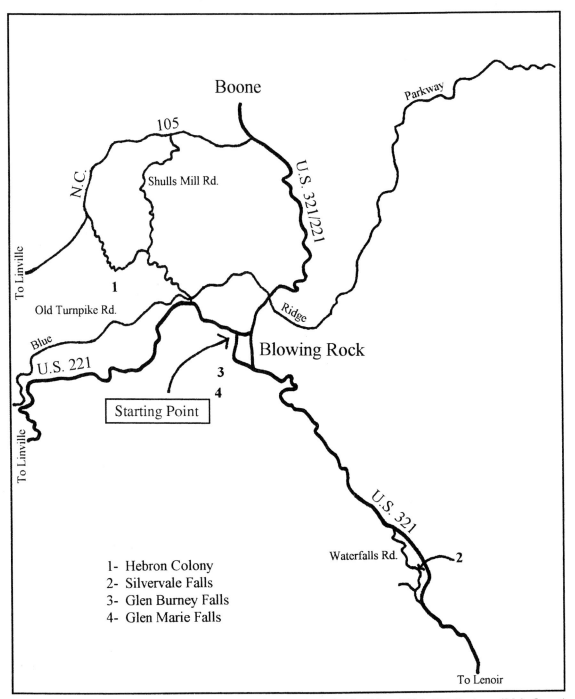

Boone

Parkway

105

N.C.

Shulls Mill Rd.

U.S. 321/221

To Linville

1

Old Turnpike Rd.

Ridge

Blue

Blowing Rock

U.S. 221

3

4

To Linville

Starting Point

U.S. 321

Waterfalls Rd.

2

1- Hebron Colony
2- Silvervale Falls
3- Glen Burney Falls
4- Glen Marie Falls

To Lenoir

The starting point is downtown Blowing Rock, at the junction of U.S. 221 and U.S. 321 Business (Main Street).

Blowing Rock

In 1752, Bishop August Gottlieb Spangenberg was commissioned by the Moravian church to find suitable land for a settlement. Upon his ascent from the valley to the site of present-day Blowing Rock, he was struck by the beauty before him. "Arrived at the top at last," he wrote. "We saw hundreds of mountain peaks all around us, presenting a spectacle like ocean waves in a storm."

Little has changed about the spectacle of the mountains since Spangenberg was inspired to write those words; little wonder, then, that Blowing Rock has become the popular resort town that it has. But unlike many tourist towns, with their neon signs and wax museums, Blowing Rock has managed to retain a natural charm. In addition to the scenery, nearby attractions include Moses H. Cone Memorial Park and Julian Price Memorial Park—both reached from the Blue Ridge Parkway—quaint shops and inns, fine restaurants, and, for the kids, Tweetsie Railroad, located on U.S. 321 between Blowing Rock and Boone.

Hebron Colony Falls
(Shulls Mill Falls, Boone Fork Falls)

River: Boone Fork
County: Watauga
USGS quadrangle: Boone
Landowner: National Park Service,
 Julian Price Memorial Park
Height: Several hundred feet of small cascades

Beauty rating: 5
Trail length and difficulty: 0.5 mile; 4–7

Directions: From the starting point, drive 1.5 miles south on U.S. 221 and turn right on Shulls Mill Road (S.R. 1552). Proceed 1.9 miles, passing under the Blue Ridge Parkway, and turn left on Old Turnpike Road (S.R. 1558). Continue 1.3 miles to a sharp left-hand switchback and park on the side of the road.
 Follow the trail that leads from the left side of the road. You will cross a small creek before arriving at Boone Fork. An obscure path leads 100 yards upstream to the falls.

Photo Tips
 This cascade does not lend itself well to wide-angle photographs, but you can climb around the falls and shoot individual cascades.
 If you want pictures of sunbathers, Hebron Colony Falls is the place to be.

Hebron Colony Falls is not a waterfall; it's merely a long series of cascades amid enormous boulders. However, it is so popular and is located in such a scenic setting that its inclusion here seems appropriate. Visit on a hot weekend when the local colleges are in session and you will be lucky to find a boulder to set your tripod on.

Hebron Colony and Grace Home, a Christian home for recovering substance abusers, is located nearby and is apparently the origin of the cascades' name. Hebron, an Israeli-occupied city, is the site of the traditional burial place of the patriarchs.

Nearby waterfalls: After visiting Hebron Colony Falls, retrace your route to U.S. 221. Turn right and follow U.S. 221 as it loosely parallels the Blue Ridge

Parkway until the two roads meet near Grandfather Mountain. Several small cascades can be seen along this route, all on the right side of the road. This route is recommended only if you have already driven the section of the parkway that it parallels; the scenery is much better on the parkway.

Silvervale Falls *

River: Tributary of Puncheon Camp Creek
County: Caldwell
USGS quadrangle: Buffalo Cove
Landowner: Private
Height: About 100 feet
Beauty rating: 4
Trail length and difficulty: View roadside
Handicapped Accessible

Directions: From the starting point, drive 1.2 miles south on U.S. 321 Business to the junction with U.S. 321. Turn right (south), drive 6.5 miles, and turn right on Waterfalls Road (S.R. 1371). Continue 1.8 miles to a view of the waterfall on the left.

Photo Tips
There is no way to photograph all of this waterfall without including the graffiti. Instead of trying to eliminate it, emphasize it, so your photograph will become a message. If you are trying to sell your work, the image may prove a highly marketable representation of the sad effects of vandalism.

I suppose it can be argued that graffiti is a unique form of self-expression and part of our culture, but that argument doesn't work with me in regard to the mountains of western North Carolina. Silvervale Falls has been ruined by vandalism.

The gravel road that passes by the falls was once part of an old toll road that ran from Lenoir to Blowing Rock. The toll road was closed in the early 1920s when the state bought the property to build U.S. 321.

Silvervale Falls
Nikon F3, 20mm lens, polarizing filter, f/22 at ¼ second, Fujichrome Velvia.

There was no way to eliminate the graffiti. Instead, I included as much as I could and will market this image as a representation of vandalism.

Glen Burney Falls *

River: New Years Creek
County: Caldwell
USGS quadrangle: Globe
Landowner: Town of Blowing Rock
Height: Over 50 feet
Beauty rating: 4
Trail length and difficulty: 1.1 miles; 7

Directions: From the starting point, drive south on U.S. 321 Business for 0.2 mile and turn right on Laurel Lane. It is 0.1 mile to Annie Cannon Park. There is a paved parking area on the left.
    Glen Burney Trail begins at the end of the parking area, near the trail board. The trail is well-marked and easily followed, but don't be fooled by the first set of cascades you come to; the main falls are farther downstream.

Photo Tip
    Glen Burney Falls does not lend itself well to photography.

According to local old-timers, Glen Burney Trail has been here forever. During the Depression, the Civilian Conservation Corps was sent to improve the trail and provide better access to the logging camps in Globe Valley. The portion of the trail that leads to Glen Burney Falls and Glen Marie Falls is the only remaining section in usable condition.

Glen Marie Falls *
(Glen Mary Falls)

River: New Years Creek
County: Caldwell
USGS quadrangle: Globe
Landowner: Town of Blowing Rock
Height: About 80 feet
Beauty rating: 5
Trail length and difficulty: 1.5 miles; 7

Directions: Follow the directions to Glen Burney Falls, then continue on Glen Burney Trail 0.4 mile to the base of Glen Marie Falls.

Photo Tip
    As with Glen Burney Falls, this waterfall is not an ideal photo subject. You might try a shot from right at the base that includes the rhododendron shrub on the right.

Although Glen Marie Falls and Glen Burney Falls are neither particularly beautiful nor particularly good photo subjects, Glen Burney Trail is highly recommended as a day-hike for those staying in the Blowing Rock area. The property has been owned by the town since the turn of the century, when it was donated by Emily Prudden with the requirement that it always be used for the recreational enjoyment of the public. A trail guide and information are available from the Blowing Rock Visitor Center, located on Main Street.

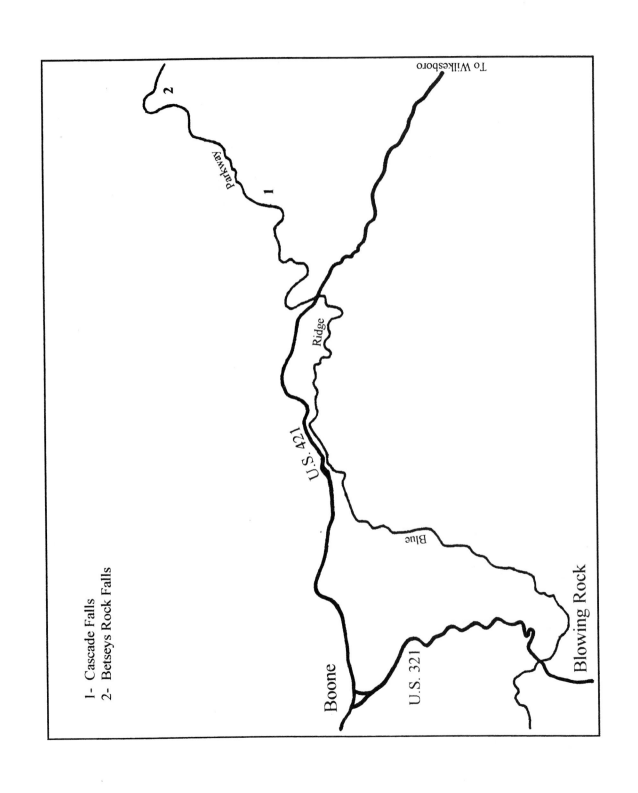

1- Cascade Falls
2- Betseys Rock Falls

Parkway

2

1

Ridge

U.S. 421

Blue

To Wilkesboro

Boone

U.S. 321

Blowing Rock

Boone

Boone, the home of Appalachian State University, is the commercial center of the northern mountains, much as Asheville is for the southern mountains. Anyone who skis in North Carolina is familiar with its many fine restaurants and hotels.

Performances of the popular outdoor drama *Horn in the West*, which celebrated its forty-second season in 1993, are offered nightly except Mondays from late June to late August. On the grounds of the amphitheater is the Hickory Ridge Homestead Museum, a "living museum" of a 1780s homestead.

Cascade Falls *

River: Fall Creek
County: Wilkes
USGS quadrangle: Maple Springs
Landowner: National Park Service, within the Blue Ridge Parkway boundary
Height: Long series of cascades and slides
Beauty rating: 4
Trail length and difficulty: 0.4 mile; 3

Directions: From the junction of U.S. 421 and the Blue Ridge Parkway, approximately 15 miles east of Boone, drive north on the parkway 4.4 miles to the parking area for E. B. Jeffress Park (Milepost 271.9). Cascades Nature Trail, a well-graded interpretive loop trail, begins at the restrooms and leads to the cascades.

Photo Tip
Save your film.

Cascade Falls is not anything to get excited about, but the walk to it is pleasant, and interpretive markers along the way offer a glimpse into the natural history of the mountain environment.

In addition to Cascades Nature Trail, the 600-acre E. B. Jeffress Park has a picnic area, along with an easy trail leading to an old cabin and church. E. B. Jeffress was chairman of the North Carolina Highway Commission and was instrumental in routing the Blue Ridge Parkway through the state.

Betseys Rock Falls *

River: North Prong, Lewis Fork
County: Wilkes
USGS quadrangle: Glendale Springs
Landowner: Private
Height: Though it is impossible to judge from the overlook, this waterfall may be over 200 feet.
Beauty rating: 4
Trail length and difficulty: View roadside
Handicapped Accessible

Directions: Follow the directions for Cascade Falls, but continue north on the Blue Ridge Parkway past the parking area at E. B. Jeffress Park. It is 4 miles to the Betseys Rock Falls overlook, on the right.

Photo Tip
It's just about impossible to get a decent shot of the falls. Visit in early spring or autumn to improve your chances.

Betseys Rock Falls is typical of waterfalls along the northern Blue Ridge escarpment. The drop is very high, but the creek is so small that the falls are insignificant, particularly in dry weather. The North Prong of Lewis Fork originates less than 0.5 mile upstream and has no opportunity to gain size before plunging over the escarpment.

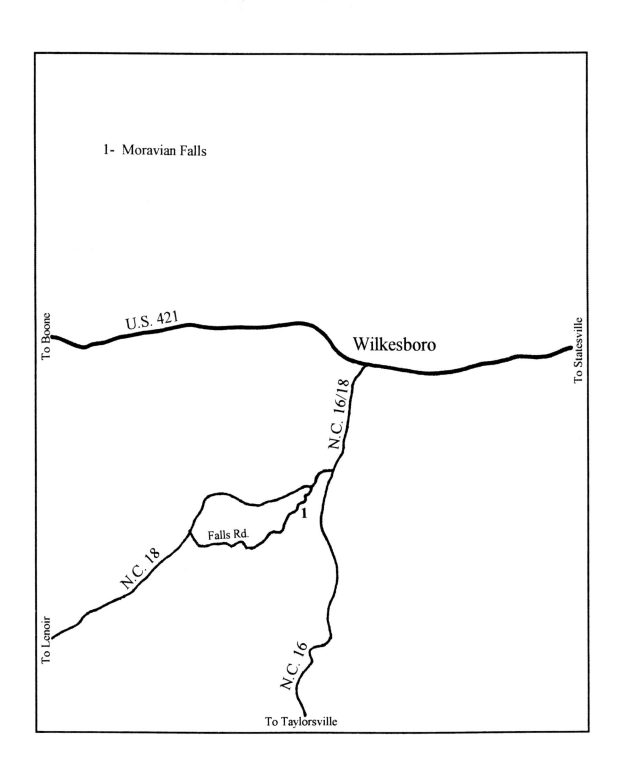

1- Moravian Falls

To Boone

U.S. 421

Wilkesboro

To Statesville

N.C. 16/18

1

Falls Rd.

N.C. 18

To Lenoir

N.C. 16

To Taylorsville

Wilkesboro

The only waterfall listed for this hub lies just outside the community of Moravian Falls, 5 miles south of Wilkesboro. Moravian Falls is nothing more than a crossroads, but it has enjoyed a fascinating history. In June 1895, on a small hand press, R. Don Laws began publication of the *Yellow Jacket*, a monthly political newspaper with the mission "to Swat Liars and Leeches, Hypocrites and Humbugs, Demagogs and Dastards." By 1902, the paper had a circulation of 20,000, and at its height of popularity, its estimated circulation was an incredible 300,000. In the paper, Laws attacked everything from communism to the New Deal. He died in 1951, and the *Yellow Jacket* died with him.

Moravian Falls *

River: Moravian Creek
County: Wilkes
USGS quadrangle: Moravian Falls
Landowner: Private
Height: The upper level is 35 feet and the lower drop 12 feet.
Beauty rating: 5
Trail length and difficulty: View roadside
Handicapped Accessible

Directions: From the junction of N.C. 18/16 and U.S. 421 Bypass in Wilkesboro, drive approximately 3 miles south on N.C. 18/16. Turn right to stay on N.C. 18; N.C. 16 continues straight. After 0.5 mile on N.C. 18, turn left on Falls Road (S.R. 1108), just beyond the crossroads of Moravian Falls. There is a sign for Moravian Falls Campground and Park. It is 0.5 mile to a view of Moravian Falls on the left.

Moravian Creek has been used as a source of power for numerous enterprises since the late 1700s. Iron forges, grain mills, and power plants have been powered by the small waterway. The mills on Moravian Creek are no longer in operation; the nonoperating mill that stands by the falls was reconstructed by the present owner to help draw tourists.

Moravian Falls
Nikon F3, 28-70mm zoom lens, f/22 at 1 second, Fujichrome Velvia.

After receiving permission to leave the road right-of-way, I spent considerable time searching for the ideal composition. The only one that worked at all is this straightforward approach, taken from eye level.

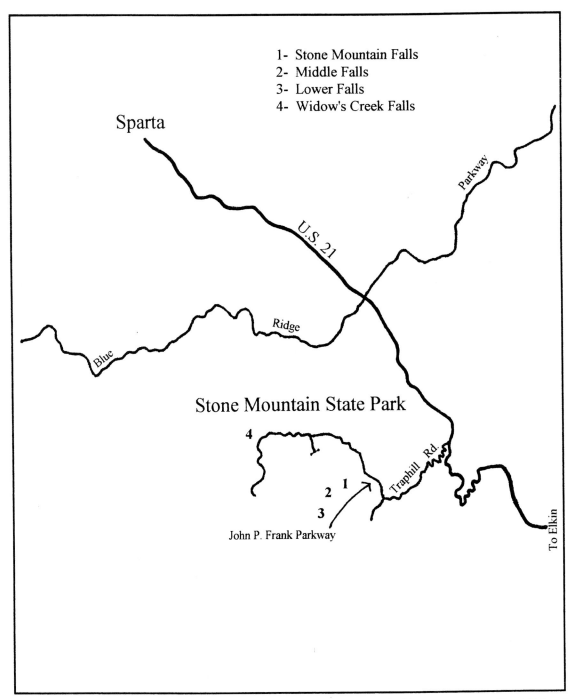

1- Stone Mountain Falls
2- Middle Falls
3- Lower Falls
4- Widow's Creek Falls

Sparta

U.S. 21

Parkway

Blue   Ridge

Stone Mountain State Park

4

1
2
3

Traphill Rd.

John P. Frank Parkway

To Elkin

The starting point is the entrance to Stone Mountain State Park. From N.C. 21, turn west onto Traphill Road (S.R. 1002) and proceed 4.3 miles. Turn right on John P. Frank Parkway (S.R. 1784); it is 2.3 miles to the park entrance.

Stone Mountain

Four waterfalls are located in Stone Mountain State Park, which is on the edge of the Blue Ridge escarpment about halfway between Elkin and Sparta, 10 miles south of the Blue Ridge Parkway. The principal attraction in the park, however, is Stone Mountain itself, a massive, dome-shaped monolith with exposed granite walls rising 600 feet from the valley floor. Its cliffs provide some of the finest friction climbing in the South. Because of the relatively smooth rock surface, a high degree of skill is required to make the ascent.

The park offers a developed campground, as well as primitive camping, trout fishing, and several miles of hiking trails, including a "safe" route to the top of Stone Mountain.

Stone Mountain is a North Carolina Natural Heritage Area and a National Natural Landmark.

Stone Mountain Falls *
(Beauty Falls, Upper Falls)

River: Big Sandy Creek
County: Wilkes
USGS quadrangle: Glade Valley
Landowner: Stone Mountain State Park
Height: 200 feet, only a portion of which is visible
   from the base
Beauty rating: 7
Trail length and difficulty: 1.2 miles; 5

Directions: From the starting point, drive approximately 2.9 miles on the park road and turn left onto a small gravel road. Follow this road 0.4 mile and park at the picnic area. If the lot is full, you will have to park at the beginning of the gravel road.

Stone Mountain Loop Trail begins and ends at the picnic area. For the shortest route to the falls, follow the loop in a counterclockwise direction beginning on the side with the picnic tables. After climbing to the top of the steps, you will enter a grassy meadow with stunning views of Stone Mountain's south face. After 0.9 mile, you will come to a junction with Middle and Lower Falls Trail, on the right. Continue straight to arrive at the base of Stone Mountain Falls. An elaborate stairway leads to the top.

Photo Tips

It's hard to eliminate the sky from the top of the falls, so shooting on an overcast day will not work. Unfortunately, the waterfall is in a deep-forest setting, so shooting when the sun is shining doesn't work well either. The best time for photos is during storm lighting, when the sky is dark gray, or during a light rain, when the sky isn't as washed out as it is on a bright overcast day. If you must shoot on a clear day, the optimal lighting is in the afternoon, when the waterfall receives the most complete illumination.

During autumn or early spring, a good vantage point is from the top, looking out over the distant mountainside.

The finest photo opportunities in the park are from the grassy meadow overlooking Stone Mountain and from the summit of the mountain itself. Stone Mountain Loop Trail gives access to both of these vantage points.

Stone Mountain Falls
Canon EOS Elan, 24mm tilt/shift lens, polarizing filter, f/22 at ½ second, Fujichrome Velvia.

This photograph provides a perfect illustration of the problem of shooting on sunny days in a forest setting. The contrast is simply too much for the film to handle. Unfortunately, because of the open sky at the top, Stone Mountain Falls is an equally unsuitable photo subject on overcast days.

The elaborate stairway leading to the top of Stone Mountain has over three hundred steps and numerous landings. Construction of the structure, which was financed by a private organization, took several months and cost over $100,000. The stairs prompted a considerable backlash from people who would like to see them replaced with a switchback trail, which would be more in character with the wilderness setting. The stairs have prevented further erosion of the fragile soils on the granite face, at least.

Middle Falls

River: Big Sandy Creek
County: Wilkes
USGS quadrangle: Glade Valley
Landowner: Stone Mountain State Park
Height: 40-foot slide
Beauty rating: 2
Trail length and difficulty: 1.2 miles; 5

Directions: Begin the hike to Stone Mountain Falls. After 0.9 mile, turn right on Middle and Lower Falls Trail, which immediately crosses a small creek. After 0.2 mile, a side trail on the right leads 0.1 mile to the falls.

Photo Tip
Save your film.

There is really no such thing as a walk in the woods that isn't worthwhile, but if you have extra time in Stone Mountain State Park, I recommend spending it on the summit or at the base of Stone Mountain, rather than hiking to Middle Falls or Lower Falls.

Lower Falls

River: Big Sandy Creek
County: Wilkes
USGS quadrangle: Glade Valley
Landowner: Stone Mountain State Park
Height: 40-foot slide
Beauty rating: 4
Trail length and difficulty: 1.6 miles; 6

Directions: Begin the hike to Stone Mountain Falls. After 0.9 mile, turn right on Middle and Lower Falls Trail, which immediately crosses a small creek. You will pass the Middle Falls side trail on the right after 0.2 mile; continue straight. You will cross Big Sandy Creek two times before arriving at the falls 0.7 mile from Stone Mountain Loop Trail. Cross the creek again to view the falls from the base.

Photo Tip
You can make a fair image by including the rounded yellow pebbles in the foreground of either a horizontal or vertical composition.

The rocks in the pool are representative of the two main rock types in the park. The fine-grained biotite gneiss of the Alligator Back Formation makes up the bulk of the park except for the domes. The domes of Stone Mountain, Wolf Rock, and Cedar Rock are composed of plutonic granite, which formed from molten rock deep within the earth. The domes were exposed as millions of years of erosion stripped away the miles of overlying rock. The yellow-stained pebbles of the pool are quartz, a common mineral.

Widow's Creek Falls *

River: Widow's Creek
County: Wilkes
USGS quadrangle: Glade Valley
Landowner: Stone Mountain State Park
Height: One drop and one slide, each measuring about 40 feet
Beauty rating: 5
Trail length and difficulty: 100 yards; 1

Directions: From the starting point, drive approximately 3.9 miles on the park road to a parking area on the left just after crossing Widow's Creek. The short path leads upstream to the falls.

Photo Tips
The best vantage point is from the base of the upper drop using a wide-angle lens to accentuate the water-carved rock. Frame carefully to exclude the fallen tree on the left.

Widow's Creek Falls is a perfect example of the erosive force of mountain streams, and the trail is so short and easy that it provides a perfect opportunity for some physically disabled persons to hike to a waterfall.

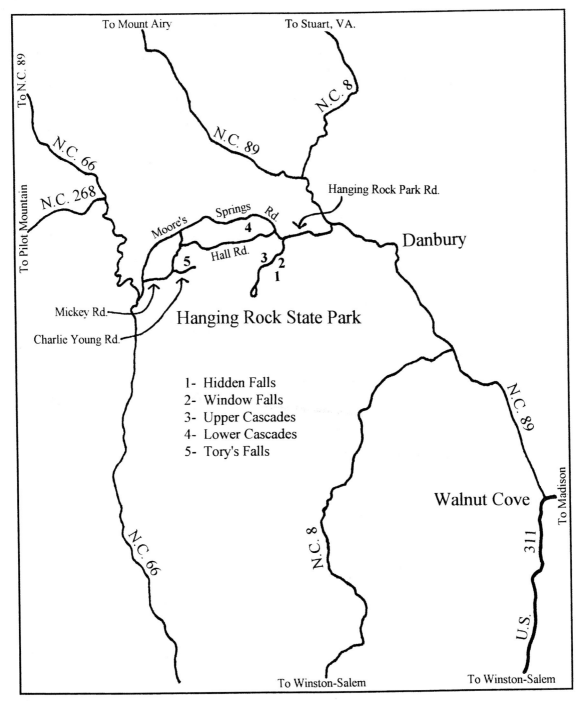

The starting point is the entrance to Hanging Rock State Park. Take N.C. 8 out of Winston-Salem. Continue past Danbury, turn left in front of Stokes Reynolds Memorial Hospital onto Hanging Rock Park Road (S.R. 1001), and drive 1.45 miles to the park entrance.

Hanging Rock

Hanging Rock State Park is located in the Sauratown Mountains, due north of Winston-Salem. These mountains are completely separated from the Blue Ridge chain, located farther north and west, and are often referred to as "the mountains away from the mountains." The park comprises some six thousand acres of the Sauratown range and offers visitors a wide range of activities, including swimming, rowboat rides, fishing, camping, rock climbing, and hiking. Spectacular views may be enjoyed from Hanging Rock and Moore's Knob, two prominent peaks in the park.

Hidden Falls

River: Indian Creek
County: Stokes
USGS quadrangle: Hanging Rock
Landowner: Hanging Rock State Park
Height: Very small cascade
Beauty rating: 2
Trail length and difficulty: 0.4 mile; 4

Directions: From the starting point, drive 1.7 miles into the park and turn left into the large parking area. Park on the far side and begin the trail, which leads through the picnic area. After about 0.3 mile, the trail forks, with the right fork leading to the falls.

Photo Tip
Save your film.

Hidden Falls is appropriately named; it is so insignificant that you may think the real waterfall has been hidden. The waterfall is listed in park literature and is easily accessible—otherwise, I wouldn't mention it here.

Window Falls *

River: Indian Creek
County: Stokes
USGS quadrangle: Hanging Rock
Landowner: Hanging Rock State Park
Height: Two levels, each measuring 15 feet
Beauty rating: 6
Trail length and difficulty: 0.6 mile; 5

Directions: Follow the directions to Hidden Falls, but turn left at the trail fork instead of right. It is 0.2 mile farther to the falls.

Photo Tips
You can shoot from in front of or behind the lower level, but the most effective angle is from the trail, looking down on the falls. Use the rhododendron leaves to frame the bottom portion of the falls.

There isn't much you can do with the upper level; the cascade and chasm are usually in shadow while the surroundings are in the light, creating more contrast than film can record. However, the bluff and the "window" make good photo subjects.

Window Falls is named for the natural hole in the quartzite bluff that overhangs Indian Creek and creates an eerie chasm for the stream to flow through. The waterfall itself is small and unremarkable, but its geological aspects are fascinating.

Upper Cascades *

Window Falls
Nikon F3, 28-70mm zoom lens, f/22 at 1 second,
Fujichrome Velvia.

I tried compositions from behind, in front, and both sides of the falls
and settled on this viewpoint looking down on the falls. The only thing
I regret is that the rhododendron were not in bloom.

River: Cascade Creek
County: Stokes
USGS quadrangle: Hanging Rock
Landowner: Hanging Rock State Park
Height: 35-foot cascade
Beauty rating: 5
Trail length and difficulty: 0.3 mile; 2

Directions: The trailhead is near the park road, on
the other side of the parking lot from the trailhead
for Hidden Falls and Window Falls. After beginning
the trail, you will immediately cross the park road.
The trail continues over a sandy ridge and curves
around to a viewing platform near the falls. Climb
down the steps to reach the base.

Photo Tips
On an overcast day, Upper Cascades is fairly
photogenic. Consider wading into the narrow
pool just downstream and using the golden-
colored water in the foreground.

After seeing the conditions at nearly three hundred
waterfalls in North Carolina, I can say that, for the
most part, nature has not been "improved" by building asphalt trails, elaborate viewing decks, concession
stands, and other man-made projects not in keeping
with wilderness settings. For many people, this type of
construction only serves to destroy the natural experience that they hoped to get out of hiking to a waterfall.
Thus, it's no surprise that I was shocked by the
multilevel deck hanging on the mountainside at Upper Cascades. What's most disturbing is that it seems
to serve no purpose. You can't get a good view of the
falls from it, and a simple handicapped-accessible

platform could have been built that would not have proven unnecessarily distracting.

The sandy ridge provides habitat for a number of uncommon species, among them turkey-beard (*Xerophyllum asphodeliodes*), a showy wildflower that blooms from May to June.

Lower Cascades *

River: Cascade Creek
County: Stokes
USGS quadrangle: Hanging Rock
Landowner: Hanging Rock State Park
Height: At this cascade, a smooth incline leads to a 25-foot drop.

Beauty rating: 7
Trail length and difficulty: 0.3 mile; 8

Directions: At the starting point, turn off Hanging Rock Park Road onto Moore's Springs Road, which remains S.R. 1001. Drive 0.25 mile and turn left on Hall Road (S.R. 2012). It is 0.4 mile on Hall Road to a parking area on the right.

The trail follows a wide roadbed 0.2 mile to a sign directing you to the left. Walk down the path 200 feet to a bluff overlooking the falls. This is an extremely dangerous area; watch your children closely. The base is reached by working your way down the bank on the right-hand side. This can be tricky even when the ground is dry, and especially when it is wet. It's suicidal when snow or ice is on the trail.

Lower Cascades
Nikon F3, 20mm lens, polarizing filter stacked on warming filter, f/22 at 4 seconds, Fujichrome Velvia.

The only way I could get the exact framing I wanted was to wade into the pool and get closer to the falls. The results were well worth a temporary case of cold feet.

Photo Tips

Bring the widest-angle lens you have and use a horizontal composition to emphasize the overhanging bluff. Pay attention to the contrast; the pool is often shaded while the top of the falls is in the light. You can minimize the contrast by framing tightly across the top and right side of the cascade, but to include much of the bluff, you will have to wade into the pool and get closer.

It is too dangerous to attempt a photograph from the top of the bluff.

Lower Cascades is by far the most scenic and photogenic waterfall in the park. If you only have time for one waterfall, this should be it.

Tory's Falls

River: Tory's Creek
County: Stokes
USGS quadrangle: Hanging Rock
Landowner: Hanging Rock State Park
Height: Series of small drops totaling about 100 feet
Beauty rating: 4
Trail length and difficulty: 0.25 mile; 4

Directions: At the starting point, turn off Hanging Rock Park Road onto Moore's Springs Road, which remains S.R. 1001. Continue 3 miles to Mickey Road (S.R. 2011). Turn left, drive 1.1 miles, and turn left on Charlie Young Road (S.R. 2028). It is 0.3 mile on Charlie Young Road to a parking area on the left. Note: If you start from the Lower Cascades parking area, continue on Hall Road 2.2 miles to Mickey Road and turn left. It is then 0.75 mile to Charlie Young Road, on the left.

Follow the trail 0.2 mile to a fork. The right fork leads to Tory's Den, a small, 30-foot cave. The left fork leads to an overlook of the falls.

Photo Tips

This waterfall is not photogenic under normal circumstances. Perhaps the situation improves during autumn or after a good snow. It is definitely best to visit when the water level is up.

Tory's Falls is in an interesting geological setting, but the waterfall itself is rather unattractive.

During the Revolutionary War, Tory's Den and other small caves in the present-day park were used as hideouts by Tories after their nighttime raids on settlers.

Appendix

Federal Agencies

Blue Ridge Parkway
Headquarters Office
200 BB&T Building
1 Pack Square
Asheville, N.C. 28801
704-271-4779

Great Smoky Mountains National Park
District Ranger Office
Box 4, Park Circle
Cherokee, N.C. 28719
704-497-9147

Great Smoky Mountains National Park
Headquarters Office
Gatlinburg, Tenn. 37738
615-448-6222

National Forests of North Carolina
Post and Otis Streets
P.O. Box 2750
Asheville, N.C. 28802
704-257-4200

Nantahala National Forest

Cheoah Ranger District
USFS
Route 1, Box 16-A
Robbinsville, N.C. 28711
704-479-6431

Highlands Ranger District
USFS
Route 2, Box 247
Highlands, N.C. 28741
704-526-3765

Tusquitee Ranger District
USFS
201 Woodland Drive
Murphy, N.C. 28906
704-837-5152

Wayah Ranger District
USFS
Route 10, Box 210
Franklin, N.C. 28734
704-524-4410

Pisgah National Forest

French Broad Ranger District
USFS
P.O. Box 128
Hot Springs, N.C. 28743
704-622-3202

Grandfather Ranger District
USFS
P.O. Box 519
Marion, N.C. 28752
704-652-2144

Pisgah Ranger District
USFS
1001 Pisgah Highway
Pisgah Forest, N.C. 28768
704-877-3350

Toecane Ranger District
USFS
P.O. Box 128
Burnsville, N.C. 28714
704-682-6146

State Agencies

Hanging Rock State Park
P.O. Box 186
Danbury, N.C. 27016
910-593-8480

Mount Mitchell State Park
Route 5, Box 700
Burnsville, N.C. 28714
704-675-4611

South Mountains State Park
Route 1, Box 206-C
Connelly Springs, N.C. 28612
704-433-4772

Stone Mountain State Park
Star Route 1, Box 15
Roaring Gap, N.C. 28668
910-957-8185

City and County Agencies

Avery County Chamber of Commerce
P.O. Box 700
Newland, N.C. 28657
704-733-4737

Blowing Rock Chamber of Commerce
P.O. Box 406
Blowing Rock, N.C. 28605
704-295-7851

Boone Area Chamber of Commerce
112 West Howard Street
Boone, N.C. 28607
800-852-9506

Brevard Chamber of Commerce
P.O. Box 589
Brevard, N.C. 28712
800-648-4523

Bryson City Chamber of Commerce
P.O. Box 509
Bryson City, N.C. 28713
704-488-3681

Burke County Chamber of Commerce
P.O. 751
Morganton, N.C. 28655
704-437-3021

Cashiers Area Chamber of Commerce
P.O. Box 238
Cashiers, N.C. 28717
704-743-5191

Cherokee County Chamber of Commerce
115 U.S. 64 West
Murphy, N.C. 28906
704-837-2242

Cherokee Tribal Travel and Promotion
P.O. Box 460
Cherokee, N.C. 28719
800-438-1601

Clay County Chamber of Commerce
P.O. Box 88
Hayesville, N.C. 28904
704-389-3704

Franklin Area Chamber of Commerce
180 Porter Street
Franklin, N.C. 28734
704-524-3161

Graham County Friends
Travel and Tourism Authority
P.O. Box 1206
Robbinsville, N.C. 28771
704-479-3790

Haywood County Chamber of Commerce
1124 Sulpher Springs Road
Waynesville, N.C. 28786
800-334-9036

Hendersonville Chamber of Commerce
330 North King Street
Hendersonville, N.C. 28739
704-692-1413

Highlands Chamber of Commerce
P.O. Box 404
Highlands, N.C. 28741
704-526-2112

Jackson County Chamber of Commerce
18 North Central
Sylva, N.C. 28779
704-586-2155 or 704-586-2336

McDowell County Chamber of Commerce
17 North Garden Street
Marion, N.C. 28752
704-652-4240

Madison County Chamber of Commerce
P.O. Box 97
Marshall, N.C. 28753
704-689-9351

Maggie Valley Chamber of Commerce
P.O. Box 87
Maggie Valley, N.C. 28751
800-334-9036

Old Fort Visitor Center
P.O. Box 1447
Old Fort, N.C. 28762
704-668-7223

Tryon Thermal Belt Chamber of Commerce
401 North Trade Street
Tryon, N.C. 28782
704-859-6236

Wilkes County Chamber of Commerce
P.O. Box 727
North Wilkesboro, N.C. 28659
910-838-8662

Yancey County Chamber of Commerce
#3 Town Square, Room 2
Burnsville, N.C. 28714
704-682-7413

Private Agencies

Bob's Creek Pocket Wilderness
Bowater
P.O. Box 7
Catawba, S.C. 29704
803-329-6600

Chimney Rock Park
P.O. Box 39
Chimney Rock, N.C. 28720
800-277-9611

Crescent Resources, Inc.
8133 Rochester Highway
Salem, S.C. 29676
803-885-3407

Foothills Trail Conference
P.O. Box 3041
Greenville, S.C. 29602
803-297-9568

Grandfather Mountain, Inc.
P.O. Box 129
Linville, N.C. 28646
704-733-2013

Great Smoky Mountains Railway
P.O. Box 397
Dillsboro, N.C. 28725
800-872-4681

Nantahala Outdoor Center
U.S. 19W, Box 41
Bryson City, N.C. 28713
704-488-2175

North Carolina Nature Conservancy
Carr Mill, Suite D-12
Carrboro, N.C. 27510
919-967-7007

Photography Sources

Most of the equipment discussed in this book is available from your local camera center. The suppliers listed below sell specialized items that may not be found anywhere else. The listed magazines have regular features that apply to outdoor photography.

Astronomical Data Service
3922 Leisure Lane
Colorado Springs, Colo. 80917-3502
719-597-4068 (This is the number for requesting a catalog; orders are accepted only by mail.)
This firm publishes the *Photographers Almanac of the Sun & Moon*, a highly recommended resource for the nature photographer.

The Filter Connection
P.O. Box 155
South Windham, Conn. 06266
203-456-3990
This firm offers a large selection of filters from various manufacturers.

Kirk Enterprises
4370 East U.S. Highway 20
Angola, Ind. 46703
219-665-3670
This firm offers a product line similar to that of Really Right Stuff, with additional, unrelated items.

Leonard Rue Enterprises
138 Millbrook Road
Blairstown, N.J. 07825
908-362-6616
This firm offers a large selection of nature-photography equipment and supplies, including the over-the-boot waders mentioned in this book.

Nature Photographer
P.O. Box 2037
West Palm Beach, Fla. 33402
407-586-7332

Outdoor Photographer
12121 Wilshire Boulevard, Suite 1220
Los Angeles, Calif. 90025-1175
310-820-1500

Really Right Stuff
P.O. Box 6531
Los Osos, Calif. 93412
805-528-6321
This firm offers a large selection of precision-machined Arca-Swiss–style quick-release clamping systems and related items.

Stackpole Books
Cameron and Kelker Streets
P.O. Box 1831
Harrisburg, Pa. 17105
How to Photograph Birds, an excellent Stackpole book by Larry West, is recommended here because of its section on exposure.

Index